THE MEDIA'S COVERAGE OF THE ARAB-ISRAELI CONFLICT

Edited by Stephen Karetzky and
Norman Frankel

Shapolsky Publishers
New York

For any additional information, contact:
Shapolsky Publishers, Inc.
136 W. 22nd Street, New York, NY 10011

First Edition
10 9 8 7 6 5 4 3 2 1

Library of Congress Cataloging in Publication Data

The Media's coverage of the Arab-Israeli conflict/edited by
Stephen Karetzky and Norman Frankel. -- 1st ed.

    1. Foreign news--United States--Public opinion. 2. Jewish-Arab
relations in the press. 3. Jewish-Arab relations--1973- --Public
opinion. 4. Public opinion--United States. 5. Israel--Foreign public
opinion, American. 6. Arab countries--Foreign public opinion,
American. 7. Jews--United States--Attitudes toward Israel. I.
Karetzky, Stephen. II. Frankel, Norman.

PN4784.F6M4 1989   956.94'05--dc19   88-29189

ISBN 0-944007-22-8

Printed in the United States of America

Credits are listed on pages 329-331

To Joanne

"Swords are in their lips"
—Psalm 59

Table of Contents

Introduction

For the first three months of 1988, seven hundred foreign journalists scrutinized the activities of eight thousand Israeli soldiers attempting to quell Palestinian riots. The stories these reporters produced dominated the news in Western countries. In contrast, greater violence seventy-five miles away in Lebanon—which resulted in more Palestinian deaths at the hands of other Arabs, including fellow Palestinians—was almost ignored. Similarly, the much bloodier conflicts in Afghanistan, Sri Lanka, The Punjab, Iraq, and Iran received little attention. And while the media roundly condemned the Israeli restrictions on newsmen in the battle zones, no complaints were made over the Western journalists sentenced to long prison terms by the Soviets who caught them trying to cover the Afghan war.

In 1988, a new level of moral, intellectual, and physical flaccidity was reached by Western journalists. In story after story and commentary after commentary, obsessed newsmen rhetorically asked whether the citizens of the Jewish state were in danger of losing their souls. As Charles Krauthammer and Norman Podhoretz observed, there was no parallel concern expressed for the Israelis' physical well-being. Journalists now openly relied heavily on easily available information proffered by Arab propaganda agencies. Thus no one should have been surprised when *The New York Times* consistently referred to P.L.O. infiltrators who commandeered an Israeli bus and killed several unarmed civilians aboard as "guerrillas" rather than "terrorists."

The purpose of this book is to provide an evaluation of the news coverage of the ongoing conflict between Israel and her neighbors. The focus of the early part of the volume is on the reporting of the so-called Palestinian Uprising of 1988. The emphasis here is on the most influential American news organs, such as *The New York Times, The Los Angeles Times*, and the television networks.

Following this is a section dealing with one particular source of news and opinion in the United States: the Jewish-American community and its media and spokesmen. Interestingly, the organized Jewish community paid almost no attention to the media's treatment of Israel until the 1982 war in Lebanon. Even in its aftermath, however, its evaluations of the press coverage have been undistinguished, incomplete efforts, which are usually seen by only a few dozen insiders or quietly discussed in closed-door meetings with newspaper or network executives. In the case of the *Boston Globe*, public silence was the price demanded by that news organ for a face-to-face discussion with concerned Jews. Interestingly, a few relatively small groups with meager resources have done some excellent work, most notably Americans for a Safe Israel with its one-hour video *NBC in Lebanon*. (It is noteworthy that even *The New York Times* gave it a positive review.)

Of special interest in 1988 was the battle fought by one Jewish newspaper in New Jersey against the dominant local daily serving approximately one million people. Like many other newspapers throughout the country, *The Record* had treated its readers to sensationalist, anti-Israel reporting for years, and excoriated Israel in its editorial and OP-ED pieces. While it is papers like *The New York Times* which set the agenda and the approach for American newspapers, it is those of the calibre of *The Record* which comprise the daily reading for most. The probing interview with one of this paper's primary editorial writers reveals much about his psychology and ideology. Like many of the "mainstream" journalists who are critical of Israel, e.g., Thomas Friedman of *The Times*, he is Jewish by birth, but more a part of the journalistic community than of the Jewish community. Information on relevant activities of the Jewish community of Bergen county are also included, since they may have effected some change in the policy of the offending journal.

Material is included from an earlier book of mine, *The Media's War Against Israel*,[1] which covers the period before and during the summer 1982 war in Lebanon. The basic approach and the specific techniques of Western journalists are essentially the same now as then. (For example, anti-government demonstrations in Israel are prominently featured on the front page of *The New York Times*, but stories of pro-government ones twice their size are buried on the inside pages.[2]) Furthermore, discussions of contemporary coverage inevitably shift to that of earlier events.

Political cartoons are included in this work because their striking images encapsulate the ideas which are disseminated elsewhere in the media. It is noteworthy that except for those of the Copley News Service, most cartoons in the past few years have been unflattering to the Jewish state. Israel has been increasingly portrayed as a brutal, militaristic nation oppressing helpless Arabs and taking advantage of its American ally. Some of the more "moderate" cartoons suggest a moral equivalence between the leader of Israel and the head of the P.L.O. A few express sympathy for the country bedeviled, and somewhat bewildered, by the constant threats to its existence.

The appendices include (1) maps of the area in question for those who are unfamiliar with it, (2) The Code of Ethics of The American Society of Professional Journalists to provide a standard by which readers can evaluate the work of reporters, and (3) a list of several organizations involved in analyzing news coverage of the Middle East.

Despite the efforts demonstrated here by some within and outside the academic community, additional research is needed. Excellent work in a related area has been done by S. Robert Lichter of George Washington University and Stanley Rothman of Smith College. As reported in their book *The Media Elite: America's New Powerbrokers*,[3] they interviewed over two hundred journalists from *The New York Times, The Washington Post*, CBS and other leading news organizations. Their findings reveal how journalists' personal views—which are far to the left of the American people—shape the news they write and the crusades they mount. (Drs. Rael Jean Isaac and Erich Isaac have also shown how newsmen think and work in *The Coercive Utopians: Social Deception by America's Power Players*.[4]) Unfortunately, the problem is not only attitudinal, but also appears to be intellectual. Irving Kristol may well have been correct when he remarked a few years ago that the only part of the newspaper

which journalists have the subject knowledge to write compe-
tently is the sports section.

By 1988 the reporters of Mideastern affairs had reached a new
professional low. As noted, radical propaganda organizations
came to be heavily and openly relied upon by the journalists for
their "news." Thus, *The New York Times* audaciously proclaimed
in its news reports that The Palestinian Press Service was the
journalists' "fastest and most reliable single source of information."[5] Included in the book's appendices is a handout openly
distributed to reporters by a similar organization, Jerusalem
Media Services. Such groups make the jobs of Western newsmen
easy. In a similar manner, there has evolved a *consistent* reliance
by *New York Times* reporters on sources such as Meron Benvenisti, a leftist Israeli professor who receives much financial support
for his "research" from the Rockefeller and Ford Foundations.

While revealing the distortion in the media—as we do in this
book—is a prerequisite to correcting it, it has not as yet proven
widely effective in and of itself. Members of the media are simply
not answerable to anyone. Journalists usually respond to criticism in one of four ways:

1. Arrogantly ignore it.
2. Irresponsibly accuse their detractors of
   "blaming the messenger for the message."
3. Illogically declare that since their critics
   on both sides of the issue in question
   criticize their coverage, their reporting
   must, ipso facto, be accurate.
4. Mindlessly dismiss it as "media bashing."

Tom Wolfe has observed that when people write about journalists as the journalists write about everyone else, "they shriek
like wienies over an open fire—they can't stand it. You're then
called a neoconservative, and if they really don't like it, they call
you a reactionary."[6]

Efforts to reform reporters and make them adhere to their
profession's own code of ethics will not only require continued
study, but also concerted action by interested groups. Reform
from within the journalistic community is probably not possible.
How can it be when Columbia University's Pulitzer Prize

Committee bestowed its award for international reporting to *The Times'* Thomas Friedman for his Middle East stories in 1983 and again in 1988?[7] As Marvin Maurer points out in this book, Friedman's reporting is tendentious, and he openly defends judging Israel by a higher moral standard then that applied to other countries. Aside from this inherently unfair double standard, one must ask why newsmen are making moral judgements at all if their job is to make objective reports.

I would like to thank Ian Shapolsky, Irving Katz, and Sally Katz for their continued encouragement and sage advice throughout this project. I am also grateful to Dr. Sherida Yoder for making available her considerable expertise on stylistic matters. Norman Frankel has been an able and congenial coeditor.

Stephen Karetzky

[1] New York: Steimatzky-Shapolsky, 1986.
[2] See March 13, 1988, p. 1; March 14, 1988, p. A12.
[3] With Linda Lichter. Bethesda, Md.: Adler and Adler, 1986.
[4] Chicago: Regnery-Gateway, 1983, pp. 251-82.
[5] March 31, 1988.
[6] *Insight on the News*, Feb. 1, 1988, p. 15.
[7] It is interesting that in 1932 The Pulitzer Prize for International Reporting went to *The New York Times'* Walter Duranty despite his attempted coverup of Stalin's intentional starvation of millions in the Soviet Union. The Committee has repeatedly refused to rescind this award.

Editors

Stephen Karetzky is the author of several books and articles on the media, the Middle East, and library and information science. He holds a doctorate from Columbia University.

Norman Frankel has written extensively on political affairs for *Midstream, Conflict Quarterly,* and elsewhere. He is on the editorial advisory board of *Political Communication and Persuasion.*

Contributors

Edward Alexander is Professor of English at The University of Washington and at Tel Aviv University and author of *The Jewish Idea and its Enemies.*

Gerald Baumgarten is a staff member of the Anti-Defamation League.

Rebecca Kaplan Boroson is Editor of the *Jewish Standard,* Hackensack, New Jersey.

The Center for Media and Public Affairs, based in Washington, D.C., is headed by Drs. S. Robert Lichter and Linda Lichter.

Judith Colp is a reporter for the *Washington Jewish Week.*

Yoram Ettinger directs Israel's Government Press Office.

Frank Gervasi is on the staff of the Center for International Security.

Rael Jean Isaac is the author of *Israel Divided* and *Parties and Politics of Israel.*

Jeane Kirkpatrick is Professor of Political Science at Georgetown University and Resident Scholar at the American Enterprise Institute.

Edward I. Koch is the Mayor of New York City.

Frederick Krantz is Associate Professor of History at Concordia University, Montreal.

Charles Krauthammer is Associate Editor of *The New Republic*.

Irving Kristol is Professor of Social Thought at New York University, Editor of *The Public Interest*, and Publisher of *The National Interest*.

Daniel Lazare is an editor and columnist at *The Record*, Hackensack, New Jersey.

Marvin Maurer is Professor of Political Science at Monmouth College, West Long Branch, New Jersey.

Micah Morrison is the Editor of *Contentions*, published by the Committee for the Free World.

Norman Podhoretz is the Editor of *Commentary*.

Eric Rozenman is the Associate Editor of *The Near East Report*.

David Sidorsky is Professor of Philosophy at Columbia University.

Woody West is the Associate Editor of *Insight*.

Eli J. Warach is, in his spare time, President of the United Jewish Community of Bergen County, New Jersey.

Ruth R. Wisse is Professor of Yiddish Literature at McGill University.

Mortimer Zuckerman is Chairman and Editor-in-Chief of *U.S. News & World Report*.

I. COVERAGE OF THE PALESTINIAN UPRISING

Israel in Crisis:
Coverage of Israel's Palestinian Problem

by The Center for Media and Public Affairs

How have our media covered Israel during the current wave of Palestinian unrest? We analyzed 375 stories on the ABC, CBS, and NBC evening news and 242 articles in the *New York Times* from the onset of protest last December 9 through April 4, 1988.

The results:

Bad News for Israel - Israel was the target of twice as much negative "spin" (judgmental reporting) as the protesters. Nine out of ten sources criticized Israel's treatment of the Palestinians.

Balancing Blame - Blame for the unrest was divided about evenly between Israel and the Palestinians. Israel's use of force was justified almost as often as it was criticized.

Video Violence - Over 1100 scenes of violence appeared on TV news in five months. Palestinian protesters were shown committing more acts of violence than Israeli soldiers. But the Israelis committed 61% of the one-sided violence.

Media Ban Backfired - The week after the army restricted press access, TV news more than doubled its coverage of Israeli violence.

3

In the Spotlight

We monitored network evening news and *New York Times* coverage of Israel from the outbreak of protest on December 9, through April 4, 1988, on the eve of Secretary of State Shultz's 1987 visit. During this period TV news ran 375 stories, averaging over three a day. ABC aired 136 stories, followed by NBC with 126 and CBS with 112. The total airtime was 10 hours 41 minutes. The *New York Times* printed 242 stories, an average of two a day. The 4276 column inches of text would fill 35 pages in the *Times* without headlines, ads, or pictures.

Focus on Israel

The newspeg was Palestinian unrest, but the main story was Israel itself. About one fifth of the coverage focused on the protests. Israel's response and other aspects of Israeli society and politics generated twice as much coverage as the protests themselves.

The media became part of the story, as 65 stories addressed questions of press access and media responsibility. The remaining coverage centered mainly on international reaction. One-sixth of the U.S. coverage concerned the reactions and opinions of American Jews toward events in the Middle East.

The networks featured stories on the riots half again as often as the *New York Times*. One TV story in five focused on violent protest, compared to one in eight newspaper articles. TV's coverage of the media's role focused on problems of access, while the *Times* devoted more coverage to media responsibility. TV carried almost three times as many media access stories as print (35 to 13), while the *Times* carried over twice as many pieces as the networks (12 to 5) on the media's role in the crisis and the quality of information conveyed.

Middle East Voices

Nearly half the 2836 sources cited (47%) were Israeli. The largest number were government officials, led by Prime Minister Shamir with 120 citations. But the military and police were also

4

cited over 300 times. Journalists and other private citizens were also well represented.

Palestinian and other Arab sources were cited about half as often as Israelis. Among them were 180 citations from Palestinian activists and demonstrators, including 64 from PLO representatives. The American response was most often presented by government sources but also included 107 citations from Jewish organizations.

Judging Israel

The major points of contention in the news concerned Israel's use of force, its justice system, and its treatment of the Palestinians. Israel's use of force against the protesters was by far the most heavily debated issue. The 164 statements coded were almost perfectly balanced, with 49% justifying Israeli force and 51% criticizing it.

The coverage was more negative toward Israel's system of justice (including both the civil legal system and military courts). Seventy percent of the 50 statements coded on this issue criticized its fairness, treatment of protesters, etc.

The most negative coverage was directed toward Israel's treatment of the Palestinians, aside from its behavior toward protesters and detainees. Among 58 statements addressing the broader social, political, or economic context of Israeli-Palestinian relations, over nine out of ten (91%) criticized Israel. And this did not include statements that addressed the Palestinians' plight without linking it to Israeli treatment.

Research shows that non-partisan sources are more influential in changing opinion than are self-interested sources. Most of the pro-Israeli viewpoints came from Israeli sources, while the anti-Israeli viewpoints on these three issues came from a wide range of sources. Among the 101 positive assessments of Israeli behavior, 94% came from Israeli sources, 4% from American Jews, and 2% from the U.S. government. Of the 168 negative assessments, 36% came from Israeli sources, while the anti-Israeli viewpoints on these three issues came from Arab sources, 15% from American Jews, 11% from other U.S. sources, and 24% from other international sources. Overall 80% of the views ex-

5

pressed by American Jews were critical of Israel, mostly about its use of force.

Casting Stones

Despite heavy criticism of some Israeli actions, blame for the unrest was divided about equally between Israel and the Palestinians. Of 148 expressions of blame, 33% accused Israel, while 31% accused the Palestinian side (including 10% that specified the PLO). Another 17% blamed the media for perpetuating or escalating the unrest. A majority of the accusations against Israel concerned underlying legal, political and economic inequities rather than the use of force against protesters.

Seeking Solutions

Much of the coverage was occupied with the search for solutions to the Palestinian unrest. The need for a negotiated settlement was mentioned by far the most often, especially after Secretary of State Shultz began his efforts toward this goal.

Israel was called on most frequently to resolve the crisis through military force or by deporting leaders of the Palestinian protests. Proposals for deportation sparked the most controversy. Of those who mentioned this policy, 46% opposed it. On the Palestinian side, the most frequent proposals were for autonomy for the occupied territories or resistance against the Israeli occupation. Fifteen sources called for violent overthrow of the occupation.

Overall, the calls for Israeli policies of force or deportation slightly outnumbered (by 66 to 57) the voices seeking Palestinian autonomy and resistance. Solutions that were only rarely mentioned included early elections in Israel and integration of the Palestinians into Israeli society.

Spin Patrol

The tone of the news can be influenced by judgmental phrasing or "spin" that introduces or concludes a story. For example: "Palestinian youths went on a rampage in East Jerusalem today...," "... what Prime Minster Shamir left behind—three months of turmoil that had divided the Israeli people and their leaders." We examined network leads and closers for spin, along with opening and closing paragraphs in the *Times*. Spin turned out to be overwhelmingly negative—90% or 114 of 126 instances coded.

Negative spin was directed at Israel twice as often as at the Palestinians. It was more prevalent (81 cases) and more anti-Israeli (70% vs. 30%) at the networks, compared to 33 cases that split against Israel by 58% to 42% in the *Times*. Israel did receive the benefit of nine of the twelve positive cases of spin.

Pictures of Protest

TV news is more than the words that are spoken. It is also, and perhaps preeminently, the pictures that appear on screen. To examine the visual impact of the coverage, we coded every camera shot taken on location. We excluded studio reports and indoor interviews. This procedure yielded 4192 "visuals." The three networks did not differ significantly in their selection of visuals.

The cameras mainly showed the protests themselves rather than the background context, e.g., refugee camps, victims of terrorism, street scenes, etc. Pictures of protesters, security forces, and detainees outnumbered "contextual" shots by 70 to 30 percent. Of the scenes that depicted the context of the unrest, the Palestinian side was seen about twice as often as the Israeli side.

Just over one on-location visual in four (26%) portrayed an act of violence, ranging from fistfights to gunshots. Of the 1103 scenes involving violence, 600 (54%) showed Palestinian protest-ers and 503 (46%) showed Israeli security forces. (When both sides behaved violently, we coded the side that was shown initiating the violence.)

When we examined one-sided violence, however, the focus shifted to the Israeli side. One-sided violence was coded only when a violent act and non-violent response were both clearly shown. One-sided violence ranged from soldiers beating civilians to protesters throwing rocks at retreating soldiers. There were 280 scenes in which one side acted in a violent manner against a person or group who did not respond in kind. The Israeli defense forces were shown committing 178 acts of one-sided violence (61%), compared to 102 acts (39%) by Palestinian protesters.

The Camera Didn't Blink

Angered by pictures of Israeli violence, the army banned all foreign reporters from the occupied territories during Palestinian Land Day protests (March 29-31), except for a small pool of reporters with a military escort. Did this "get tough" policy change the coverage? To find out, we compared TV coverage of the week that included the ban (March 29-April 4) with coverage of the week preceding the ban (March 22-28).

The result: After the press restrictions, the cameras produced more negative images of Israel than before. The focus of coverage did not shift away from the riots, but expanded to include the issue of press access. Instances of negative spin toward Israel also increased. (There was no negative spin toward the Palestinians during the two-week period.)

Most striking, pictures of violent acts not only increased, they shifted decisively toward the Israeli side. The week before the ban, only 21% of the violent visuals featured the Israeli Defense Forces. The next week, 64% focused on Israeli violence. Before the ban, only 33% of the one-sided violence shown was committed by Israelis. Afterward, the Israeli share increased to 86%.

Times, TV Play It Anti-Israel

by Jeane Kirkpatrick

"Ten die in PLO Fighting," the *New York Times* reported on May 3 in a small headline on a short story on page 13. It began: "Three days of gun battles between Palestinian guerrilla factions in a refugee district in southern Beirut have left 10 people dead and 40 wounded." The understated report on this latest violence in Shatila between Yaser Arafat's PLO and the breakaway "PLO Intifada" stood in stark contrast to repeated front-page accounts of one or two or three Palestinians killed by Israeli troops in what the *Times* dateline regularly terms "The Occupied West Bank."

Why, I wonder, is the now familiar low-level war on the West Bank more newsworthy than the new outbreak of violence between Arafat's Fatah and its sometime ally, Al Fatah Intifada? The question is particularly interesting considering that the PLO in-fighting occurred at the same time that Arafat and Syrian President Hafez Assad were negotiating a reconciliation.

A good many devoted *Times* readers—and friends of Israel—have reluctantly concluded that the paper has a marked bias against Israel in its reporting on the current disturbances. Compare, they say, the way the *Times* and the *Washington Post* began their Page 1 stories describing an Israeli operation in Lebanon on May 4.

The *Times* lead: "At least 1000 Israeli soldiers in tanks and armored personnel carriers stormed through parts of southern Lebanon today, searching homes, questioning Lebanese villagers and distributing warning leaflets."

The *Post* lead: "Hundreds of Israeli troops conducted house-to-house searches in several southeastern Lebanese villages today in a hunt for Palestinian guerrillas and weapons caches that brought the soldiers within a few miles of Syrian military lines."

The *Times* is not the only news organization that has been charged with unfair reporting on the conflicts in Gaza and the West Bank. The television networks are similarly accused.

Now, finally, there is evidence against which to check these impressions and accusations. The Center for Media and Public Affairs, directed by Dr. Robert Lichter, carefully analyzed coverage of the Israeli-Palestinian conflict by the networks and the *Times* from Dec. 9 through April 4. The findings have just been released in the *Media Monitor* issue of May 1988.

Significant findings include:

> "A negative spin was directed at Israel twice as often as [at] the Palestinians" (far more so among the networks than at the *Times*).
>
> The uprisings were frequently used as a point of departure for a broad criticism of Israel's politics and society. Nine of every 10 comments on these broader issues were critical.
>
> Eighty percent of the reported comments by U.S. Jews were critical of Israel.

In other words, commentary was heavily slanted against Israel, even though news pictures of violence were more or less evenly divided, as were explicit judgments as to "who's to blame."

So far, however, negative reporting on the uprisings has had little impact on American support for Israel, according to a new study reported in *Public Opinion* magazine (May/June 1988).

Comparison of a national opinion poll conducted by Penn and Schoen Associates in late January 1988 with a similar 1981 study indicates that the friendship of U.S. citizens toward Israel has not been affected by reports on the uprisings.

Penn and Schoen found that Israel "continues to be seen as a strong and reliable ally in a volatile and unfriendly region," even though 36 percent of Americans believe its anti-riot measures have been "too harsh."

The Penn and Schoen study also revealed that most Americans:

Regard the PLO as a terrorist organization.

Oppose establishment of an independent Palestinian state under PLO auspices.

Believe Arab states share with Israel responsibility for the Palestinians in Gaza and the West Bank.

Though there is broad consensus on support for Israel, the broadest support of all is for a negotiated settlement to the conflict: 78 percent believe an international conference should be convened, and 74 percent think the PLO should be invited to participate.

What can we conclude from this array of evidence?

First, the networks and the *Times* emphasize the negatives in reporting on Israel and use violent events as an occasion for airing broad criticisms of Israeli society.

Second, on this (as on many other subjects), the perspectives of our liberal network news organizations run counter to those of a majority of Americans, and that so far the anti-Israel media "spin" has had only a limited effect on popular support for Israel or opposition to the PLO.

These data confirm once again Americans' faith in reason and negotiation as tools for foreign policy. Just as Will Rogers never met a man he didn't like, a majority of Americans never see a conflict that cannot be negotiated.

11

"Explaining" the Media's Anti-Israel Bias

by Marvin Maurer

In the first few months of 1988, front page headlines and prime time television news provided a steady stream of news about Israeli forces killing, beating and tear gassing innocent Arab women and children. Dominating the press are such headlines as "Jewish Settler Kills an Arab Amidst Continuing Disorder" or "Israel's 'Iron Fist'... Betrays Nation's Highest Moral Principles." Political cartoonists thrive on using the Nazi analogy. One cartoon depicted an Israeli in a Nazi SS uniform, with a Star of David emblem on the cap, a whip in hand, declaring: "Hey! We don't shoot them—we're humanitarians." Another shows a stereotyped elderly Jew in traditional garb holding a "Free Soviet Jewry" placard while standing on the back of a grovelling Palestinian. Another portrays a powerful, laughing Israeli soldier shrugging off the pebbles thrown at him while blazing away at Arab kids.

News about the riots are packaged so that rock- and Molotov-throwing street toughs are presented as would-be Davids facing up to their Goliath-like tyrants. Photographs of many rioters wearing fashionable clothes and fancy wrist watches and looking healthy and well-fed inadvertently suggest another reality of life under Israeli rule. While detailed accounts are provided of selected Arab victims—usually children—the media virtually ignores the fate of Jews who have been beaten, stoned and murdered. To drive home the persecution theme, prominently displayed photographs invariably juxtapose armed Israelis alongside aged Arab shopkeepers or women and children.

Much has been made of the excesses committed by Israelis who happened to have had virtually no training in riot control.

13

The media has failed to investigate which particular Israelis committed such excesses as the attempted burial of Arab youths. Were they the sons of the forgotten (by the media) 700,000 Jews expelled from the Arab states after 1948? (Would Israel have gotten the same mileage from the media had they kept the Jews from the Arab states in camps—as did the Arabs and the UN? Probably not. Reporters such as the *Times'* David Shipler made it a point to condemn Israel for not providing *instantaneous* equality for these newcomers in all areas of life.) Expelled from ancient lands after centuries of oppression, these troops would have the incentive to hate Arabs and be tempted to reply in the way Arabs customarily treat their opponents. These Sephardic Jews now comprise the majority of the Jewish population in Israel. Once Israel trains effective riot control forces and understands media tactics, such excesses are not likely to occur again.

Absent are the compensating news and photographs of Arabs and Jews living and working together or the stories of Arabs and Jews attending college classes or union meetings. One cannot learn from the media whether Israel is awash in chaos or whether the disturbances are confined to relatively small numbers of people. Sensationalizing incidents throws events out of perspective making relatively minor ones appear to represent the total picture. However nasty the limited efforts by Israelis to defend themselves against the rocks, they are mild compared to what takes place in the Arab Middle East. (It has not dawned on the Middle East pundits that Israel's crude and pathetic effort at riot control by troops poorly trained for such duties suggests that for forty years there was no need for such forces.) This includes the Arab massacres of tens of thousands of Arabs in Lebanon since 1976 or King Hussein's killing and exiling of some twenty thousand Palestinians in 1970. During the current riots, Jordan, Egypt, and Morocco suppressed riots and demonstrations without eliciting editorial or pictorial responses in the mainline media. There have been no photographs of many of these occurrences, and no on-the-spot interviews with civilian survivors by investigative reporters.

Surveying how the media packages news from Israel and the Arab world provides a strong clue of how they perceive problems in the region. For example, on January 18th, 1988, ABC's evening news anchorman Peter Jennings spent eight minutes comparing selected Israeli policies with those of South Africa. He concluded that the blacks in South Africa were making more progress than the Arabs in the administered territories. Would not a fairer evaluation include comparison of the Israeli record on human rights with that of its neighboring Arab states? Given South Africa's moral standing in the media, comparing it with Israel is a form of crude victimization aimed at undermining Israel's moral credibilty.

Not surprisingly, the media deny that their Middle East coverage is slanted or fosters implicit values and agendas, but inadvertently—and even overtly—some elements reveal their strong bias. At a Tel Aviv conference on recent media coverage of the riots, CBS news correspondent Bob Simon called the charges that Israel is covered by a different standard "a crock." He recalled, according to *The Jewish Week* (2-26-88), that the U.S. government was also subjected to intense media pressure during the Vietnam War just as Israel is now. Isn't that the point? The media select a target that they believe needs pressuring and then wage advocacy journalism, i.e., the packaging of news to achieve a strongly held moral goal.

In an article syndicated widely in Jewish newspapers (for example, *The Jewish Standard*, 1-29-88), Judith Colp of *The Jewish World* compiled the reactions of prominent journalists to charges of media bias. Rather than blame *The Washington Post, New York Times* or the networks, *Washington Post* columnist Richard Cohen argued that "these things are really happening. They [the critics] never had the same complaints when the violence was coming from the Arab side and they showed Israeli women mourning their dead or shrieking." He explains that Israel looks bad because it is "an occupation power doing what occupation powers do...." Ted Koppel, the highly regarded anchor of ABC's Nightline, denies that the news about Israel is purposely slanted: "The American media has always been tough when it perceives injustice.... I have no embarrassment... no constraints about criticizing Israel since I felt no embarrassment and no constraints about criticizing my own country." Israel, he concludes, confuses the source of its troubles with the presence of the cameras.

15

It is important to understand that Koppel is defending the media's provision of news based on their moral values rather than on objective criteria. Therefore, explored below is the central issue implied in Koppel's defense that the media's coverage is based on the perception that Israel is the immoral party in this struggle, in short, "the bad guy" or the Goliath. It follows that once this main assumption is made, those in the field have to send home the appropriate copy and/or expect their coverage to be edited to fit in with the perceived injustice. This includes giving full coverage to the moral claims of the supposed victims and participating in, and staging, events. For example, the as-of-now aborted PLO propaganda attempt to simulate the 1947 *Exodus* sailing with Jewish refugees included about one hundred Arabs seeking to return to Haifa accompanied by over three hundred media personnel with their full regalia of cameras. The world media thus enlisted to become a crucial part of a PLO propaganda offensive.

The New Republic's Charles Krauthammer sees the issue differently from Koppel. He recognizes that the media dramatize and hype the news "by simply showing the confrontation rather than any background." He gives an example of how moral issues are ignored or made. On January 2, Brazilian troops massacred about one hundred protestors and the next day an Israeli soldier accidentally shot an Arab woman. The latter story was emblazoned on page one of the *Washington Post* and the former buried on page twenty-seven. *The New York Times,* according to the *Jewish Week* (2-12-88), like the television networks, did not carry the Brazilian story at all.

On occasion, someone in the media comes forth and concedes that news related to Israel is packaged according to pre-conceived perceptions. In an August 1982 *Jerusalem Post* interview, NBC chief Reuven Frank admitted that the media hold long-term biases about Jews and Israel which determine how the news is presented or packaged. He explained that, for a time, memories of the Holocaust and the influence of Jewish lobbyists allowed the Jews to enjoy the status of the underdog, but after the 1967 Israeli victory in the Six Day War a shift occurred so that the Palestinians were perceived as the underdogs.

16

Thomas L. Friedman, then Jerusalem bureau chief for *The New York Times*, commented on Frank's explanation in his February 1, 1987 *New York Times Magazine* article entitled "The Focus On Israel." He attempts to explain why Israel is covered by different standards than are other countries. Readers of his coverage of Israel and Lebanon, and now on the riots, would have little trouble recognizing his portrayal of Israel as the bully of an oppressed Arab population.

Agreeing with Reuven Frank, Friedman writes that while Jews "historically enjoyed the moral strength of the weak, they now wrestle with the responsibilities of the powerful." He contends that it is the historical presence of Israel which accounts for the media reaction whereby the "Jew is transformed from the victim to the victimizer." (Note his use of "victimizer" rather than, say, "a proud, free people.") In an article on April 15, 1984, he explained that Israel is powerful because it occupies Arab lands and has the means to suppress Palestinians. Should Jews become transformed from the "powerful" to the "ultimate cosmopolitan" or universal brother of all, then they would find the media tilt in their favor.

His February 1st article, however, admits no guilt or duplicity on the part of the media. Instead, it attributes "the special response" by the media to their perception of Jews and Israel. He frankly acknowledges that he and the *Times* utilize these special responses when processing news about Israel. He wonders aloud why Israel receives almost as much coverage as the Soviet Union and why "sometimes I find myself reporting on minor incidents on the West Bank and wondering why editors defined it as news." Friedman recognizes that the media have flooded Israel with foreign journalists. The riots have resulted in hundreds more to cover the riots. He fails to add that the Arab states—and Western states engaged in military action—regulate the number and actions of foreign and domestic correspondents and carefully monitor their output. Covering Israel, an extremely open society, a journalist like Friedman can give full vent to his predispositions. His counterpart in Damascus, only a few miles away, would do so only at great risk. Israel pays a heavy price for its open press policies.

17

He concedes that many of the incidents in Israel which are frequently given front page coverage in the United States would not even be considered newsworthy if they occurred elsewhere. The news from Israel is processed on the basis of a series of "interrelated factors" or ideological perceptions. These include the media's "attraction and aversion" to Israel, their obsession with biblical lore, their belief that Israel is the preeminent power in the region and their premise that Israel goes out of its way to curry favor with the United States.

Friedman declares that the media and their Christian readers are enthralled with biblical lore and perceive any event from the Holy Land as part of an overall "superstory." The return of the Jews is covered as a sequel to the New Testament. The accuracy of his assertion is arguable, but what is important is that Israel appears as a failure and betrayer of the tradition, having not yet earned its proper place in the enfolding "superstory."

Israel receives special media attention because of its need "to satisfy a deep longing to be accepted and to prove its worthiness... to the United States." While other small states regularly, and understandably, curry favor with the big powers in the pursuit of their interests, he implies that when Israel does so it is a form of sycophancy that irritates the media. Friedman cites Abba Eban's explanation that "the world is only comparing us to the [high] standards we set for ourselves," and declares that the media are merely judging Israel by these same standards. Again quoting an Israeli (a practice he frequently employs to support his views), Friedman explains that it is neither shocking nor newsworthy when "the French or the Germans behave cynically..., but when the Jews with their moral record of preaching behave cynically, now that's news." Friedman fails to consider whether it is professional to permit a particular subject's alleged values to be the criteria for judging its behavior while all others are judged by less demanding criteria.

Singling out Israel by judging it according to a strict moral code has the effect of putting Israel in a permanent adversarial position. One might ask Friedman how Israel could persistently live up to this code and avoid committing national suicide at the same time? Its media disadvantage is magnified further because its foes are judged in restrained terms—not only because they can censor and monitor the foreign media, but because their actions are judged in terms of "causes," "contingencies," and "understandable" responses, such as historical grievances.

Friedman does not advocate that the "special responses" to Israel's actions be discontinued. Confronting the critics of media bias, he avers (speaking through an Israeli again) that they really don't want to change for "deep down they realize the day Israel is boring to the world, the day it is covered like Norway, is the day the world no longer expects anything of it...." Friedman admits that media people find "something satisfying about watching the Jewish state behaving improperly...." He refers to "the shock and relish which many news organizations have reported Israel's role in shipping arms to Iran...." Furthermore, it is made clear that so long as Israel fails to resolve the Palestinian grievance, he and his colleagues in the media in general will press the aggressor-oppressor theme in their coverage.

At other times in his February 1st article, however, he berates Israel for behaving differently from other nations, especially when it nurtures what he calls its "superman complex." For evidence, Friedman cites Israeli political columnist Gideon Samet: "Nothing is beyond our reach..., however tiny and poor a country we are, our mastery of intrigue is unsurpassed...; our achievements have gone to our head...." The complex, Friedman maintains, is also manifested in the Israeli government's public relations campaign to flaunt its achievements. However, the general coverage found in the media suggests that Israel's efforts to publicize forty years of progress have had no impact in this arena.

He contends that this "superman complex" led Israel to become "indirectly involved in such horrors as the Sabra and Shatila refugee camps..." and that Israel's propaganda campaign against terrorism made the slaughter in the camps all that much easier. This is surprising because Friedman covered the Lebanese beat before his Israel assignment, so he should be well aware that the killings in the camps were typical of how the different Arab factions deal with one another.

Friedman's coverage of riots in the territories takes the same approach as his other reporting. In an October 7, 1984 article he explains that Arab violence (murder and stabbings) stems from

Israel's insensitivity towards the Palestinians. On April 15, 1984 he attributes the "youthful acts of rock throwing Palestinian Arabs to their frustration with the continued occupation." He adds that "it seems [that] so long as the vast majority of the Palestinian people have no homeland there are going to be Palestinian guerrillas."

Friedman and the others covering the riots for the *Times* cast their story in terms of two people fighting for the same piece of land. The terror and rock-throwing are merely expressions of nationalist yearnings. Intent on proving that the Palestinians are acting on impulse, Friedman cites West Bank Data Project Director Meron Benvenisti's claim that Palestinian violence is largely carried out... by individuals and groups who spontaneously express their feelings, undeterred by the consequences of their actions." Because of their singular belief that what is seen is true and highly suitable for reporting, reporters on the Israeli beat fail to delve into the question of how determined groups harness the media for propaganda warfare.

Is Friedman conscious of the implications of his astonishing revelations that the media are fostering a simplistic portrait of the struggle in Israel? Apparently he is. He explains that the Palestinians are mistaken if they believe their front page coverage is due to their grievances. They are only objects of attention because Israel is involved. Were they under another power, he declaims, they would receive as little attention as the Kurds. It is assumed that under normal media coverage it is the nature of the event that determines the degree of coverage, but this is certainly not true in the case of Israel, as Friedman admits. He notes that the shooting of one West Bank student by Israeli troops is plastered on the front pages while the shooting of twenty Palestinian Arabs by Jordanian troops is buried in the inside pages. However, he places the responsibility on Israel, not the media, because so much more is expected of Israel than of Jordan!

His own accounts of occurrences involving Israel reflect his lack of objectivity and judgment. For example, in his October 7, 1984 article, "The Power of Fanatics," he equates the 1982 Syrian army massacre of 20-30,000 Syrian civilians in Hama to Rabbi Meir Kahane's advocacy of expelling Arabs from Israel. He also finds congruence between Jordan's censoring coverage of The

Holocaust with some shortcomings alleged by protesting Israelis of their country's television coverage of abuses experienced by Arabs. By repeatedly comparing Arab actions to verbal excesses or lapses by some Israelis he reduces Israel to the level of the brutal Arab dictatorships. Nowhere does Friedman indicate that the Arab rioters act the way they do is because the civil liberties orientation of the Israelis emboldens them to perform before the cameras and take actions they would not dare contemplate if they were in Jordan or Syria. In short, these strained comparisons are unaccompanied by favorable comparisons of life in Israel with life in the Arab world.

Friedman's agenda allows for only one set of rational actors—the Palestinians who riot and kill for the "just" cause of national liberation—an all too familiar refrain heard on behalf of many national liberation groups these past two decades.

From its inception, Israelis learned the Arabs would not settle for any compromise in Palestine. Repeatedly, Palestinian spokesmen have stated that any piece of land granted for statehood is but a step towards recovery of all of Palestine. Friedman, however, ignores the record and instead characterizes the rioters' totalist demands as a reaction to more recent claims made by Israel. (Here he confuses statements made by some Jewish groups with the official policy of the Israeli government.) Since the Jews perceive the land as a single entity "so the Palestinians, including the Israeli Arabs, have come to see it as single territory...," and they are no longer after the "territories... but all of Palestine." Thus, he blames the Jews for setting an agenda of totalist battle over the land. Contrary to long-standing evidence, he states that the Arab fathers of the rioters and Yassir Arafat were "ready for a peaceful settlement with a Jewish state provided a Palestinian state was created alongside." Friedman virtually denies the centrality of the long-standing Arab refusal to concede any land for a Jewish state.

While Friedman and many in the media portray the riots as spontaneous, there are some clues that is not the case. Moderate or passive Arabs have been forced to participate. It is difficult to imagine Arab shopkeepers staying closed for weeks on end without some organized coercion. An Arab bus driver was stabbed in the face for taking Arab laborers to work. Another Arab was lynched for allegedly collaborating with Israelis. No photos were taken of this last incident, nor did it inspire any investigative reporting. Only in bits and pieces is the story of these "spontaneous" riots being revealed.

Friedman himself describes how "boys gathered along the roadside... pelting the bus [holding Arab workers] with stones, shattering windows and driving the passengers inside onto the floor" gave Arab workers a clear message to join in "the spontaneity" and express what this journalist calls the "fire inside the hearts of the people." In the process of jumping on Israel, a *Times* editorial refers to the role of "PLO provocateurs" in fomenting riots, and a February 1, 1988 article briefly mentions how well-organized Palestinian groups are "shepherding reporting crews to the trouble." Only part of the story has been told of how the media and the rioters have colluded to make dramatic news. Similarly, there has been no in-depth probing of the role played by the thousand or so Arab terrorists freed from Israeli prisons in exchange for a few Israeli prisoners. To what degree did they provide the infrastructure to sustain the riots for months on end? A thorough revelation of the organizational underpinnings of the riots would counter the simplistic "spontaneity" thesis.

With pride the media claim that they mirror realty, provide the facts, and fulfill their mission by bringing the truth to the public. On many occasions, the American media do a credible job. However, they often fail to acknowledge some of their shortcomings, including limitations imposed by dictatorships and unacknowledged biases. Certainly Amman or Damascus would never let the media play a role in fostering a dissident's agenda by allowing batteries of photographers and rioters to create photo opportunities. Since the media must select and edit the copy and photographs sent in by their reporters and news services, in effect they tell the public what is important and what is not. In the case of Israel, the importance of Friedman's article on reporting in the Middle East is that in it he acknowledges that news about Israel is processed to fit preconceived beliefs. Friedman denies that the media are engaged in either advocacy journalism or a media war against Israel, since Israel is to blame for the judgments meted out by reporters.

Crucial to an understanding of events in the Middle East are background reports about Israel's democratic welfare state and how its Arab enemies still dream of Israel's demise. Unfortunately, these are absent in American newspapers. Also missing, but equally germane to an understanding of the rioters' goals, is a review of the Palestinian record when they governed the state-within-a state in Lebanon. Even the PLO's most ardent supporters concede that it ran a lawless, bandit operation prior to the 1982 war.

Friedman arrogantly warns Israel that its status in the media will not change unless it accords justice to the Palestinians and abandons its "superman" complex. Futhermore, he openly defends the media's simplistic and erroneous assumptions concerning the region which he contends provide the correct underpinnings for covering the Israeli-Palestinian conflict. Contrary to this reporter's assertions, the day the media is prepared to cover Israel as they do Norway, they will have taken a giant stride towards fulfilling the journalist's credo to report accurately and fairly.

The *Los Angeles Times'* Coverage of Afghanistan, Gaza, and the West Bank; A Comparison

by *The Committee On Media Accountability (COMA)*

Through distortion and manipulation, the *Los Angeles Times* minimized and trivialized the eight-year Soviet occupation of Afghanistan while sensationalizing out of all proportion to their size, duration, and violence Israeli riot-control actions in Gaza and the West Bank. This was accomplished through:

1. Disparate employment of story size, frequency and display.

2. Manipulation of headline size and language.

3. Selective use of photos, editorials, op-eds and columns.

The *Times* devoted more front page stories and photos to four weeks of Gaza violence than to the entire eighth year of the Soviet assault on Afghanistan, where over one million civilians have died and 3-5 millions became refugees. As a result, this newspaper's manipulation of the news placed the limited Israeli action in Gaza at the top of the national agenda, while concealing and suppressing the slaughter of more than a million Afghans.

At the end of 1979, the U.S.S.R. invaded Afghanistan with the massive military war apparatus only a superpower could muster—tanks, planes, bombs and tens of thousands of soldiers. The invasion was in response to the rejection by the people of Afghanistan of the Marxist, Soviet-sponsored takeover of their government. There the Russians have remained for eight years, inflicting so much agony that one out of three Afghans has already fled—to create 3-5 million refugees in nearby Pakistan and elsewhere—and over a million Afghans were killed. It is by far the biggest, most brutal military campaign of the decade.

Eight years after the Soviets invaded Afghanistan, in December of 1987, riots broke out in the Israeli-held Gaza strip and West Bank. In response, the Israeli Army stepped in to restore order. By January of 1988, some 40 Palestinians had been killed, and less than a dozen were threatened with expulsion.

In spite of the enormous differences between the two events in terms of brutality, bloodshed and sheer magnitude, the *Times* ran more front page stories on the violence in Gaza in three weeks than on the entire eighth year of the Soviet depopulation and devastation of Afghanistan. Although the *Times* ran hundreds of stories about the Soviet Union in 1987, only 89 full-length reports dealt with the destruction of Afghanistan, slightly more than the 63 prominently-headlined stories on just 3-4 weeks of unrest in Gaza. And for that whole eighth year of the Soviet invasion, the *Times* ran just 17 photos from Afghanistan—none of them on Page 1—compared with a saturation coverage of 21 photos in almost as many days, six of them on page 1, from Gaza and the West Bank.

Of still greater impact on public awareness than the discrepancies in size and number of stories on the two conflicts was the disparity in story placement and headline language. No other component of the *Times* coverage is as revealing. From the beginning of the upheaval in Gaza and the West Bank, the *Times* kept a body-count of dead and wounded Palestinians in the headlines: "2 Palestinian Girls Wounded in Gaza as Israeli Fires On Stone Throwers" (11-12-87), "Four West Bank Youths Wounded Protesting Palestinian Partition" (11-30-87), "1 Killed, 8 Injured In New Gaza Violence" (12-15-87), "Israeli Soldier Kills Arab Women; Inquiry Ordered" (1-4-88), "Palestinians Slain, 26th in a Month. Shamir Calls Persistent Protests 'New' Kind of Arab Battle" (1-9-88).

On days when there was no new violence the *Times* kept the Gaza story alive with news-page headlines containing reckless and unsubstantiated rumors, and fanning the flames of conflict:

"PLO Asks End to 'Massacres' in Occupied Zones" (12-15-87), "Rumors Helping to Fuel Unrest in Gaza; (subhead:) Killings in Hospitals, Poisoned Water Supplies Alleged" (12-17-87), "U.S. Dispute With Israel Unlikely to Hurt Relations" (12-24-87), "American Jews Distressed, Divided; (Subhead:) Scenes of West Bank, Gaza, Violence are Embarrassment" (1-8-88), "Robertson Criticizes Israel as Using 'Excessive' Force in Arab Unrest" (1-8-88). Throughout the Gaza confrontations, *Times* headlines consistently placed responsibility for the violence and killings on Israel, portraying it as an "aggressor" and "occupier."

About Afghanistan, on the other hand, the *Times* presented a very different picture of victims and aggressors. In all of 1987, not a single *Times* headline made a direct link between Russian troops and any civilian killing, bombing or maiming. Instead of body counts and details of civilian suffering, *Times* headlines portrayed the Afghan violence in broad military terms, devoid of any reference to the killing of over 1 million Afghans: "Soviets Heavily Deploy Armored Units Around Afghan Capital" (1-15-87), "Soviet Armored Units Take Up Positions at Major Intersections in Afghan Capital" (1-17-87), "Soviets Reportedly Open Heavy Attack on Afghan Guerrillas" (2-5-87), "Soviets Reported Destroying Towns on Afghan Border" (4-22-87).

In just one headline did the *Times* finally link the Soviets with a civilian killing, but it promptly ameliorated the message by stressing it was all a "mistake": "Soviets Reportedly Bomb Post by Mistake, Kill 100" (5-6-87). Through an entire year of unrelieved violence against civilians by the Red Army and the Soviet-backed Afghan Army, there was no attempt by the *Times* to place responsibility on the Soviets for a single Afghan death. Quite the contrary—the *Times* consistently attributed whatever aggression existed in Afghanistan to the rebels, turning victims into aggressors: "Afghan Rebels Again Reject Truce" (1-18-87), "Afghan Guerrillas Shoot Down Plane; 30 Killed" (2-15-87), "Afghan Rebels Said to Down 24 Aircraft" (4-1-87), "Rebels Down Afghan Plane, Killing 15" (9-15-87), "Rebels Shoot Down Afghan Plane, 53 Die" (6-11-87). As if to make sure their readers didn't miss it, the *Times* printed the story again the next day: "Afghan Plane Downed by Missile, Killing 53" (6-12-87). While portraying the

27

Afghan rebels as aggressors, *Times* headlines actually pictured the Russians as victims: "Soviet-Made Plane Downed by Rebels; 43 Dead" (2-9-87), "Afghan Rebels Attacked Soviet Post, Tass Says" (4-19-87), "Soviet Casualties in Afghanistan Rising Due to U.S. Arms, Kremlin Aide Says" (7-17-87), "Soviet Veterans Face Scorn, Pravda Says" (8-6-87).

Although Soviet-backed Afghan Government troops used Soviet-supplied war planes to conduct the fighting—and attack refugee camps—no *Times* headlines made the connection: "Afghans Accused of Bombing Pakistan Village, Killing 35" (2-27-87), "Afghan Bombers Strike Pakistan Again; 31 Die" (2-28-87), "Afghan Air Raid Kills 51 in Pakistan Border Village" (3-24-87), "80 Killed in Afghan Air Strike on Iran, Pakistan Border, Rebels Say" (3-24-87). But, in marked contrast to its Gaza coverage, the *Times* ran no human-suffering interviews with any of the millions of refugees in the easily-accessible, bombed-out refugee camps in Pakistan.

In fact, even as their assault on rebel strongholds escalated throughout 1987, *Times* headlines managed to portray the Soviets as peace-seekers. Promoting a peaceful Soviet image began right from the start of the new year: "Soviets Link Afghan Pullout and Truce" (1-7-87), "Soviet Forces Begin Unilateral Truce" (1-15-87), "Soviets Pushing for Afghan Peace; (Sub:) Recent Moves Indicate Soviets May Be Serious About Ending War" (1-21-87), "Soviet Hopes for Afghan Pullout Beset by Troubles" (5-14-87). *Times* headlines kept up the Soviet peace campaign clear to the end of the year: "Gorbachev May Bring Afghan Pullout at Summit" (12-1-87), "New Afghan Pullout Plan Reported; (Sub:) Soviets to Leave in Year if Aid to Rebels Ends, Kabul Says" (12-1-87).

In *Times* headlines, Russia's peaceful intentions reached far beyond Afghanistan to span the entire globe: "Soviets Offer Pact on Missiles, Drop Link to 'Star Wars' (Sub:) In Major Shift Gorbachev Proposes New Agreement on Europe Weapons" (3-1-87), "Soviets Formally Present New Plan to Ban Missiles in Europe" (3-2-87), "New Arms Offer Made by Soviets (Sub:) Gorbachev Proposes Eliminating Short-Range Missiles In Europe" (4-15-87, Page 1), "Gorbachev Proposes Double-Zero Option; Asia as Well as Europe" (7-22-87, page 1), "Gorbachev Yields on Mid-Range Missiles" (7-23-87, page 1). This peace-seeking image was consistent with the *Times'* glowing reporting of Gorbachev's "new" Russia: "140 Dissidents Free, 140 More May Follow" (2-10-87), "140 Political Captives Free in Eight Days, Kremlin Reports" (2-11-87), "2 Soviet Activists Freed" (2-25-87), "Soviet Dissident Released After 4 Years in Siberia" (3-19-87), "An Apparent First for Soviets: Secret Ballot and Real Election" (2-11-87), "Soviets Publish Crime Figures for the First Time" (10-10-87), "Rumbles of Change Stir Soviet Union" (10-25-87), "Soviet Paper Decries Psychiatric Abuses" (11-12-87), "Czechs Cheer Gorbachev as a Symbol of Hope, Reform" (4-10-87, page 1), "Gorbachev Ally Says Exporting of Revolution is Outdated" (7-11-87), "Capitalists and Comrades Mix" (2-17-87, page 1), "1st American-Soviet Rock Concert Held" (7-5-87, page 1).

What the *Times* did not tell us, in any way that mattered, was that even as it ostensibly sought peace around the world, the Soviet Union was turning Afghanistan into a desert, ravaged and depopulated. While the *Times'* singularly intense coverage of Israel's actions in Gaza, though incomparably briefer and less bloody, isolated her in world opinion, its underplaying of the carnage in Afghanistan allowed the Soviet aggression to continue unchecked, unexposed and unaccountable. Incredibly, *Times* headline writers even found ways to make light of the suffering and decimation there: "Forget Pebble Beach—Try Golf In Afghanistan" (5-10-87). And, in what was clearly the most morbid, noted that "Humor a Casualty... Afghan Capital Loses Its Playfulness" (5-27-87).

In a recent CBS special report titled "The Battle for Afghanistan," Dan Rather, one of the few reporters attempting to draw attention to the story, observed that "in foreign affairs, the story the Soviet Union most wants suppressed is that of Afghanistan." In this respect, the *Times* has been of invaluable help. By reversing the techniques through which it kept the Gaza story alive—page 1 stories and photos, sympathetic headlines and human interest interviews—the *Times* successfully concealed and suppressed the agony of Afghanistan from its readers.

Totals:

	Gaza/West Bank two month's coverage	Afghanistan one year's coverage
Victims	under 100	1,000,000
Stories: All	119	87
Page 1	36	14
Column Inches	3,122	1,667
Photos: All	91	17
Page 1	8	0
Editorials	4	2
Op-Eds	18	8
Letters	30	3

Nightly News—Skewed

by Eric Rozenman

"The numbers for January are incredible," said an Israeli in Washington. "And I doubt that the numbers for February will be much different."

He was referring to saturation coverage of the clash between Israel and the Palestinian Arabs, as measured by minutes of air time on the three commercial networks' nightly news shows. Not only was the conflict the major news story in January 1988 for ABC, CBS and NBC—but on each it left the rest of the news far behind.

According to A.D.T. Research, a media analysis firm in New York, ABC's "World News Tonight" gave 67 minutes to the uprising in the Gaza Strip and West Bank and Israel's response. A distant second, with 21 minutes of coverage, was the Central American peace plan. Third, with 17 minutes, was the story of questions on Vice President George Bush's role in the Iran-Contra affair. A possible Soviet pullout from the Afghan war tied for fourth—with five minutes of air time.

NBC's "Nightly News" allotted 50 minutes to the uprising.

CBS's "Evening News" gave the clash between Israelis and Palestinian Arabs 48 minutes.

In other words, 165 minutes—23 percent of the time given to the top 30 stories—went to the violence in the territories. "It's not that anyone is trying to blame it [the damage done to Israel's reputation by pictures of Israeli troops shooting at and beating Arab rioters] on the messenger," an Israeli said. "And no one expects to be treated like Jordan or Syria," where news media access ranges from strictly controlled to nonexistent. "But what's really startling is the proportion."

Or better, the lack of proportion. With approximately 700 reporters covering 5,000 troops (the latter number probably increased during Secretary of State George Shultz's visit), the media itself became an actor.

It is simplistic to claim, as at least one Israeli Cabinet member did, that without the presence of camera crews there would be no riots. But it is foolish to insist on the opposite, that television plays no role in intensifying the unrest or in exaggerating its news value.

A majority of Palestinian Arabs may well despise Israeli control and support the uprising. But what television turned into January's major story was, according to the Israeli, the work of groups of 200 to 300 people at the most, in four or five locations throughout the territories, on any given day.

This exposes once again the cardinal principles of television news: pictures dictate stories, and the more arresting the picture, the more important the story. Conversely, no picture, no story.

Tight U.S. press control in Grenada and British censorship during the Falklands war came with no apologies. And difficult or impossible access to the large-scale fighting in Afghanistan or between Iraq and Iran seems to diminish these stories' worth.

"The first and only serious attempt on any network to try to give a wider perspective [to the Uprising] was CBS's '48 Hours,' " the Israeli said. "It tried to give some context.... But other than that, we learned again, if another lesson was needed, how shallow, superficial, and powerful television news is."

The history of the Gaza Strip and West Bank did not start on Dec. 9, when the violence erupted. And *Al-Quds Radio*, "the foremost propaganda tool of the uprising," according to Israel's *Davar* newspaper, does not demand negotiations, or even a Palestinian state on the West Bank and Gaza Strip. Its demand "clearly encompasses all parts of the country, which would amount to the elimination of the state of Israel."

But American viewers of the networks' nightly news might never know that. In a sense, they are being treated to the 1980's video version of the 1920's newspaper tabloids, the medium which defined mass market sensationalism.

An Ally Pelted by the Media

by Woody West

It is Israel's turn to be roasted over the searing flame of American outrage. Not even during the wildly skewed press coverage of the Israeli invasion of Lebanon in 1982 was criticism so acidulous as it has been since the current Palestinian riots erupted. The government's use of the army to prevent the riots from swelling to insurrection is not good for the morale of the soldiers or the self-esteem of the army, but the force used (occasionally and unhappily excessive) hardly has amounted to authoritarian repression.

Three times Arab armies have failed to destroy this genuine democracy, a form of government as rare as a speed-skating camel. What is going on now is a sanguinary effort to ignite a fourth war against Israel, an internal conflagration the containment of which may severely test the values of a humane society. Assaulted from within, Israel must also reckon with tendentious U.S. television broadcasts of Palestinians firing rocks from slingshots and Israeli troops hurling tear gas, wielding batons and, from time to time, resorting to gunfire. The incessant pictures of violence, with their implications of Israeli culpability (though for what is never made clear, of course), are beginning to establish in this country what was beyond the power of terrorists and invading armies: a portrait of the Israelis as the bad guys.

This perverse characterization is twisting a good many American Jews into knots of ambivalence, especially those multitudes who traditionally perch on the liberal left and are thus easily susceptible to the pious Third Worldism and the "give peace a chance" gibberish that passes for political thought in trendy neighborhoods. The Palestinian deaths in the rioting obviously are awful, but the toll would be far higher in almost any other country. The news media's saturation coverage has not been useful to anyone, substituting sound and fury for any attempt to explain the tangled dimensions of the issue. (The fixation of the press with violence recalls George Will's mordant observation that if there'd been television cameras at Gettysburg, we'd be two nations today.)

The Palestinians have a remarkably unhappy recent history and a not encouraging future under any set of conditions. But it must be recalled that Arab leaders twice rejected proposals to partition the land and share historical claims to it with the Jews, a tragic myopia. This has been compounded for 40 years by the Arab world's callousness in using the Palestinians as pawns in their own savage politics—as one result of which the West Bank, the Gaza Strip and the Golan Heights became "occupied territory."

But that was then, and now is now. It is inconceivable (or nearly so) that the United States ever would withdraw its moral and material commitment to the state of Israel. However, it is increasingly apparent that the status quo cannot be indefinitely extended—it is too flammable, for Israel and the world. Something must be done and that something can only be done by an agonizingly divided Israel, firmly nudged by the United States.

Secretary of State George Shultz can rent an efficiency and remain in Israel until the Reagan administration expires. But nothing will happen unless the Israelis both put a lid on the riots and concede the utter necessity to commit to an initiative. That initiative must of course emphasize security and recognize joint and mutual claims of equity. Trading land for security is too glib a formulation, though it is as feasible an assumption to contemplate as evidently exists. But no matter who says what in the region, keep in mind that neither Jordan nor Syria is keen to see an independent Palestinian state emerge to jostle the precarious arrangements of present sovereignties.

Probably the only eventual direction of a compromise would be total demilitarization of the West Bank, or a significant portion thereof, with local autonomy and shared security with Jordan, which is part of the fragile U.S. proposal. If such an equation is at all possible, it isn't going to be fashioned rapidly. Camp David only works once. And an international conference, as Henry Kissinger wrote recently, is likely only to provide a forum for the parties to "exhibit their incompatibilities"—and permit the Soviets entree to the Middle East and opportunity to create destabilization, St. Gorby's peaceful protestations to the contrary notwithstanding.

The Palestine Liberation Organization will be a fanatic opponent to any compromise prospect, as it is to Israel's existence. But the Israelis must mobilize their immense ingenuity and courage to fashion a reasonable accommodation with the Palestinians in the West Bank and Gaza despite the PLO and despite the implacable hostility of much of the Arab world.

That is the moral burden a democratic society must bear. And if not now, when?

TV's Incomplete Picture

by Mortimer B. Zuckerman

Television loves action. It is focusing often these days on the action in Gaza and the West Bank. When Israeli soldiers swing clubs among rioters, TV news gets a lot of what it likes best—great moments. They shock the viewer; they compel attention. When action is the essence of the story, as it is most simply in something like a sports event or an earthquake, the moments can add up to a truth. In the West Bank and Gaza riots, the moments have added up to a lie.

Television has polluted the public debate because it is inherently difficult for pictures to give context, history and meaning to events. It is asking too much for pictures in a half-hour news program to summarize 40 years of the history of Israel, or the history since 1967 or since the Yom Kippur War, or even the history that forced Israel to occupy the West Bank and Gaza. Words are necessary. The disturbing feature of the TV reporting of the West Bank and Gaza is not only that the words have been inadequate; some of them have been inflammatory. They have compounded the lie.

I refer in particular to the reporting by ABC television last month and its comparison of the Gaza uprising to riots in South Africa, suggesting an odious moral equivalency between the two. There is a superficial resemblance in Israeli soldiers swinging clubs and South African police swinging clubs, between disenfranchised blacks and West Bank Arabs without full political rights in their own land. But these are facile comparisons. It is the job of journalism to take such comparisons as a starting point, not a conclusion. And the conclusions in comparing Israel and South

Africa are dramatically different in substance from those that have been suggested by the TV images.

Israel is an open democracy, the only one in the Middle East, and it is being made to suffer for that. Even though the TV pictures are doing it damage in world public opinion, it has not closed its borders, deported journalists and imposed the kind of censorship South Africa has imposed.

For ABC to compare the Arabs of Gaza and the West Bank to blacks in South Africa is not only unfair but ignores history and reality. The blacks in South Africa are an overwhelming majority whose rights are denied. By contrast, the Arabs within Israel have full political and civil rights. (The exception: They cannot serve in the Israeli military.) It is only the Arabs in Gaza and the West Bank who lack these rights, because they are subjects of a military occupation as the result of a war in which the Arabs tried to destroy the very state of Israel. It is because of this threat to Israel that Israel must curtail their political rights. By contrast, the blacks want to be full partners in South Africa. In South Africa, the white government refuses to negotiate with the blacks; in the West Bank, it's the Arabs who refuse to negotiate directly with Israel. The blacks are oppressed because of the color of their skin; Zionism rejects racial superiority and indeed was founded in response to discrimination in the West. The blacks in South Africa have not stated their intention to drive the whites into the sea; the PLO leadership has proposed such an end for the Jews. Unlike the South African blacks, the Arabs of Gaza and the West Bank have an alternative. They suffer—and no one denies that they suffer—because they and their leaders have made a choice. This is the crux of the matter, and it requires spelling out a little.

The choice they have made is not to live in peace with Israel. They want the Jewish state to disappear, whatever its boundaries. A recent poll of the Palestinians in the West Bank by *Al Fajr* found 17 percent of the inhabitants favored the establishment of a Palestinian state in the West Bank and Gaza Strip—but 78 percent wanted a Palestinian state in what is now Israel. In their more conciliatory public statements, the PLO leaders now reject the idea of driving the Jews into the sea and would permit the Jews some kind of role in a future "secular and democratic Palestine." But in their charter, in their writings and in their speeches, their demands are not only for the areas Israel conquered in the war of 1967 but for the end—and often the violent end—of Israel as a political entity.

Both the PLO and its more extremist wings have taken or threatened to take the lives of Palestinians who want to negotiate. Today's TV images do not recall the 1983 assassination of Issam Sartawi, a PLO member and leading advocate of reconciliation with Israel, whose murder by extremist Palestinians became symbolic of the systematic assassination of conciliatory Palestinians.

So what the Palestinians have is a political leadership in the PLO that has consistently blocked any attempts at peace with Israel since 1948, when the Arab states refused to accept the United Nations plan for the partitioning of Palestine. Intransigence continued up to 1967, when Israel pleaded with Jordan's Hussein not to enter the fighting. After the 1967 War, Israel was prepared to give back the West Bank and Gaza for peace. The war was in June; in September, the Arab states met in Khartoum and issued the famous three "Noes": "No peace, no recognition and no negotiation" with Israel. To this day, the Arab leadership continues to be unwilling to talk directly with Israel or to risk the realistic political compromise that would relieve the lot of the Palestinian people. Israel is forced to rule over the Arabs largely because these Arabs have left no other choice.

It is easy enough to say there is a simple choice: that Israel should walk away from the occupied territories in the hope that this gesture would produce enough Arab good will for peace. History and geography counsel against such a gamble. There is a greater likelihood that Arab extremists would use these territories as a terrorist base that would ultimately constitute a threat to Israel's very existence. Look at the map, as Israel's soldiers say. To drive from the Jordan River of the West Bank to Tel Aviv on the Mediterranean takes about 90 minutes. If Israel abandoned the West Bank, a Jordanian or Palestinian Army would be about 10 miles from Tel Aviv—as close as Bethesda, Md., is to the White House. Even if the West Bank were demilitarized like the Sinai, an Arab army could cross the river in the afternoon and control the ridges overlooking Tel Aviv by the same evening, well before Israel's citizen army would have time to mobilize. The unacceptable risk is that this territory could be a source of destabilization not only for Israel but even for Jordan itself. Jordan, being 60 percent Palestinian, would be threatened by a militantly Palestinian West Bank—a threat King Hussein is known to recognize.

No wonder Israel argues against the simple idea of exchanging territory for peace. The reality is that Israel will stay on the West Bank for a long time even though its presence there will continue to be challenged. Many Israelis and others view that prospect with grave misgivings. Violence will continue at some level, though probably not the kind of unrelenting civil war some predict. But whatever the problems and tensions, they can be endured because the real alternatives are worse.

It is necessary for statesmen, and especially the Arabs, to focus less on the future of the occupied territories and more on the future of the Arab inhabitants. During the years when Moshe Dayan was Minister of Defense in Israel, there was a policy of minimal Israeli intervention in Arab domestic matters that included the avoidance of provocation and the attempt to improve the standard of living. On balance, life measured in health, incomes and education has improved for the Arabs in the West Bank and Gaza compared with that of their fathers and grandfathers. Teddy Kollek, as mayor of Jerusalem, has demonstrated how a potentially hostile Arab population can be treated with respect and political skill, making it possible for this city to work for both Arabs and Jews—in ways utterly inconceivable in South Africa.

Israel should not be discouraged or panicked by reaction to the Gaza riots. Israel should continue quiet, confidential relations with Jordan in what has been called an "adversarial partnership," wherein both parties encourage the West Bank's residents to accept their status as Jordanian subjects in all civil matters, leaving the security issues of the territory under Israel's military control. Only in this way can Israel, Jordan and the West Bank Palestinians be assured that PLO extremists will not make the West Bank into another Beirut. Until there is a fundamental transformation of the political and ethnic hatreds in this area, this is the best hope among many lesser alternatives.

The question is not one of instant solution. There is none. To talk of one is to encourage expectations that can only be dashed by the historic enmities of that tragic region. The tragedy of glib comparisons to South Africa is that they incite the resentments of the viewers and stimulate the false hopes that there are simple solutions.

Violent Disobedience is an Act of War

by Mayor Edward I. Koch

As an American, I am concerned first and foremost with what happens in this country and what happens outside America that has an impact on our security. But, as a Jew, I am also concerned about what occurs in the land of my ancestry, Israel.

Because Israel's security has remained such a volatile issue for the past 40 years, American Jews find themselves in a quandary.

If they rush to the defense of Israel without giving careful thought to what they are defending, they convey a sense of blind trust in that nation's government, which itself has outspoken critics in Israel.

No government is immune from criticism, nor should it be. On the other hand, for American Jews simply to join in the chorus of criticism now being leveled at Israel by some who are well-intentioned and by others whose ideology has caused them to constantly oppose Israeli policies would make no sense.

I have a special affection for Israel, but I also try to remain objective. I believe it is in the national interest of the U.S. to support Israel because it is the only democratic country in the Middle East we can rely on.

Israel's current problems stem from the new strategy that Palestinians in Gaza and on the West Bank have adopted to obtain their political objective. That objective is to achieve a separate Palestinian state by casting Israel in an unfavorable moral light in the eyes of the world.

It is profoundly regrettable that the new strategy is achieving its desired results. Because while the goal of a new homeland may be acceptable, the violence which now propels the issue is not. Especially when Israel is forced to play the villain's role and Egypt, Jordan and Syria are let off the hook.

Those countries have as much obligation to help break the impasse as anyone. Yet they do nothing to help their Arab brethren in the territories.

There is an important difference between violent insurrection and non-violent civil disobedience. The latter cannot be lightly dismissed, nor should it be suppressed by force. Those who engage in non-violent disobedience expect to be arrested and hope to shame those in power into making changes.

Those who engage in violent disobedience, particularly people who live in an occupied zone captured in war—as in Gaza and the West Bank—are in a different situation. Such violence is seen simply as a continuation of war—in this case, of the war that ignited the Arab-Israeli conflict 40 years ago, with the goal of destroying Israel and driving the Jews into the sea.

If the Israeli government allows the rioters to succeed, it will lose in the streets what it won on the battlefield. Thus, it uses whatever force is necessary to keep the rioters from winning.

The situation is complicated by the power of the international press corps, in particular television. Street violence provides 30 or 45 seconds of news that's tailor-made for the camera.

Israel is a democratic country with a free press. There is some limited censorship on matters involving national security. But you'd never know it from reading the print media and watching television.

Selective news coverage of the Palestinian street violence creates the false impression that Israel is an oppressive society. A case can be made that by allowing television to cover every violent confrontation in Gaza and the West Bank it promotes further confrontation and is a disservice to peace.

Edwin Newman talked on a recent Ch. 13 program about the impact of TV on current events. He noted that when Iran took American hostages, the mobs would chant in the language of the countries where the report was to be shown that night on television—in English for the American TV crews, in French for the French viewers.

In other words, the mobs tailored their actions and rhetoric to the TV crews taping them. This is not news. This is acting.

The Israeli government should seek to work with producers and correspondents to reduce provocations caused by the presence of cameras. TV journalists should be cautioned to exercise great care not to manufacture or aggravate confrontations. More sensitive TV coverage will make rational discourse more likely.

Arab boys with slings are trying to kill or injure Israeli soldiers or Israeli citizens, and have done so. The victims of Arab violence are only occasionally shown.

CBS's "48 Hours" was very impressive in its fairness. Two scenes left a lasting impact on me.

One was of an Arab, face covered with headdress, advancing on an Israeli soldier with a stick in his hand. The Israeli soldier with a gun in his hand retreated. I thought, he is undoubtedly retreating because there is a TV camera focused on the scene. And the Arab is advancing because he knows the soldier will retreat because the camera will record the confrontation.

I think the soldier erred and should have used whatever force was required to subdue the stick wielder.

The retreat reinforced the belief that Israeli soldiers will be shamed and stop fighting back. I don't think they will, and I don't think Israelis should be subjected to insults and slander by ideologues who denounce them for defending themselves.

Indeed, most criticism of Israel is laced with hypocrisy. Where were the defenders of human rights when Syria crushed an insurrection in the city of Hama, killing a reported 20,000 people? Were there protests in the U.S., sanctions against Syria? No. Only silence.

More recently, Moroccan security forces suppressed a demonstration of 2000 university students in Fez, leaving three dead, 80 wounded. At a similar demonstration at Yarmouk University in Jordan, military action left at least 8 students dead.

Who in the West even knew, let alone raised a voice in protest? Were these Arab lives worth less than the lives lost in demonstrations against Israel?

A second scene in "48 Hours" showed a correspondent interviewing a group of Arabs. He asked if the troubles could be solved by Israel leaving Gaza and the West Bank.

The answer was "no." The Arabs said that Israel cannot exist. They said all land from the Mediterranean to the Jordan is

45

Arab land. They were repeating, in effect, the PLO "covenant" which says all Jews who came to Palestine after 1917 had to leave.

Those interviewed were very clear that they believe the street violence is part of a fight to the death.

So what should Israel do? I believe it must continue to meet force with force.

Israel is Subjected to a Double Standard

by Mayor Edward I. Koch

One recent Sunday, I took the time to go through the Sunday papers from cover to cover. As I read the stories concerning the troubles in Israel, it struck me that Israelis have every right to believe they are being subjected to a double standard by the world press. They see their actions in the occupied territories of Gaza and the West Bank—those that are totally defensible and those that are not—attacked daily on television screens and on the front pages of newspapers. The coverage seems intended to harass and intimidate them, to get them to change tactics and comport themselves in a manner acceptable to columnists and editorial writers.

In the same news columns were many stories from other countries, where brutality is the order of the day. The articles were small, non-judgmental, and not even critical of the brutal events in those countries. They simply presented the facts.

For example, a March 5 article stated that "hundreds of Moscow youth battled each other with sticks and iron bars in a street fight last month and 18 people were arrested. But the Moscow police denied local rumors that ten people had been killed or seriously injured in the brawl Feb. 20."

Does anyone believe the Soviet press is telling us exactly what happened in that incident? Are there any television cameras covering that incident and reporting it on our screens?

Do we see television reports on the bloody clashes in Soviet Armenia and Azerbaijan? The Soviets say dozens of people were killed and injured. We can't be sure of the actual death toll because there was no independent press coverage or television reporting from the scene.

Another story that received little attention came from Prague: "The Communist authorities rounded up human rights advocates on the eve of a Catholic pilgrimage aimed at pressing for greater religious freedom in Czechoslovakia, dissidents said today. Thirteen people were arrested, including the playwright Vaclav Havel and the Charter 77 human rights movement spokesman, Stanislav Devaty. Six others were briefly detained."

That is the entire article. Was there anything on television about this incident? I don't recall seeing it.

Also from the Sunday papers: "In Sri Lanka a Tamil rebel mine killed 19 Sri Lankans and wounded 17 today in the Trincomalee district, military officials said." That same article states that the Tamils "shot to death 14 Sri Lankans and a Tamil last Wednesday."

Does anyone believe that the Sri Lankan government reported all of the killings taking place on that island? Do we know what the Indian Army—which is not exactly known for its benign attention to human rights—is doing in response? Has any of this violence been reported on television? I don't recall seeing it.

In the same news section was this article on Korea: "Hundreds of protesters demanding the release of political prisoners today threw rocks and firebombs at policemen, who responded by firing tear gas to disperse the crowd."

Not long ago, scenes of anti-government street violence in Korea were being shown nightly on American television. Rocks and firebombs were thrown at Korean policemen. Clouds of tear gas drifted through Seoul. Confrontations of this kind make compelling segments on the evening news. A sort of symbiotic relationship develops between the demonstrators and the television reporters. The reporters get dramatic footage for network news programs. The demonstrators get exposure for their cause. Television coverage of the Korean riots helped pressure the administration in power into holding an election. When the opposition lost the election, American television coverage stopped. Are there now fewer assaults by the Korean cops on students, or by students on the cops? We don't hear much about Korea these days because our television newsrooms have decided it wasn't interesting anymore.

One paper carried a news article on Africa. The opening line read: "The arrests and unrest last week in the wake of Senegal's elections were another reminder of the continuing decline of Western-style democracy in Africa."

Do you recall stories about Senegal's problems in the press? Have we seen the arrests and unrest on television? In fact, one-party government is becoming commonplace throughout Africa. Generally, that means small tribes are being assaulted and their rights reduced. Do we see such events covered in the press? Do we see them on television? I don't think so.

Have we seen reports on what the People's Republic of China is doing to the Tibetans? A Sunday news article did mention that rioting broke out in Lhasa on March 5. The article went on to say: "The outbreak of violence is apparently the first anti-Chinese disturbances since three violent protests in October in which at least a dozen people were killed, some by Chinese policemen who fired automatic weapons into crowds of Tibetans."

I don't remember seeing that on television. Do you?

Focus on Arab Protesters Misses the Point

by Yoram Ettinger

The process of selecting what the readers read involves not just objective facts but subjective judgments, personal values and, yes, prejudices. Instead of promising All the News That's Fit to Print, I would like to see us say—over and over, until the point has been made—that the newspaper that drops on your doorstep is partial, hasty, incomplete, inevitably somewhat flawed and inaccurate.
     —Journalist David Broder in his book *Behind the Front Page*

In light of David Broder's candid assertion, one may examine the recent focus, by the media, on teen-agers and women ostensibly dominating the unrest in Judea and Samaria (also known as the West Bank) and the Gaza Strip. Being relatively unfamiliar with the political scene in the Mideast, much of the media have failed to note the cardinal role played there (e.g. Iran, Lebanon, Egyptian campuses, etc.) by youth and women in the process of mob mobilization—fomenting violence, recharging revolutionary zeal, and the diversion of attention away from the identity and objectives of the behind-the-scene instigators.

These elements have also featured prominently in the production of excitement and unconventional scenes eagerly sought after by the Western media, so conveniently exploited by the orchestrators of violence throughout the Mideast (the takeover of the U.S. Embassy in Tehran, the hijacked TWA plane in Beirut, etc.) and of the unrest in Gaza, Judea and Samaria.

In fact, by and large the media have tended to romanticize the subject, conveying an impression that Israel is challenged by

51

a bunch of daring boy scout-like youths employing reasonable, desperate means to gain civil rights, political freedom and peace.

Does the public get a fairly complete and accurate perception of the role played by the rioting teen-agers? Does the media's focus on the youth of the rioters advance comprehension of the motivation and intent behind the unrest? It is the sort of distinction herpetologists would know about: they have to be wary of deadly coral snakes, which look much like harmless skipjack snakes. Both share similar colors, but there is a lot of difference.

In their attempt to dramatize the story, to draw moral and idealistic conclusions from the unrest, and to partake in the shaping of foreign policy, some of the media have ignored the extracurricular activities of these would-be modern-day Davids. For instance, the director of Nasser Hospital in the Gaza Strip and his deputy were brutally assaulted (the latter losing a leg and an arm when hit by a grenade) by local youth condemning their joining Israeli doctors in the treatment of wounded Palestinians. They would rather generate false rumors about Israeli brutality, which would in turn fuel the machine of violence. A "collaborator" was lynched in the village of Qabatiyya, and many "non-cooperating" Palestinians are systematically intimidated and terrorized by youthful gangs.

Such violence is consistent with the agenda of PLO and Moslem fanatic youth movements. They engage in radical education and orientation and specialize in the arts of mob deployment, incitement of violence, and assembling bombs and Molotov cocktails.

A Texas colloquialism says, "The roosters crow, but the hens deliver the goods." Examining the hens that deliver the goods (while the youthful roosters crow in Gaza, Judea and Samaria) sheds light on the nature of the unrest and its regional context.

There are five major fanatic Moslem organizations activating the demonstrators. Their steps are severely restricted in Jordan and in Egypt. Some (the Islamic Decency Association) are connected with the murderers of Egyptian President Anwar Sadat; others (al-Salfiyyun) are involved in the attempts to topple the Saudi regime through violent means, while the Islamic Jihad regards Khomeini as its role model.

Their common denominator is the rejection of Western culture, modernity and political order; the pursuit of revolution rather than evolution in the resolution of conflicts, and in the replacement of secular Arab regimes by Islamic republics; the inadmissibility of a Jewish—or *any* non-Moslem—state in the Mideast, and the activation of the Jihad (holy war) until the liquidation of any such state is achieved.

The focus on the age and sex of the demonstrators has also concealed their connection with the PLO and its Shabiba youth movement. It has allowed their behind-the-scenes leaders to perpetrate violence unchecked, unexposed and unaccountable, and has clouded the impact of the unrest on the peace process. Thus, PLO ringleaders have intimidated Palestinians lest they meet with Secretary of State George Shultz during his October 1987 and March 1988 visits to the area. The PLO has claimed responsibility for a car bomb intended to kill Shultz and deto-nated by the Israeli police. Furthermore, 429 Palestinians were killed and 3,110 injured by the PLO during 1967-1986.

The actual intent and character of the demonstrators—armed with Molotov cocktails, homemade bombs, knives, dag-gers, iron bars and rocks—may be seen through a study of the daily leaflets distributed by the ringleaders of the unrest—leaflets that have determined the pace and shape of the riots. A Jan. 15 PLO leaflet reads: "... Kill and fight with anything that comes to hand: a knife, a stone, a Molotov cocktail... for the dowry of Palestine is bought with blood...."

One may conclude that the unrest in the area does not constitute a cry of outrage against the failure to resolve the conflict with Israel. Rather, it is a cry of outrage against the *existence* of Israel, and against those who attempt to bring about coexistence.

(Mis)Perceptions Shape Views of Israel

by Yoram Ettinger

Some friends of Israel might be tempted to use that candid assertion by *Washington Post* Associate Editor David Broder in his book *Behind the Front Page* to castigate the news media for their portrayal of Israel as the aggressor in the current disturbances in Judea and Samaria (often referred to collectively as the "West Bank") and the Gaza Strip. However, rather than resort to ill-advised charges of media bias, it is better to examine certain perceptions and misperceptions affecting the molding of public opinion and the formulation of policy that have been recently perpetrated by some of the media.

For instance, conventional (mis)perception implicates Israel as the party responsible for the distressing poverty in the refugee camps, which in turn is supposed to nurture the current riots. However, almost unnoticed went a U.N. General Assembly resolution last Oct. 30 "reiterating strongly its demand that Israel desist from the removal and resettlement of Palestinian refugees in the Gaza Strip...."

That annual condemnation—approved initially in 1971—expresses U.N. disenchantment with a 1970 Israeli initiative attempting to eliminate the squalor and misery that have been institutionalized in the refugee camps ever since their establishment in 1949 by the U.N., Egypt (in Gaza) and Jordan (in Judea and Samaria). In fact, it is the U.N. Relief and Work Agency (UNRWA) that still administers the social, educational and economic environment of the camps; Israel's authority is limited to the security aspect alone.

The Israeli initiative consists of nine housing projects—including infrastructures of water, electricity, sewage, roads,

55

health clinics, schools and mosques—built outside the camps for some 10,000 refugee families. That the initiative earns a positive response from some of the refugees has been most impressive in view of repeated U.N. denunciations, brutal Arab pressure and a systematic campaign of intimidation and terror against the refugees by the Palestine Liberation Organization and Moslem fanatics lest the refugees acquiesce to the Israeli "conspiracy." Such opposition apparently stems from concerns that alleviating personal plights may deprive radicals and terrorists of an instrument that fuels the machine of violence.

The (mis)perception of Israel as an aggressor was reinforced following its decision to expel a few of the leading organizers of the recent disturbances. Observing the volume and the tone of the resulting protest, one would think the personal freedom of Mother Theresa-like human rights activists was at stake. Actually, the current expulsion saga evolves around some senior operatives whose record is much closer to that of Jack the Ripper.

All of them are veterans of planning and execution of terrorism and incitement on behalf of the Moslem fanatics and the PLO. They are intimately connected to elements responsible for hijackings and mid-air bombings of planes and for systematic intimidation and killings of innocent bystanders. Their colleagues have frequently been deported—for justifiable security reasons—from Egypt, Tunisia and Jordan. (Yasser Arafat's first deputy, Abu-Jihad, was deported from Amman, along with many of his lieutenants in July 1986.)

However, no condemnation by the U.N., Western media, or policy makers followed those expulsions. Unlike their colleagues deported by Arab regimes, those expelled from Israel have recourse (while still in the country) to a judicial consultative committee and then to the Supreme Court.

Long before expulsion, they had been warned by the authorities, then (when the warnings were ignored) placed under administrative detention, sentenced to various prison terms—including life imprisonment (when the fomenting of violence continued)—and then released on condition that they refrain from engaging in subversive activities, a condition they violated repeatedly.

Contrary to common (mis)perception, Israel's major concern in activating expulsion as a last resort is deterrence rather than punishment. At stake is the safety of the population in the area, rather than any satisfaction that might be derived from severe retributions, such as capital punishment or life imprisonment, which could be applied against the instigators. International law-watchers may note that, according to the Geneva Convention, the Jordanian law—which allows for expulsions—should be adhered to in Judea and Samaria.

Misperceptions add fuel to the fire in an already unstable reality. Thus, a misperception is formed by focusing on the rather young ages—rather than on the actions—of some of the demonstrators who throw Molotov cocktails, homemade bombs, iron bars, knives and rocks at civilians and soldiers. It certainly dramatizes the story; it also tends to draw moral and ideological conclusions. But is it relevant? Is it constructive?

The ancient Greeks would not allow children to partake in their famous plays, lest emotions prevail over logic in observation of the play. Is a Molotov cocktail lobbed by a teen-age demonstrator less lethal than the one used by an adult? Are the demonstrators involved in a human rights sit-in or in a riot with the intent to injure and kill?

Teen-agers and women have been used as a political tool of convenience in the attempt to cloud the ideological identity of the major instigators (the PLO and fanatical Moslem ringleaders) involved in the unfolding drama in the Gaza Strip, Jordan, and Samaria. They have also been employed by the instigators in an attempt to disguise the underlying goals of the current disturbances.

The PLO has been known to exploit this technique in its subversive activities in Lebanon and Jordan, especially during periods of drastic decline in its political fortunes. Thus, experiencing a low ebb following its July 1986 semi-expulsion from Jordan, the November 1987 Arab Summit and the December 1987 Reagan-Gorbachev Summit, the PLO is once again trying to revive its political stock at the expense of Palestinian lives.

Iran's Ayatollah Ruhollah Khomeini, just like the Moslem fanatics in Gaza, has realized the potential of teen-agers as an emotionally recharging instrument in the attempt to maintain the religious and military zeal of his troops. Are the Iraqis to be condemned for firing at the assaulting Iranian teenagers?

The responsibility for the killing of some demonstrators does not lie with those who are torn between the need to ensure public safety and the equally critical need to avoid casualties, which escalates violence. Rather, it lies with those who exploit them for violent political ambitions.

A basic misperception has been perpetrated by those who depict Israel as being short on resilience in the face of violence, and low on patience in view of the absence of an Anwar Sadat-like Arab leader willing to stick his neck out in order to advance the chance of peace.

Furthering such misperceptions may add to the drama of news presentations. However, it may feed the forces who believe in their ability to defeat Israel through violence; it may undermine moderate elements who subscribe to political negotiations as a means of resolving conflicts; and it thus may result in a setback to the cause of stability.

American Journalists Defend the Media Message

by Judith Colp

Washington journalists and columnists agree that in the past month and a half, the intense media coverage of the violence in the West Bank and Gaza has seriously eroded Israel's image, portraying Israel as a brutal occupying power instead of as an underdog surrounded by enemies. Yet the recently interviewed journalists disagree about how fair the coverage has been.

"The great danger is that it is the Palestinians who are being shown day after day after day after day as victims of the Israeli Jews," said Ted Koppel, anchorman of ABC's Nightline, in an interview with Shimon Schiffer, Kol Israel Washington correspondent, broadcast recently in Israel. "Victims of strong young men carrying weapons, some of them in armored personnel carriers, some of them in jeeps, firing bullets against a crowd of people who appear to be armed with nothing more than rocks. Those images are doing incredible—and I'm afraid long-lasting—damage to Israel."

Washington Post columnist Richard Cohen voiced a similar view. In an interview with the *Washington Jewish Week*, Cohen said, "From the point of view of Israel it's been a bad story, because it's been a bad situation. Israel doesn't look good because Israel is an occupation power doing what occupation powers do, which is not nice, not pretty. If [people] don't like what Israel is doing, they ought to do something about it, rather than blaming it on *The Washington Post, New York Times,* or the networks. These things are really happening. They never had the same complaints when the violence was coming from the Arab side and

59

they showed Israeli women mourning their dead or shrieking. There isn't one rule for Arabs and another for Jews."

But Charles Krauthammer, a syndicated columnist and editor of *The New Republic*, called the coverage "extremely shallow" for not reporting the background causes of the Palestinian violence.

"I don't think it's been malicious," Krauthammer told this reporter. "It's just a question of trying to dramatize a story which is dramatic and making it more dramatic by simply showing the confrontation rather than any background. People just don't know about Gaza—that for 20 years, before 1967, the Egyptians prohibited the residents from working and traveling. Israel has given them that."

Krauthammer's magazine, *The New Republic*, noted that on Jan. 4 *The Washington Post* ran a front-page article headlined "Israeli Soldier Kills Palestinian Woman," while on the previous day, a massacre in Brazil in which state troopers may have killed a hundred protestors was relegated to a two-paragraph article on page 27. "It is not what you do, it's where you do it," ran the magazine's headline.

Wolf Blitzer, Washington correspondent for *The Jerusalem Post*, noted in a recent column that such intense news coverage is a result of Israel's giving journalists free access and the country's being of interest to American readers. He said the correspondents in Israel are veteran journalists who are not anti-Israel or anti-Semitic and who even Israeli officials acknowledge are doing their job.

"This very real double standard can be of little comfort to Israel and its supporters. It cannot conceal the short-and-long-term impact that the west bank and Gaza unrest is having on Israel's image in America, and that once very popular image cannot forever withstand the assaults without a serious erosion setting in. There are limits to the basically strong reservoir of support which has been generated for Israel in the United States over the years."

Win Meiselman, president of CAMERA (Committee for Accuracy in Middle East Reporting in America), a Washington-based organization that monitors press coverage of the Middle East, told the *Washington Jewish Week*: "The pictures are so powerful, if you play catch-up for the rest of the year you simply don't catch up." Meiselman called the networks "unscrupulous in presenting a one-sided picture" of events in the west bank and Gaza.

CAMERA also noted problems in newspaper coverage and pointed to a *Washington Post* story headline: "Israeli Police Storm Temple Mount." The fact that the raid was precipitated by protestors' attempting to drag an Israeli policeman into the mosque was not made explicit, Meiselman said. "The headline just as easily could have read Israeli policeman pulled into mosque," said Meiselman.

Washington Post ombudsman Joseph Laitin said reaction to the newspaper's coverage of events in Israel "has been emotional," as it always is on Middle East issues. Callers have complained about the photographs and lack of historical perspective in articles.

"I can understand that an American Zionist would get upset at every day seeing a picture of an Arab lying on the sidewalk with an Israeli soldier," said Laitin.

Koppel, in his Kol Israel interview, denied media coverage in Israel has been purposely slanted. "The American media has always been tough when it sees what it perceives to be injustice," he said. "It was very tough on the Johnson administration and the Nixon administration [during Vietnam]. I have no embarrassment and I have no constraints about criticizing Israel since I felt no embarrassment and no constraints about criticizing my own country....

"The Israelis make a mistake when they confuse the source of the violence, the source of the frustration, the sources of the anger with the presence of outside television cameras. We are a convenient tool that is used by some of the enemies of Israel right now just as we have been used as a tool by the enemies and friends of the United States. Everybody tries to use and misuse television."

Three Eyewitness Accounts

Debi Ledeen:
There is enough news taking place in Israel today but some journalists don't seem to feel that way. They have to stage their own to get "just the right picture."

Such an event occurred recently in the Gaza strip. What began as an organized tour of the strip by the Israel Defense Forces Spokesman's office turned into an attempt to stage a stone-throwing session using some Arab teenagers. There are enough real stones thrown at members of the IDF stationed in Gaza; there is no need to ask youngsters to "pretend."

On Sunday, Feb. 7, a small group of reporters was taken on morning rounds with members of the Givati Brigade.

Two months had passed since the "disturbances" began, and according to pamphlets distributed among the residents the day was declared one of strikes and demonstrations.

At 8:30 a.m. our group hopped into jeeps and trucks along with bleary-eyed, hungry soldiers, some of whom were finishing their breakfast. Right away one of the trucks carrying two reporters from Kol Israel radio was diverted to a trouble spot. Those of us who were in the jeeps continued deeper into the city itself. Burning tires could be seen on several occasions, as well as rocks and other debris in the street. A Molotov cocktail had been thrown at a jeep earlier and the soldier displayed it—he had managed to catch it before it ignited.

But all in all it seemed relatively quiet. Children in school uniforms were seen walking through the streets. All the stores were closed due to the general strike, but many Gazans had left early in the morning for work within Israel.

From a lookout high above the city we could see children playing in a school field and women hanging out their wash: a bit of normality in an otherwise abnormal situation.

But the calm was broken. Because of a call on the radio, our tour was abruptly terminated. Trouble was brewing in a section of the city and in one of the camps. The soldiers dropped us off and left quickly, the officer shouting instructions over his radio.

This reporter joined two correspondents from France. We headed into the city because, as one of the reporters said, "I've been here for days and have yet to see a stone thrown."

The Frenchman spotted some idle teenagers on the side of the road and we pulled over. After a few words in Arabic, they donned their keffiyas and began setting rocks in the street—a makeshift roadblock. A moment later the youths, with stones in hand, were about to have their pictures taken when from down the street came two IDF patrols, their tear gas gun aimed in our direction. With shouts of "Don't take a picture," the gun was fired. The youths, however, were long gone; they must have felt the patrol was close by. Soon after the soldiers drove away, the youngsters returned, waving and smiling at us.

The tear-gas smell was horrid, but not as horrid as the event that had just taken place, the staging of violence merely for the sake of a picture.

World public opinion is affected by what is shown on television and written in the papers. But how can people formulate their own opinions if what they see is not really what is happening?

As a journalist myself, I can't help wondering how much of what we see is not helped along by the presence of the media.

Rabbi Yechiel Leiter:

I am an American, born in Scranton, PA, now living in Hebron, Israel, with my wife and young child. On Feb. 5, 1988 I was a victim of Arab violence.

On that Friday at 4 p.m., I was driving home from Jerusalem just before the Sabbath, along the Jerusalem-Hebron road. About a mile south of Bethlehem, I passed the Dehaishe Arab refugee district, which the road skirts on its way to Hebron, about 12 miles south. Israeli soldiers were patrolling the northern areas of the district.

Passing the southern section, I noticed an Arab boy about 14 years old standing next to a building beside the road. As my car approached, he gave a waving hand signal and immediately 10 or 12 youths roughly the same age rushed forward, hurling large rocks at my car. The rocks hit their mark. One crashed through and shattered the windshield, cutting my face in several places. Another hit me in the jaw. I carry a firearm with me in the car. Upon being hit, I got out of the car and fired shots in the air, causing my attackers to retreat. Then I noticed several adults in the background behind my attackers, egging them on and urging them to resume the stoning.

As I stood injured beside my car, within five minutes, maximum, there arrived on the scene three news crews in three cars. One car was marked "foreign press" and another "television." No soldiers were to be seen. They parked very close to me and emerged with television cameras. I stood in the road with blood streaming down my face, beside my car with its shattered windshield, and not a single newsman or cameraman approached to talk to me or inquire what had happened or offer assistance. Not a single camera was pointed in my direction. A passing motorist stopped and hailed some soldiers up the road. As the soldiers arrived, the stone-throwing youths returned, showing no fear and began pelting them with rocks as well.

The soldiers responded by firing tear gas and giving chase to the rioters. This was what the newsmen were waiting for. Cameras rolled, capturing for television viewers the familiar picture of well-armed Israeli soldiers chasing and firing at unarmed Palestinian youths. Unfortunately, as in my case, the Israeli victims of Palestinian violence—and there are many—are rarely, if ever, shown. When I returned to Hebron, I reported the incident to the police.

The press crews apparently knew that there was going to be a stone-throwing attack on that road and at that time. Otherwise, there is no way they could have arrived at the scene within a few minutes—even before the soldiers got there. They were simply waiting for the "news" to happen.

Ehud Yaari, quoted by Thomas L. Friedman:

"I was in Al-Amari refugee camp last week with a lot of foreign cameramen as well," said Ehud Yaari, Israel Television's Arab affairs correspondent. "Israeli soldiers were standing off at a distance, facing a big violent crowd of Palestinian demonstrators who were throwing rocks, bottles, Molotov cocktails. The following conversation took place between the cameramen and the Israeli officer in charge: The officer said, 'We are not going to go in. We are not going to do it for you.' And the cameramen said, 'You will have to go in, so you might as well do it now.' Everyone understood his role very well. Eventually the soldiers went in and as soon as they started breaking into homes to capture rioters who had fled, the cameras all started to roll."

The Mideast as Moral Disneyland

by Charles Krauthammer

Saul Bellow once wrote that the Middle East has become for the West what Switzerland is to winter holidays—a "moral resort area." It's high season now. With Palestinian rioting soon to enter its third month and Israeli attempts to suppress it becoming increasingly desperate, there has never been a better time for striking moral poses about the Middle East.

Woody Allen set the tone on *The New York Times* op-ed page last week. He wrote, "I'm not a political activist. If anything, I'm an uninformed coward." His mind inclines "to more profound matters: man's lack of spiritual center, for example—or his existential terror. The empty universe is another item that scares me, along with eternal annihilation, aging," etc. You think, you hope, that Allen is doing a parody of the self-obsessed neurotic. No such luck. "Now after months of quiet in my own life, another situation has arisen"—he refers here to his previous public stands against the twin evils of apartheid and colorization—"and a stand must be taken."

The artist's repose having been disturbed by nettlesome, if distant, Semites, he feels compelled to speak out. He addressed the Israelis: "I mean, fellas, 'Are you kidding? Beating of people by soldiers to make examples of them?'" Won't you cut it out? The man is trying to wrestle with God, make his movies, parent with Mia—and you disturb his domesticity with distressing pictures.

Since, writes Allen, "I prefer instead [of politics] to sit around in coffee houses and grouse to loved ones privately about social conditions," he has no suggestion to offer Israelis about either how more humanely to control Palestinian violence in the short run or how to escape the dilemmas of occupation in the long run.

That he leaves to others. Jonathan Schell once wrote a 244-page book describing in graphic detail how nukes make your eyeballs fall out and your skin melt and thus must be abolished. Exactly how? That "awesome, urgent" task, he wrote, "I have left to others." To his credit, Schell did follow up a couple of years later with an attempted solution. We await Allen's. In the interim, having made his courageous stand, he can return to his table at Elaine's.

At the other tables, the moral vacationers are deeply concerned about Israel's soul. There is great nostalgia for the Israel of yore, the noble, vulnerable Israel so suddenly beloved of its critics. The cover of the current *Economist* captures the mood perfectly. It quotes the prophet Hosea: "When Israel was a child, then I loved him."

Why loved then, not now? Because, as Oriana Fallaci once complained to Ariel Sharon, "You are no more the nation of the great dream, the country for which we cried." Israel as victim, Israel on the brink of annihilation was so easy to love. It required only pity and a handkerchief. It is, after all, no moral effort to love a charity case. "My goodness!" writes Woody Allen. "Are these the people whose money I used to steal from those little blue-and-white cans after collecting funds for a Jewish homeland?"

They are. What happened to them? Forty years of continual attack from every conceivable quarter: Arab armies, terrorists and now angry Palestinians over whom Israel never sought to rule, but for whom no one, other than those committed to destroying Israel, wants responsibility. Under these terrible circumstances, Israel has committed terrible sins: Sabra and Shatila being the worst, the beatings of Palestinians in the territories being the most recent.

The beatings are a horror and blot on Israel. They represent the kind of brutality a desperate army resorts to and for which there is no excuse. It is a relief to learn that Defence Minster Rabin has issued orders restricting the use of violence to stopping rioters in the act of rioting, and not otherwise.

It is perfectly legitimate to express revulsion at the beatings. And perfectly frivolous to stop there. For a moral critique to be serious, it must show concern for principle, not for parties. Serious ethics, like justice, is blind.

At a moral resort, however, it is not. So much concern for Israel's Jewish soul. Do Arabs, too, not have souls? When they prick, should our hearts not bleed? When the government of Syria killed 20,000 people in the 1982 Muslim Brotherhood uprising in Hama, where were the anguished editorials about the Arab soul? In 10 days in 1970, plucky little King Hussein killed 3,400 Palestinians in putting down a PLO uprising. (In the last two months about 40 Palestinians have died at Israeli hands.) No concern about the state of his soul. Or that of the Palestinians themselves. After Sabra and Shatila 400,000 Israelis turned out to protest. How many Palestinians protested the murder of the Israeli Olympic athletes?

A second characteristic of the moral vacationer is that he feels obliged to offer only indignation, not alternatives. No country can give free rein to rioters. Even an occupying power has an elementary responsibility to keep order. How to subdue rioters who know that the threat of death or deportation is almost nil? How to stop rock throwing and fire bombing without at least the threat of violence? Surely the police of New York and Paris don't know.

Israel's critics, so concerned about its soul, would have a little more credibility if they displayed equal concern for Israel's body. After all, it is that body—its right to mere existence—that has been the burning issue for 40 years now. Israelis don't crave the tears of the West's moral vacationers. They crave life. Any Arab negotiating partner who, like Sadat, fully declares that life to be an absolute given, will soon find across the table the kind of Jewish soul for which the moral nostalgics so ostentatiously pine.

Woody Allen in Black and White

by Micah Morrison

America's chief funnyman recently discussed some very unfunny business on the op-ed page of *The New York Times*. As usual, he wrote with self-deprecating wit and charm. Who else would begin a piece in the Paper of Record with the declaration that he was "an uninformed coward, totally convinced that a stand on any issue from subway fares to the length of women's skirts" would ultimately lead him "before a firing squad"?

Who else but Woody Allen? In "Am I Reading the Papers Correctly?" (January 28, 1988) Mr. Allen takes the reader on a short tour through the odd precincts of his moral universe. The essay was occasioned by the recent turmoil in Israel; in particular, by the Israel Defense Forces' use of harsh tactics to quell the disturbances.

Now, Mr. Allen would be the first to admit that he is no expert on the Mideast. Yet being those of one of our premier filmmakers, his words can fairly be said to have no less, if not more influence in shaping public opinion than, say, the familiar gallery of pundits and experts who lately have turned their attention to this new phase of a very old conflict. Evidence of Mr. Allen's influence on the climate of opinion—a thing itself almost impossible to define with precision—may be found in the fact that many television stations and newspapers around the country carried reports of his pained remarks.

Mr. Allen's article is interesting not simply as a demonstration of intellectual posturing but also for what it reveals about a certain type of easy moral indignation—the type, all too familiar these days, that makes a platform of outrage yet eschews the search for answers. At least Mr. Allen has the partially saving grace of viewing his condition of ponderousness and self-absorption with some degree of humor.

He is frank: he is "not a political activist" and would prefer "to sit around in coffee houses and grouse to loved ones about social conditions." He is "apathetic to political cross-currents" because he has "never felt that man's problems could be solved through political solutions." Whenever talk turns to "ameliorating mankind's condition," his attention shifts to "more profound matters: man's lack of a spiritual center, for example—or his existential terror." Or "the empty universe," or "eternal annihilation," or "aging," or "terminal illness," or "the absence of God in a hostile, raging void."

We get the picture. Not for Mr. Allen the grubby little realities of everyday politics at home or abroad—he is above all that, he is an Artist, concerned with the Philosophic Condition of Man. This retreat into pious generalities is of course a familiar gambit. Truth is in the details, as Mr. Allen surely knows, but then the particulars are often so bothersomely paradoxical.

Bowing to the tin gods of Alienation and Apathy, Mr. Allen hurries on to point out a few political landmarks that have indeed stirred his restless soul. These are the issues of movie colorization and South Africa. To be sure, Mr. Allen does not place the two issues on the same moral plane—but they intruded, he says, on the prized quietude of his life, and the urge to speak was upon him. On the matter of the colorization of black-and-white movies without the director's consent, Mr. Allen was "amazed" at the "lack of support" his position received. On South Africa, he was so "infuriated" by the treatment of blacks that he proclaimed he would not allow his films to be played there "until a total policy change" was agreed to. "This," he notes, "unfortunately failed to topple the existing regime...."

Still, it was a "gesture" and he hoped it would "stir others." And as a supporter of Israel, Mr. Allen felt is was necessary to make another "gesture" when Israel resorted to some extremely tough tactics—beatings—to stop Palestinians from attacking Israeli troops with knives, stones, and Molotov cocktails in the West Bank and Gaza.

Israel, of course, is in a no-win situation. Simply to withdraw from the troubled camps and cities would be to turn over control to Arab extremists who have no intention of living in peace with the Jewish state and who would soon set about murdering their less extreme brethren in battles for political control, until events turned their attention back to the matter of murdering Jews. Whatever actions the Israeli army takes—whether it is the use of live ammunition, or rubber bullets and tear gas, or physical intimidation—Israeli democracy allows the world to watch, and many people, including Mr. Allen, do not like what they see.

But image is not everything, and tragedy, after all, is tragedy precisely because certain facts have an inexorable logic. Israel's need to maintain control over the territories while waiting for a sane negotiating partner is such a fact; and so, tragically, is the simple truth that one usually survives a beating but usually does not survive a bullet in the brain. As *Contentions'* readers know, these are the hard truths that Israelis and Palestinians live with. Unlike Mr. Allen, who by his own account has only recently been roused from pleasant apathy (a condition, to judge from recent events, he shares with a good many Americans), Israelis and Palestinians know full well that they are in a life-and-death struggle—talk about "existential terror"!—and that the struggle between them can often turn, *has* often turned, cruel and evil.

Obviously, though, Mr. Allen had something to get off his chest—his own pain was the central subject of the essay, not the Palestinians', not Israel's. Naturally, he was not alone in this; the papers are full of the fulminations of armchair ethicists casting stones toward Jerusalem. Breastbeating and garment-rending might, however, be a tad more responsible if critics such as Mr. Allen paused to offer a contribution to resolving the tensions in the area, or at least a clear explanation of the roots of the dilemma, or perhaps simply a bit of sustained attention.

Alas, attention wanders, and apparently having survived his latest spasm of moral indignation Mr. Allen is now back in his favorite coffee house, sitting around and grousing to loved ones. Maybe that's where he truly belongs. On the other hand, maybe a two-week vacation in the Gaza Strip would provide him with striking subject matter for a new film about existential terror and other profundities so long in fashion among the shapers of contemporary culture.

II. POLITICAL CARTOONS

Drawing Lines

By Rebecca Kaplan Boroson

Political cartoons have been around since the stone age. And for good reason. A well-thought-out, cleverly drawn cartoon can point up flaws in actions, policy, personality, and ideology with an immediacy and verve that can't be matched by a page full of words.

And cartoons often communicate a wry slyness that makes you nudge your neighbor and say, "Did you see that? Did you see what Oliphant drew this week?"

But for all those reasons, and more, a political cartoon can be more damaging than that page full of words. Of necessity, it can show only part of the picture; though strictly speaking drawn in two dimensions, a cartoon can never be anything but one-dimensional. Whence comes it power—and its potential for doing ill.

We were distressed last week to see two shocking, distorted drawings on the disturbances in Israel's territories. One, by Don Wright, a Pulitzer Prize winner, was reprinted in *The Record* after having appeared in the *Miami News*. It was also syndicated to hundreds of papers across the country.

It showed a Star of David made of barbed wire, within which a miserable mass of people was confined. The caption was "THE PALESTINIANS."

A similar cartoon was reprinted in Sunday's *New York Times* Week in Review section. That one, by Ed Gamble, syndicated from *The Florida Times-Union* (Jacksonville) by King Features, the largest newspaper syndicate in the world, showed a figure—labelled and standing in for "PALESTINIANS"—caged by barbed wire and shackled. A big bully in a soldier's uniform is labelled "Israel." He carries a club and a rifle, as well as pouches of ammunition. He snarls at the imprisoned Palestinian, "You can't protest while we occupy your land!" In the background, another bullying Israeli soldier, poking a gun at Uncle Sam—let's say that again; poking a gun at Uncle Sam—says, "Is that clear?" Uncle Sam can only say "But... but... but... er... perfectly!"

These are reminiscent of the vicious cartoons common during the Deyfus affair, in which Jews were depicted by some of the most famous French artists, including Toulouse Lautrec, as groutesque and venal. Those who visited the recent Dreyfus exhibit could not help being struck and repelled by these cartoons which helped to inflame the French public against Dreyfus and against the Jews in their midst.

We're concerned that such cartoons as the ones appearing in the *Times* and *Record* could have a similar effect, that they will foster a cartoon state of mind, where history and background are ignored and only the most simplistic message is delivered.

Paul Johnson, the learned non-Jew who has compiled a most impressive one-volume history of the Jews, comments that, "One of the principal lessons of Jewish history has been that repeated... slanders are sooner or later followed by violent physical deeds." Yes, of course.

Israeli Flag

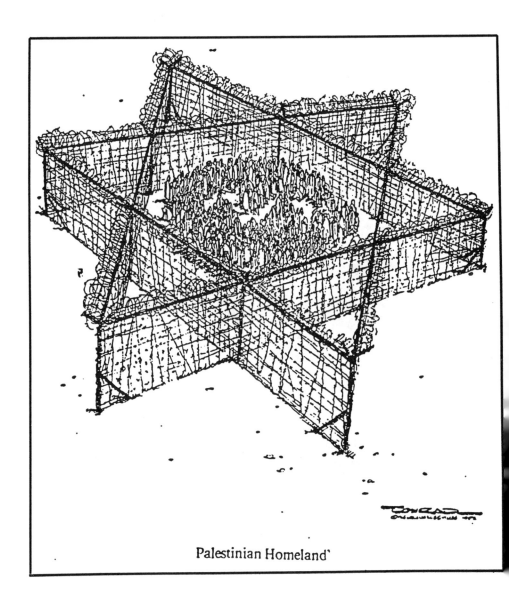

Palestinian Homeland`

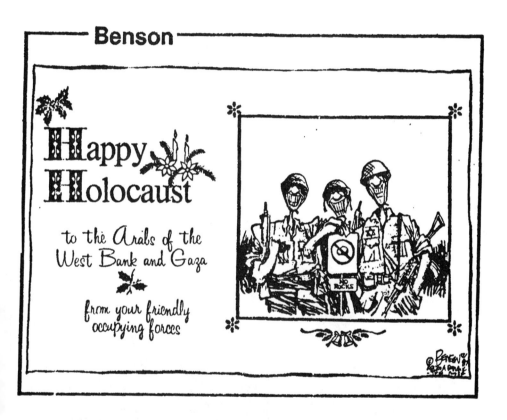

THREE MORE WERE KILLED YESTERDAY NEAR BETHLEHEM
IN CONTINUED VIOLENCE. – NEWS ITEM

Shamir and Waldheim

III. COVERAGE THROUGHOUT THE 1980's

INTRODUCTION

by Rael Jean Isaac

The issue of media bias toward Israel came to the fore in the summer of 1982. In reporting the war in Lebanon, the media behaved like a lynch mob, with print and TV reporters, columnists and cartoonists vying with each other in misstatement and calumny. The analogy of Israel to Nazi Germany became a familiar one.

The media performance was so execrable that several studies were published in response, documenting the pattern of misrepresentation. A most detailed account which analyzed the specific performance of major newspapers (*The New York Times* and *Washington Post*), the newsmagazines, and each major network was Joshua Muravchik's "Misreporting Lebanon." It appeared in *Policy Review. Commentary's* editor, Norman Podhoretz, titled his essay "J'accuse," evoking the powerful echo of Emile Zola's indictment of anti-Semitism in the Dreyfus affair. Similarly, the title of Edward Alexander's essay in the English journal *Encounter* summed up his theme: "The Journalists' War Against Israel: Techniques of Distortion, Disorientation and Disinformation." Martin Peretz, editor of *The New Republic*, went to Lebanon during the war and indignantly contrasted the media's portrait of massive destruction in southern Lebanon with his own eyewitness testimony.

There were also studies focussing on specific performances. There was agreement that NBC had been seized by an even higher degree of anti-Israel fervor than CBS and ABC. A film, "NBC in Lebanon," and a pamphlet, "NBC's War in Lebanon" by Edward Alexander, were sponsored by Americans for a Safe Israel. And because the *Washington Post* was more poisonous than the *Times*, Leonore Siegelman analyzed the *Post*'s coverage in "Did the *Washington Post* Tell It?" a pamphlet published by the Zionist Organization of America.

To be sure, disapproval of the media's performance was not universal. The media was well pleased with itself. The influential *Columbia Journalism Review* assessed the media's product during the war and concluded that American journalism "reported what it saw for the most part fairly and accurately and sometimes brilliantly, provided balanced comment, and provoked and absorbed controversy. For performance under fire, readers and viewers could have asked for little more."

Most American Jews were taken aback by the virulence of the media attack on Israel. There was a vague sense among Jews that media support for Israel had slipped considerably after the Yom Kippur War of 1973. *Time*'s bias was so glaring that it drew particular attention. Jews were shocked in 1977 when *Time* introduced the name of Menachem Begin, the newly elected Prime Minister of Israel, with the words "rhymes with Fagin." (There were no lack of other "rhymes *Time* might have used—how about "rhymes with Reagan?") Martin Peretz was sufficiently disturbed by *Time*'s pattern of distortion that in 1980, two years before the war in Lebanon, he asked this writer to do an analysis of *Time*'s coverage. This was duly published in *The New Republic* as "*Time* Against Israel." In analyzing *Time*'s coverage over a twenty year period, I found that coverage was reasonably balanced until 1970, tilted against Israel after 1973, and became venomous after Begin's election in 1977. While the post-1973 tilt was leavened with a certain disarming frankness about the impact of the oil weapon on changing the views of Israel's "friends," *Time*'s reporting after 1977 was equally distant from fairness and reality. Indeed, I devoted a section of the article to "*Time* vs. Reality" showing how frequently and blatantly *Time* departed from the facts in a randomly selected five week period. The departures from fact were in a consistent direction, designed to convince the reader that the PLO wanted peace and that Israel blocked a settlement.

If the American Jewish community had been less liberal politically, it might have been better prepared for the media onslaught in 1982. While little had been written about media bias specifically toward Israel, considerable attention had earlier been focussed on the media's bias toward the left. The Media Institute had chronicled the pattern of media bias against business and nuclear energy. Since 1972 Accuracy in Media has been publishing a bimonthly newsletter, *AIM Report*, documenting media misreporting on both domestic and foreign issues. The most detailed single study of media distortion was Peter Braestrup's massive two volume study *Big Story*, published in 1977. It dealt with the way the American press and television reported and interpreted the 1968 Tet offensive in Vietnam, converting a decisive defeat for the Communists into an American defeat.

Relatively few Jews were interested in these matters. Had the media misreported the Vietnam War? The war was long over and most Jews had been opposed to it anyway. The conservative outlook of most media critics prevented many Jews from taking the criticism seriously. And there was another factor: conservative groups concerned with media bias had neglected the subject of media bias against Israel. Indeed, the first time Accuracy in Media paid attention to this problem was during the Lebanon war when, to its credit, it came out with a hardhitting issue titled "Lies About Lebanon."

The upshot then was that for many Jews the media assault on Israel in 1982 seemed to come out of nowhere. Unaware of the pattern of hostility that had been developing over the years, many Jews initially accepted what they were being told in their newspapers and on their TV screens and blamed Israel.

The importance of Stephen Karetzky's study is multifold. First, it covers the months of February, March and April of 1982, in other words, a period *before* the war in Lebanon. This enables us to see how the pattern of distortion characteristic of news coverage prior to the war determined the way the war would be covered (and, one might add, how Israel has been covered since the war). Second, this study spotlights *The New York Times*, the most important and influential source of news in the United States. The *Times* is familiarly referred to as the bible of the media and it sets the news agenda of the electronic as well as the print media. (Russ Braley, a longtime foreign correspondent for the *New York Daily News*, reports his dismay when he was reassigned to New York and discovered that the night editor was required to listen to the *New York Times* radio station WQXR, at 9 p.m., when the next day's headlines are revealed, and then match every story on the *Times'* front page in at least a paragraph or two.)

The *Times* was treated too lightly in the exposes of media coverage of the Lebanon war. Joshua Muravchik wrote that the *Times*, "notwithstanding some notable lapses, maintained higher standards of journalistic objectivity than did any of the other news outlets covered by this study." But as Muravchik himself documents, the lapses were indeed notable. Bias was not merely apparent on the editorial page, where a stand against the war was legitimate, but on the Op-Ed page (where seventeen of the first nineteen essays on the war were hostile to Israel) and, most significantly, on the news pages. There were the familiar, wildly exaggerated casualty figures and a lengthy tribute to Yassir Arafat by Thomas Friedman which contained not a whisper of criticism. There was an endless stream of stories by Marvine Howe, many of them based on nothing but mere speculation: "growing fears" that Israel was planning a drive against Tripoli after it was through with Beirut, "fears" that the rights of PLO prisoners were not properly guaranteed, etc.

Muravchik dryly remarks that "Ms. Howe's reports gave the impression that she had travelled Lebanon looking for stories with an anti-Israel twist." In his hostility to Begin, the *Times'* Bernard Nossiter actually doctored his words. When Begin at the UN praised the "*right* of self-defense as the noblest concept of the human mind," Nossiter reported in the *Times* that Begin had called "*wars* of self-defense the noblest concept of the human mind." This made Begin sound wholly ridiculous. Far from correcting the statements, the *Times* repeated it the following day.

Professor Karetzky is forced to compare the *Times* with a range of other papers that were less biased on specific stories. For example, he finds that the *Washington Post* did a better job than the *Times* in reporting the slaying of two Arabs at the Dome of the Rock by a crazed Jewish gunman. Yet, overall, the *Post's* coverage of Israel is abominable, with some of the most anti-Israel reporters in the business employed there, including Loren Jenkins (who compared Israel to the Nazis in a *Rolling Stone* interview) and Jonathan Randal (whose animus led him to make such bizarre claims as that Sharon and Begin "gloried in the polarization of Israeli society produced by the Lebanese War"). Since the *Post* makes no effort to separate fact from opinion, the attitudes of its journalists strongly color its stories, even if its anti-Israel reporters make some of their most outrageous statements in other forums. In taking on the influential *New York Times*, Dr. Karetzky has made the right choice. He shows how poorly the best of our newspapers serves us.

Finally, Karetzky's study is important because it provides a model that can be used in studying other newspapers. He analyzes the ways in which papers can distort material: misuse of photographs, inappropriate use of sources, false analogies, misleading terminology, and so on. The reader can use these categories as a means of evaluating how a given newspaper performs on a specific issue.

What emerges from his study, as from the studies of media coverage of the war in Lebanon, is that Israel is judged by a double standard. Occasionally a reporter or columnist will be frank about this. For example, Anthony Lewis has written: "Yes, there is a double standard. From its birth Israel asked to be judged as a light among the nations." (To Anthony Lewis it is plain that the only light Israel emits is a hellish glare.) Or there is the ever-censorious (of Israel) Nick Thimmesch: "The media employs high standards to measure Israel... because Israel always claimed high standards for itself." It is true that Israel sets for itself a high standard of behavior. But this does not entitle journalists to set wholly different standards as *appropriate* to Israel and the Arab states, and to give Israel an "F" on the basis of one standard and Arab states an implied "A" on the basis of a totally different one or worse yet to apply *no* standard to Arab states. For example, just because brutality is to be expected from the Syria of Hafez al-Assad does not mean that journalists should shrug off as of no interest or consequence repeated demonstrations of that brutality, like the slaughter of thousands of civilians at Hama. In his book *Double Vision*, Ze'ev Chafets, former director of the Israeli Government Press Office, notes that what is really at work is a *double* "double standard." Israel is not simply judged on a basis that is inapplicable to her Arab neighbors. Israel is judged by standards more exacting than those applied to other democracies. Surrounded, beleaguered and attacked, Israel is nevertheless expected to behave like democracies *at peace.*

Karetzky documents the mechanisms of the double standard; he does not address the fascinating, if necessarily speculative, question "Why?" In the case of the *Times* there are specific historical factors that may have some bearing. The *Times* has remained the property of the Ochs family, which is of German Jewish Reform background, assimilated, and self-conscious regarding its Jewish origins. (Some of the family now style themselves "Oakes.") Both the German Reform background and the assimilationist attitudes have shaped the *Times'* views and attitudes toward Israel over the years.

As Russ Braley observes in *Bad News,* the first major study of the *Times'* misreporting of foreign events since the Suez Crisis of 1956, the Ochs family were so opposed to Zionism that in 1946 when Truman advocated that 100,000 survivors of the death camps be permitted to immigrate to Palestine, a *Times* editorial condemned Truman's interference in British affairs. In a commentary, James Reston dismissed the plight of Jewish survivors: "It is generally conceded in the capital that the plight of the Jews in Europe is only one aspect of the melancholy story of the displaced persons of Europe, of whom the Jews are a minority." Apparently it never occurred to Reston that the murder of six million Jews had something to do with their being a minority of the survivors and that this might entitle them to special attention in the "broader" context of displaced persons.

The anti-Zionism of the *Times* faded as Israel became an increasingly well-established fact, but the uneasiness with Israel remained, manifested, for example, in the care the *Times* took to avoid sending a Jewish correspondent to report from Israel. Chafets relates how, in 1979, *Times* executive editor A.M. Rosenthal proudly informed a meeting of the paper's editors that a new man had been assigned to Jerusalem and he was glad to report that the *Times* had become mature enough to send a Jew. The "Jew" was David Shipler—a WASP. Shipler's replacement, Thomas Friedman, *is* a Jew, "seasoned," to be sure, by his five-year stint in Beirut. (Of course, being Jewish has done nothing to mitigate hostility toward Israel; for example, second to none in his antagonism is Jonathan Randal, whose mother is Jewish.)

More significant in the long run, certainly for the tenor of the editorial page, is the tradition of liberal Jewish reform which still gives the *Times* its distinctive stamp. Daniel Patrick Moynihan attributes to that tradition the "universalist, even deracinated air" that marks the *Times* editorial page. It has been observed that if the United States had consistently followed the advice of the *Times*, it would probably no longer exist. But even if the U.S. could have weathered the almost consistently bad advice of the *Times*, there can be little doubt that Israel would no longer exist had she shown the perennial restraint and readiness to accommodate Arab demands urged upon her by the *Times* over the years. In the world of *Times* editorials, there are no irreconcilable conflicts or savage animosities. If the Arabs show fanatical hatred of Israel, then it is up to Israel, by undeviating good will, generous territorial and other concessions, and the saintly turning of cheeks, to set an example of reasonable behavior that the Arabs will feel impelled to emulate.

That the media performed so poorly during the war in Lebanon was owing to a set of specific circumstances. Since Israel swept quickly through southern Lebanon but remained for so long outside Beirut (intent on forcing PLO forces to leave the city), the focus of media attention for many weeks was the siege of Beirut.

Israel was inflicting death and destruction on the television screen, with all the suffering made immediately accessible to viewers. This inevitably worked against Israel. The PLO refused to leave the city and refused to allow civilians to leave, using them as hostages in the "media war" precisely because civilian bombing casualties made Israel look bad. But the Beirut-based reporters, who dominated coverage in this period, did not explain this to the American public. To understand why, one must understand that the reporters in Beirut were, on the whole, a special group.

Chafetz documents in *Double Vision* that reporters in Beirut were subject to a pattern of intimidation since the civil war of 1975. Murder and the threat of murder taught reporters to practice self-censorship and not send home stories unacceptable to either Syria or the PLO. Reporters uncomfortable with self-censorship found Lebanon an uncongenial post and were glad to find another assignment. Those who thrived in this atmosphere did not need to be intimidated because they identified with the PLO, seeing them as "progressive" heroes whose cause deserved support. These newsmen congregated at the Commodore Hotel in Moslem West Beirut. (Chafets reports the dismay at the ABC bureau in Beirut when it was learned that former ABC producer Barbara Newman, who had come to Lebanon in 1980 to film a documentary, was planning to stay at the Christian-run Alexandre Hotel in East Beirut. To ease the situation, the documentary's correspondent, Geraldo Rivera, booked rooms in both places and commuted from one side of the city to the other.) At the Commodore, newsmen interacted with one another, learning to engage in "group think."

Newsweek's Tony Clifton authored *God Cried*, perhaps the single most venomous book to be published by a U.S. newsman following the war. He throws considerable light on the process by which the news consensus was formed during the war. When the Israeli invasion began, the media rushed to the scene whatever hands they had available. Clifton, who has openly referred to the PLO as "our side," complains that reporters swallowed Christian "propaganda" and dispensed it as news. He notes that it took a few weeks before the "old hands," i.e. those who had covered the civil war, were sent to Beirut. The "old hands" of course were the pro-PLO hands.

One exception was Kenneth Timmerman, whose failure to toe the PLO line led to his "arrest" (French consular authorities eventually arranged a trade for his release). In an article in *Commentary* in January 1983, he observes that the PLO carefully screened journalists who were sent and "no newspaper or other medium would commit the error of sending in to West Beirut someone who had adversely reported in the past on the activities of the PLO or the Syrians, for fear of him simply disappearing." Ironically, the Western reporters in Beirut became actors in the drama, prolonging the siege and destruction. By acting as a PLO sounding board, the media fanned Arafat's hopes that Israel could be stopped by the pressure of public opinion, and that PLO forces would not have to leave the city.

The peculiar mind-set of the *Times* and the special circumstances in Beirut do not explain the pattern of anti-Israel bias that made itself felt after the 1967 war, growing worse after 1973 and worse yet after Begin's accession to power in 1977. Moreover, events in Israel, which these years demarcate, merely reinforced attitudes in the media whose source had nothing to do with Israel, its wars or its choice of Prime Minister.

The real explanation lies in intellectual trends in the West which led many—including a majority of the media elite—to elevate the Third World to a position of moral authority and to see Western democracies, especially the powerful United States, as colonialist-imperialist oppressors. Countries like Israel (that identified with Western political values) were seen as extensions of Western imperialism, while Third World countries (or groups within such countries) that struggled against the West were *ipso facto* virtuous freedom fighters. Moreover, an aura of inevitable success rested upon the insurgents, while the Goliaths of the West were doomed to military helplessness before those on the side of both morality and history, the Davids of destiny.

The conflict between Israel and the Arab states was reconceptualized in terms of these attitudes. Israel was seen as an extension of iniquitous Western power. The central role of the Arab states in the conflict, long taken for granted by the media, was now minimized. The PLO assumed center stage. Once defined as a terrorist organization, it was reinterpreted as a progressive movement of Third World liberation. The PLO was guilty of occasional "excesses" perhaps, but its goal of "national self-determination" and anti-Western credentials definitely put it on the moral side of history. The media dismissed as rhetoric the problem posed by the PLO's repeated insistence that Palestinian self-determination could only be built on the ashes of Jewish self-determination, effectively pretending that the PLO did not really mean what it said.

That transferring the role of "good guy" from Israel to the PLO gave freshness to reporting a stale conflict was no doubt a welcome plus. But beyond the attraction of fresh news copy, Israel and the PLO changed roles to conform to a broad new agenda that many in the media had embraced.

95

As the media increasingly assumed an adversarial posture on a host of issues, it began to see itself as a high court, sitting in judgment on the political realm. The publication of the Pentagon Papers by the *Times* was a watershed in the confrontation between the media and the political realm, changing the correlation of power between them. As Harrison Salisbury put it: "The *Times* has come to fulfill a new function; it has become that Fourth Estate, that fourth co-equal branch of government of which men like Thomas Carlyle spoke." As Braley notes in *Bad News*, the Pentagon Papers were but a prelude to the media's exercise of more formidable muscle. To quote Salisbury again: "One can imagine the Watergate break-in without the Pentagon Papers affair; one cannot imagine the Watergate exposé, the whole debacle of the Nixon presidency, without the Pentagon Papers."

This adversarial stance toward the political sphere, with the assumption of superior moral virtue and the taste of power, produced an immense arrogance in the media. Reed Irvine, who founded Accuracy in Media, told me that when he started the organization in 1969 he was convinced that research on media inaccuracies would force those responsible to admit errors, issue corrections, and be more careful in the future. Irvine ruefully observed that it did not work out that way. The media refuse to admit the most egregious mistakes, for if they have become a fourth branch of government, it is a branch which—unlike the others—is subject to no checks and balances, one which can behave irresponsibly without fear of consequences.

Increasingly, injured individuals, seeing no other recourse, have turned to the libel suit in the hope of forcing media accountability. The most dramatic recent suits have been those brought by General William Westmoreland against CBS and by General Ariel Sharon against *Time*. But U.S. libel law is so stringent as to make libel extremely difficult to prove. In *The New York Times v. Sullivan,* twenty years ago, the Supreme Court ruled that for a public figure to be "libeled" he or she must prove not only that the material published was defamatory and false, but also that the paper *knew* that is was false or published it with "reckless disregard" as to its truth. "Intent to defame" turns out to be almost impossible to prove conclusively. As a result, when juries have ruled that there was malicious intent, their verdicts have mostly been overturned on appeal. Indeed, barely one in four jury verdicts establishing libel have survived on appeal, judges ruling the jurors did not properly understand the law.

Given the often multi-million dollar price tags and the extremely remote chances of victory, why do cases continue to be brought? It is because the libel suit at least offers the opportunity to hold the media accountable in the court of public opinion. In the absence of any other mechanism to make the media accountable, only the libel suit forces the media to disclose for public scrutiny the way it collects information, the way it verifies it, and the way it edits—and edits out—what it gathers.

The Sharon case revealed that the much vaunted *Time* editorial procedures were a humbug. Steven Brill, editor of *The American Lawyer* and a civil libertarian who opposes all libel suits on constitutional grounds, has provided a long, detailed and devastating analysis of what the trial revealed of *Time's* procedures. In an "open letter" to *Time* editor-in-chief Henry Grunwald, Brill acidly observes that "it seems from the testimony of your own people that *Time* made up its story [about Sharon]— that's right, simply made it up." Brill studied not only the trial but the pre-trial record as well. (*Time* had tried to persuade the judge to dismiss the case prior to trial on a number of grounds, including the ploy that Sharon's reputation was so bad that he was "libel-proof.") On the basis of both studies, Brill concluded that the record "reveals an arrogant, bloated bureaucracy in which the reporter of the paragraph that Sharon is suing about is biased to the point of being a near-fanatic, your chief of correspondents isn't much of a chief and has a suspiciously selective memory when he's under oath, your managing editor (the supposed boss of *Time*) doesn't know much of anything about what goes on in his shop, your much-vaunted research department is a sham, and your system for weeding out unreliable reporters is nil." Brill wryly noted that "nobody ever admits a mistake about anything" during the whole sorry process.

Even if *Time* printed its story about Sharon believing it was true, a few days after publication *Time's* bureau chief in Israel, Harry Kelly, was told by Knesset member Ehud Olmert (at a dinner party) that *Time's* story was false. Olmert had seen the secret appendix to the Kahan commission report investigating the massacres at Sabra and Shatilla. (It was this document which *Time* claimed had details of Sharon's visit to the Gemayel family where he "discussed" the need "for revenge" for Bashir Gemayel's assassination.) Kelly asked Olmert to confirm this and make sure. Olmert did so and testified that he called Kelly and told him, "There is nothing in this that resembles your story." Kelly did not deny that these events took place, but in his deposition said he did not consider this to be "news." In other words, a false story was "news." Indeed, *Time's* public relations department felt it had such a "scoop" that it circulated a press release to accompany the story. It claimed that Sharon had "urged" the Lebanese to send Phalangists into the camps. But evidence that a *Time* feature story was false was "not news" and Kelly never even bothered to file a story. Brill, in preparing his *American Lawyer* article, asked Louis Slovinsky, the chief *Time* spokesman, why *Time* did not acknowledge and correct facts that it discovered to be wrong on its own. He was told: "You sound like a total ass just to ask a question like that. Why should we do that? We don't have to, and we haven't had to for sixty-two years."

So much for journalistic responsibility at *Time*.

Brill contrasts *Time's* behavior with the behavior it would expect of a president or governor or corporate president in similar circumstances. If *Time* were covering the story it would expect a politician to admit the mistake and fire those responsible. On the contrary, *Time* has cast itself as a hero under fire, protecting free speech against a menacing onslaught. The judge in the case, Abraham Sofaer, has a comment to make about this posture. In denying *Time's* request that Sharon's case be summarily dismissed without trial, Sofaer stated: "*Time* has refused to issue any correction or to print plaintiff's denial. Only through the litigation process has plaintiff been able to uncover and publish the evidence from which *Time* claimed to have learned the contents of the Commission's secret appendix.... *It would be pure fantasy to treat "Time" in this case like some struggling champion of free expression, defending at great risk to itself the right to publish its view of the truth.*" [Italics added.]

Time "won" the trial in the sense that the jury failed to find intent to tell a lie. CBS won the Westmoreland case in that

General Westmoreland withdrew from the case before it reached the jury. The danger then is that while these trials deservedly undermine the media's credibility with the public, they can reinforce the media's sense of invulnerability. The "cost" of a trial, it is sometimes argued, will have a "chilling effect" on smaller papers and TV stations, which will be afraid to publish articles critical of public figures. But by the same token, the "cost" of a trial will seem prohibitive to an injured party if it is clear that damages cannot be ultimately collected. The Sharon case cost the firm of Shea and Gould over a million dollars, only a third of which has been covered through fund-raising appeals. Organizations like *Time* and CBS have libel insurance: the worst they have to anticipate is higher premiums.

Certainly, the reaction of *Time* to the suit's conclusion is not encouraging. The jury took the unusual step, in announcing its verdict, of issuing an amplifying statement that declared the jury had found certain *Time* employees had acted "negligently and carelessly." *Time*'s managing editor, Ray Cave, subsequently dismissed the jury's criticism, saying he "disagreed" with it. In an official statement on behalf of *Time* he reaffirmed the truth of the story that the jury had found to be false and stated, "We are totally confident that the story is substantially true" and professed "the utmost confidence in our editorial staff and our editorial procedures."* *Time* editor Henry Grunwald, interviewed on the David Brinkley program on ABC on January 27, even announced that *Time* planned to keep David Halevy on its staff. This was despite the fact that Halevy had previously been suspended by *Time* for filing a false story and had been singled out by name in the jury's statement as guilty of negligent and careless reporting.

While day-to-day reporting on Israel is rife with the subtle kinds of distortions that Stephen Karetzky analyzes in his work, the media's negative underlying attitudes against Israel persist, ready to surface at any crisis.

Just such an opportunity arose in March 1985, when CBS unjustifiably attacked Israel in the world press. When two Lebanese cameramen working for CBS were killed in a shelling incident, the company's response was all too familiar. Within hours of the incident CBS News President Edward M. Joyce fired off a telegram to Israeli Prime Minister Shimon Peres accusing

Israeli forces of "outrageous behavior."A subsequent telegram spoke of "deliberate fire" on "unarmed and neutral journalists." CBS promptly announced that as a "matter of principle" it was cancelling plans for a weeklong Eastern television broadcast from Israel on the CBS Morning News. Not to be outdone, ABC News President Roone Arledge fired off his own telegram to Peres, calling the killings "an appalling act."

Once Israel had been roasted in the court of public opinion for the deliberate murder of journalists by the three major networks, CBS belatedly decided to send someone to investigate what had actually happened. An embarrassed vice president of CBS News in Jerusalem, Ernest Leiser, was then forced to admit that the tank which fired the fatal shell was more than a mile away and that the Israeli action "was certainly not a deliberate attempt to fire guns against our camera people."

A senior Israeli official remarked caustically: "CBS had a gut reaction. They came to their verdict, called us every name in the book, punished us, and then they said they were sending someone over to investigate what happened." The hasty, hysterical attack on Israel must be contrasted with the simultaneous failure of any of the networks to use their Beirut-based reporters for an exploration of the Syrian-Lebanese role in the kidnapping of Americans and others in Beirut.

Needless to say, CBS did not apologize for its earlier unfounded attacks on Israel. Indeed, Joyce managed to substitute a new attack for an apology. He expressed "regret" that Peres planned "no measure which could prevent a recurrence of last week's tragedy." CBS gave no indication that it planned to take any steps to safeguard the lives of its freelance Lebanese crewmen by keeping them out of combat areas that Israel had explicitly warned were dangerous and should be entered only with Israeli military escorts. By permitting their unescorted employees to enter this active combat zone, it was more accurately CBS which was responsible for the reckless endangerment of their lives.

The CBS cameramen fiasco notwithstanding, Central America distracted some of the media's attention in 1985. The media elite's Third World enthusiasms were transferred to the Sandinistas and, to a lesser extent, the guerrillas in El Salvador.

(The election of socialist Napoleon Duarte as President seemed to dampen media enthusiasm for the guerrillas.) Arafat, temporarily at least, was out of favor as a heroic figure. Although his forces left Tripoli, as they had left Beirut, with a victory sign, his exit this time did not go down triumphantly with the press. This may have been because he was forced out by other Arabs. In any event, outrage was focussed once again on the supposed malice of the U.S. Government in supporting repression and counter-revolution in Central America.

Israel can derive little encouragement from such phenomena. As long as those who set journalistic standards retain their self-righteous, adversarial elitism, any respite Israel enjoys from media obloquy will be brief. The process of misrepresentation goes on, which, in the long run, may do more to undermine support for Israel than concentrated bursts of outrageous reporting, such as accompanied the war in Lebanon. The drop of water technique can be more effective than crasser methods.

While there are no easy solutions to the problem of media distortion of the news, this brief survey would not be complete without mention of one encouraging development. That is a new willingness on the part of the media to criticize one another. Although still rare, it is no longer taboo for one newspaper to attack another for inaccurate and distorted reporting.

It is an enormously healthy development when the media look skeptically at each other rather than hunt in a pack. What if ABC's *20/20* had decided to do its own study of CBS after CBS had aired its documentary on the alleged "conspiracy" by General Westmoreland to deceive the President? What if *Newsweek* were to reexamine questionable stories published by *Time* and vice versa? There would then be no question of a "chilling effect" on free speech, but rather a genuine exercise of press freedoms and responsibilities. No one likes to be exposed by his peers, and the prospect should help journalists to achieve balance and accuracy in reporting. If the media act to monitor one another, the need both for libel suits and for media monitoring organizations would be reduced.

Without the criticism that the media have experienced in the last few years, there would not even be the very small harbingers of change now visible. Stephen Karetzky's study is a valuable contribution that hopefully will bring about some much needed reform.

* Judging from a 1969 book, *Evidence* by Robert and Dale New-man (Houghton Mifflin), *Time*'s editorial procedures have not changed much over the years. The study notes that while on a typical newspaper the story is basically a product of the man at the scene, at *Time* "copy filed from reporters in the field is primarily stimulus to editorial imagination. Testimony on this point from defectors from the magazine is unanimous." After chronicling the account of a former *Time* writer on what was done to his story on Marilyn Monroe, the authors note that if such changes "are made in stories where the ideological impact would be minor, one can only imagine what happens when the magazine's biases are touched."

Of course in the Sharon case, the reporter's biases and the editorial biases were in the same direction. Thus Halevy's report that Sharon had given the Gemayel family "the feeling" that he understood their need for revenge was changed by the editor to become Sharon's "discussing" the need for revenge. Both were wrong, but the editor's version made Sharon's supposed behavior even worse.

THE CANNONS OF JOURNALISM: *THE NEW YORK TIMES* PROPAGANDA WAR AGAINST ISRAEL

by Stephen Karetzky

Introduction

The most prestigious and influential newspaper in the United States has been presenting an inaccurate, tendentious picture of developments in Israel and its neighboring territories. These developments comprise the most significant foreign news story in the world that is open to relatively easy coverage by the Western media. This low quality coverage increases the chances of major war in the Middle East, with another disruption of Western oil supplies and another major confrontation with the Soviet Union. It threatens the continued existence of the only Western, democratic, stable, reliable American ally in that strategically important region, the only country there of any significant value to the United States in a military confrontation. The present coverage also exacerbates the widespread anti-Americanism overseas—especially in Arab countries—because of its negative attitude towards Israel: Israel is often erroneously considered to be a client state of the United States for whose actions America is ultimately responsible.

The impact of New York Times news stories is great. There is a widespread assumption that they are objective, intelligent, complete reports of the most significant developments; and they are read by a large number of the influential and educated in the United States. People of significance in other countries also read them. In addition to the relatively widespread and strategic

103

national and international distribution of the Times itself, its stories are also featured in the *International Herald Tribune* and in the hundreds of newspapers and broadcasting agencies which subscribe to the Times thru online computer services. On microfilm and computer print-out, the Times will be a prime source for future historians, and of course it is now widely used by contemporary researchers. The quality of the Times reporting is also important because it is the most respected American newspaper, and one *expects* that it adheres to the canons of the journalism profession. It sets a standard for the entire journalistic community, a major component of the nation's democratic system.

The major interrelated elements in the Times' distorted news coverage and analysis have been the following:

1. The unbalanced and prejudicial use of personal and written sources.
2. Misperception and misconception of phenomena. A gross incapacity to evaluate sources and data.
3. Phantasy.
4. The use of biased and incompetent sources for news accounts and opinions.
5. Factual errors.
6. Misrepresentation.
7. Distortion through false analogies, playful and inaccurate inversions, and spurious ironies.
8. The use of inaccurate, misleading and prejudicial terminology.
9. Inaccurate labelling of people and phenomena.
10. Manipulative wording and phrasing of sentences.
11. Misleading headlines.
12. The use of photographs to confirm a biased view through the selection of subject matter, the frequency of themes, the size of the photographs, and their placement in the newspaper.
13. The selective cropping of original photographs.
14. Inaccurate and biased photo captions.
15. Biased foci: the unreasonably intense scrutiny of particular subjects, and the omission or under-coverage of others.

16. The selective repetition of particular themes, words and stories.
17. The biased emphasis or deemphasis of particular stories by their physical placement in the newspaper.
18. The selective substitution of melodrama and pathos for objective analysis.
19. The selective substitution of subjective, glib discussions of the psychological and/or near-spiritual for concrete, factual analyses.
20. The intrusion of moral judgments. The unfounded nature of these judgments.

An accurate picture of the Times news coverage requires the close analysis which follows. The focus is on the news stories of February, March, and April, 1982. (The stories examined appeared in the early edition of the Times. They rarely varied in later editions.) Several noteworthy events occurred during this period (which received much world attention): rioting on the West Bank, an armed attack in the Dome of the Rock Mosque, and the final withdrawal of Israeli troops and civilians from Sinai in accordance with the Camp David accords. These developments were the focus of attention in newspapers throughout the Western world. Some warranted the attention accorded them, others did not. Nevertheless, they dominated the front pages until the conflict in the Falkland Islands. The reporting before and after this period appears to use the same methods and has the same general thrust. During the summer 1982 war in Lebanon and its aftermath, the quality of the journalism declined further.

The Portrayal of Israel as a Suppressor of Innocent Arabs

One of the major elements of the Times news reports during these months was the presentation of Arabs as helpless, innocent victims; civilians who were in the middle of a terrible situation they bore no responsibility for creating; people being brutalized by calculating, cruel, anti-democratic, voracious Israelis. The Arabs, one is lead to believe, used force only when compelled to by the Israelis. An interesting element accompanying this portrayal was the unstated assumption that both the New York Times journalists and the Arabs could look into the minds of the Israelis, discern their innermost thoughts, and foresee their complicated, long-range, nefarious plans.

In "The West Bank Occupation Now Resembles Annexation" (3/28, p. E3) by David Shipler, head of the Times news bureau in Israel, he discussed the "tough handling of stone-throwing Arabs, who were protesting the Government's replacement of elected local officials with Israelis." This was a perverted version of events. In actuality, the Arabs were killing and maiming people, and to characterize the Israeli response as "tough" was a distorted, subjective judgment rather than objective news reporting. (This subject is dealt with at length later.) He noted that six Palestinians had been "shot to death" by soldiers, while "one soldier died when his jeep was hit by a grenade." The very wording here misrepresented the situation. Palestinians were "shot to death" but the blowing up of an Israeli was presented as incidental to the denouement of an almost non-violent occurrence—the effect of a grenade on a jeep, rather than an attack by an Arab on an Israeli. In this, as in most other Times reports, Shipler failed to explain or describe the events surrounding the shootings of the Arabs, e.g., the menacing of vastly outnumbered Israeli soldiers who had shown a great deal of restraint. The actions of the Palestinians were made to appear virtuous compared to those of the Israelis: they were "protesting the replacement of elected local officials with Israelis." The reasons for the dismissal of the mayors were not given here, and the *Arabs* were presented as people who were fighting for democracy.

In Shipler's article, the New York Times correspondent adopted the Arabs' claims concerning the Israelis' activities and aims on the West Bank (note the headline), although it would seem to have been unwarranted to take such a position given the limited evidence available on this complicated, ever-changing situation. The article stated: "From the perspective of the Arabs in their stone villages amid vineyards and olive groves, the Israeli takeover is self-evident and relentless. Not only are Jewish settlements seizing and purchasing tracts of land...." In the second sentence here, the journalist had overtly assumed the distorted perspective of the Arabs, and the view was presented as the accurate one. It would seem that the claim that the Israelis were "seizing" land, i.e., taking land forcefully (and by implication, illegally), would have required some evidence. None was presented in this piece or in any other in the Times during the period under consideration here.

Shipler's unrestrained story went on to describe some of the Jewish settlers as terrorists, and claimed that "these vigilantes have brought a frightening spirit of lawlessness to the West Bank." This was an unusually harsh condemnation, and it was unsupported. It was mentioned that settlers were "vandalizing electric-generators," but no evidence was provided for even this relatively minor charge. (It was later repeated—as a fact—in one of the many anti-Israeli contributions by the regular Times columnist Anthony Lewis.) In contrast, the Times did not confront the undeniable, tangible facts of Arab violence and riots on the West Bank, and their relationship to any possible "frightening spirit of lawlessness." These are blatant examples of selective perception and the application of a double standard.

Explanations or justifications for the settlers' presence on non-religious grounds (e.g., military, social) were rarely printed in the New York Times in this three-month period. Mention was sometimes made that such settlements in the West Bank were first put up when the secular, socialist Labor Party was in power.

It was not pointed out that the settlement policy (and the democratically elected government) was supported by a public which is perhaps only 20-25% religious, a far smaller percentage of "believers," incidentally, than one finds in the United States. Nevertheless, the focus of the Times was on the fundamentalist, religious impulses for West Bank settlements which could easily be misinterpreted by secular Times readers as being merely a Jewish version of Middle Eastern religious fanaticism. A pretence of objective news gathering and "going to the sources" was made by having the religious reasons come out of the settlers' own mouths. Thus we are provided (Shipler, 4/1, p.A3) with declarations such as: "We're acting under orders here. We have the Bible and the Bible says that this is our land; and it commands the Jews to settle the land of Israel."

It was not mentioned in Times articles that vital Jewish settlements existed for the past several centuries on what is now sometimes called the West Bank (such as in Hebron), in addition to those in ancient times. These were evacuated due to massacres by Arabs in the 1920's and 1930's, and in the voluntary—albeit painful—exodus brought about by the 1948 U.N. partition plan for "Palestine." (Many Israelis, such as the former Prime Minister Yitzhak Rabin, were born and brought up on the West Bank.)

The Jews on the West Bank were consistently presented to Times readers as merely being recent interlopers. In news stories, it was always mentioned when one of them formerly resided in the United States, and the name of the American city he or she came from was given. The sly attempt here was to heighten the contrast between that far-off Middle Eastern territory and the well-known American place to make it appear incongruous that a person (albeit a Jew) who has been here is now there. Since it is difficult for American Times readers to imagine themselves moving to the Middle East, they might naturally assume that these settlers also do not belong there, and that their presence there is absurd and wrong. There was a brief interview with "Era Rappoport, 37 years old, a native of the East Flatbush section of Brooklyn." (Shipler, 3/22, p. A3. It was *not* reported that Rappoport had moved to Israel *eleven years earlier.*) Shipler wrote of "Yorucham Leavitt, a lanky 41 year-old who came to Israel from Cleveland three years ago," (4/11, p. A3) but in the same article Shlomo and Orna Shkedi and Jacqueline Elliaz were also interviewed, and no mention was made of where they came from or when. Apparently, noting that a settler originally came from Jerusalem, Morocco or even the West Bank, or that he had immigrated many years ago, was not useful to the general thrust of the stories and was thus omitted. The use of this technique for propagandistic distortion becomes even clearer when one sees that the man responsible for killing many Arabs at the Dome of the Rock in Jerusalem, who had emigrated from America to Israel a few years ago and was in the Israeli army for only ten days, was usually identified in the Times as an "Israeli soldier." (This will be dealt with later.)

The myths of Arab innocence and of Arab persecution by Jews who desire to force them from their land were extended in the Times back to 1948. The reader was apparently supposed to believe that there was a parallel between the recent developments and the events of that time. Shipler wrote: "Some Palestinians think they [the Israelis] are laying the groundwork for the expulsion of the Arabs or the flight of the Arabs in a future war, as occurred during Israel's 1948 war of independence." (3/28, p. E3) In a melodramatic news report one month earlier, "Boys on the West Bank Arrested at Night for Weeks of Questioning by Israelis," (2/27, p.5) Shipler had presented the same view, which is the very same, self-serving, paranoid one generally put forth by the Arabs. He reported that in 1948 "many Arabs were driven out by the Israelis or fled to escape the battle." It was not indicated that many of the Arabs within Israel—some of whom now live on the West Bank and Gaza Strip—were the frontline fighters of the Arab armies in 1948. The men were well-armed by the departing English and the surrounding Arab countries, and often had excellent strategic positions close to the Jewish areas, sometimes in the very same towns and cities. The Jews in cities like Jerusalem and Haifa were almost entirely surrounded. It was the Arabs who were confident and armed-to-the-teeth. One percent of the Jewish population was killed in this long, bloody war. The Arabs were not driven out, but rather had been asked to stay and live in peace in the new country. Most who left did so on the orders of the surrounding Arab countries to facilitate the envisaged massacre of the Jews.

Another Times story (Shipler, 3/22, p. A3) reported the Arab claim that Israelis on the West Bank were trying to set up the same psychological atmosphere that allegedly existed in 1948, an atmosphere designed to drive them out. This claim received no critical evaluation, and tended to be supported by the other elements put forth in this report. As I note briefly elsewhere, Times opinion columns and editorials were umbilically connected to such news stories. Thus, Anthony Lewis (4/5, p. A23) repeated a statement by "Elias Freij, the gentle moderate who is Mayor of Bethlehem," which had been quoted a few days before in a David Shipler news article (3/31, p. A16): "The rate of settlement in the area is driving people crazy, and the heavy hand, the censorship, the arrests. People are ready to explode, they feel so oppressed."

As already mentioned, David Shipler's news article of February 27, 1982 had the damning headline: "Boys in the West Bank Arrested at Night for Weeks of Questioning by Israelis." The article was later complimented as objective reporting in an Anthony Lewis column, and referred to in a major Times editorial. In truth, the so-called "boys" were actually teenagers or young adults: *all* were fourteen years or older according to David Shipler and Anthony Lewis. (A careful reading of another Shipler story headlined "West Bank Boy Dies as Israeli Forces Fire on Arab Protesters" [3/21, pp. 1, 12] uncovers that fact that this "boy" was seventeen. Incidentally, Israelis—male and female— are drafted into the army after high school and some undoubtedly were serving on the West Bank during this period. No attention was paid to *their* difficulties in the Times.) The news story was a manipulative, melodramatic piece calculated to evoke sympathy for the teenagers and their families. We were presented with a picture of sensitive "boys" who struggled to hold back their tears when relating their stories to a Western newsman. The piece was an attempt to evoke disgust for authorities who, the reader was supposed to believe, arrested ("at night," no less, with its "knock on the door" connotations) and incarcerated teenagers indiscriminately. Shipler described in detail some of these teenagers and their arrests. He chose as his final sentence the words of a mother whose some had been arrested: "All these soldiers for taking a child?" Thus, the Times ended its article by implying an unneeded and irrational brutality against *children.*

111

The possibility that some of these "boys" may have actually been guilty of some of the violent acts by Arabs so common on the West Bank—and which were *occasionally* reported by the New York Times—appears to have been inconceivable to Shipler and Lewis. This was in spite of the fact that a recent series in the Times had shown that a great many of the murders, rapes and other violent crimes in America are committed by teenagers. Shipler blamed the *Israelis* for any extremism which existed among the Arabs. He said that the situation "indicates that boys are being forced by harassment to become radicals."

Shipler claimed (3/30, p. A12) in another article that "Israeli military censorship, based on the 1945 emergency regulations of the British mandate in Palestine, is always stricter with the Arab press than with the Israeli or foreign press, officials explain. Arabic papers must submit all material to the censor." Stories for Israeli and foreign newspapers, he affirmed, are inspected only if they concern military matters. Here, as elsewhere, Shipler did not mention who these "official" sources were. The nature of the censorship regulations were made to appear sinister and ridiculous by claiming that they are based on the emergency regulations dating from the British mandate. For some reason, this minor historical sidelight was stated often in the Times, and one wonders whether it was done to imply that while the Jews were once oppressed by a colonial, military rule in this area, they have now adopted a position analogous to their former oppressors. (Such false analogies, inaccurate inversions, and wild attempts to portray spurious ironies have become popular recently among political commentators to the point where Israelis, i.e., Jews, have been put forth as the modern-day Nazis.) It should be explained that when Israel became independent in 1948, it was sensibly declared by the government that all laws and regulations then in force would remain in effect unless rescinded. Thus a great number of the laws now in force are British in origin, and many even date from the time Turkey ruled the area. In addition, the particular Times report in question erroneously distinguished between the "Arab" press and the "Israeli" press: Arabs in Israel are full-fledged Israeli citizens with the same rights of freedom of speech and press. The *radical* Arab press, geared largely towards West Bank residents but distributed throughout

Israel too, are published in Jerusalem and are protected by Israel law. Charges against them must usually follow a lengthy, tortuous route through the court system. The worst fate that any of them had ever faced (*Al-Fajr*) had been a one month suspension. (In an article in the *Columbia Journalism Review* by an American observer, Milton Viorst, he expressed great surprise at what he found was allowed to be printed in these newspapers, which are, he pointed out, the freest, least-censored Arabic-language newspapers in the Middle East.)

The Times article was incorrect when it claimed a great difference in the procedures in the censorship of the Arabic-language press and the "Israeli" (i.e., Jewish) and foreign ones. The contents of the Hebrew language papers are *also* closely scrutinized, in part because many seemingly harmless stories have military implications. It is known that the Israeli press is closely examined by Israel's enemies. Thus, a seemingly innocuous story shortly before the 1973 war about the sending of holiday cakes to Israeli soldiers on the Golan Heights indirectly and inadvertently signaled to the Syrians how many soldiers were there.

During this period, a highly significant story was made public to the world press by the Israeli government. It revealed that reporters from Western media had been physically intimidated in Lebanon and elsewhere by the P.L.O. in an attempt to make them report more sympathetically on Arab activities. (See Shipler, 2/14, p. 9.) However, Shipler's Times article on this revelation left out the fact that New York Times reporters had been involved. (See "Special to the N.Y. Times," 2/18, p.A4. This information had not been censored from the Times story appearing in the European-based *International Herald Tribune*.) When this omission was pointed out by the Israeli government, the Times denied that a P.L.O. kidnapping of its reporters and the direct threats made in this and other instances had had any effect on the work of its journalists. Craig R. Whitney, the deputy foreign editor and soon-to-be chief foreign editor, made the absurd claim that the facts had never been published in the Times because they had never been considered newsworthy! John Kifner, one of the Times journalists in Beirut who had been kidnapped, then publicly shrugged off the incident as a mere "mistake" by the P.L.O. (See his Times story 2/22, p. A4) Thus, any fear, error, dishonesty, censorship or secret agreements were never admitted to by the Times. (See also Shipler, 2/24, p. A3.)

In contrast, reports concerning Israeli censorship were common in the Times. (See, for example, "Special to the N.Y. Times," 2/26, p. A11.) The temporary banning of reporters from the Golan Heights—part of the successful attempt by the Israeli government to avoid precipitating violent clashes—received a good deal of attention. (For example, 3/24, pp. 1, A6.) The reasons for these restrictions were not generally reported. No comparisons of these policies with those of other countries in comparable circumstances were made.

The Arab population within Israel has thrived since 1948, and their villages, towns and cities are vital. Yet in a description of Israel (3/21, sec. 10. pp. 14, 20), David Shipler neglected to mention these places but instead noted that there are "Arab refugee camps." Of course there are no such camps—they exist only in Shipler's head. He has a fixed and distorted picture of the area in his mind, and it appears that he is unable to see anything that does not fit into this phantasm.

A common practice in the Times during this period was to portray the mayors of the towns on the West Bank and Gaza strip as "moderates." Among these were the mayors who were dismissed for not cooperating with the moves to change from military to civilian rule. They were held up as heroic elected officials who were being unfairly victimized. In a news article (Shipler, 3/29, pp. A1, A4) Shipler described Elias Freij of Bethlehem and Rashad al-Shawwa of Gaza as "two relative moderates." (In a column from Paris on March 8, Anthony Lewis had also called Freij and al-Shawwa "moderate.") In another article, Shipler quoted Freij—the least radical of the handful of mayors expelled—at length about the alleged suffering of the Palestinians and about Israeli oppression. He also quoted Freij's description of himself: "I will not be a yes man, and I will not be an extremist. I will continue to follow my line of moderation." (3/31, p. A16) There was no critical evaluation of any of Freij's absurd claims. As previously noted, a few days later Lewis quoted some of the very same statements on Israeli oppression in his column, and described the man as "the gentle moderate." (4/5, p. A23) There were no discussions anywhere in the Times of the other former mayors, like Bassam-al-Shakr, and their very extreme political activities. Covering the *same* events concerning the mayors in the *Sunday Times* of London (3/21), reporter David Bundy mentioned the links between these West Bank (and Gaza) mayors and the National Guidance Committee, the coordinating body of pro-P.L.O. forces in the West Bank and Gaza. Ibrahim Tawil, one of the dismissed mayors, was most often described in the New York Times as the intended victim of an unsuccessful bomb attack whose perpetrators have never been found by the Israeli authorities. (For example, see Shipler, 3/26, pp. 1, A4.) The implication was always that the act was done by Jewish terrorists whom the government had no sincere desire to catch. (However, it was usually noted that Israeli soldiers alerted Tawil about a possible assassination attempt, that they found a bomb in his car, and that an Israeli soldier was blinded when he tried to defuse it.) The British journalist Bundy noted in his *Sunday Times* story that Tawil "has close links with a Marxist-Leninist P.L.O. faction, the Democratic Front for the Liberation of Palestine." (The D.F.L.P. is a "rejectionist" group; that is, it rejects *any* intercourse with Israel, including even the arrangement of cease-fires. It is more radical than Yasser Arafat's P.L.O. group, El Fatah.)

While the New York Times corespondents had nothing good to say about the *true* Arab moderates on the West Bank, and gave them little coverage, David Bundy acknowledged their existence and their significance. He noted that in contrast to the urban areas with their radical mayors, the Palestinians who lived in the countryside and constituted 60-65% of the West Bank population were relatively apolitical. The New York newspaper paid scant attention to these people. It also had nothing positive to say about the Village Leagues the Israeli government and the new civilian governor, Menachem Milson, encouraged in the countryside to offer the residents an alternative to the P.L.O. Although far from impressed with these Leagues, Eric Silver of the British newspaper *The Observer* noted (3/21, p. 5) that "His [Milson's] policy of sponsoring village leagues had made indisputable headway in the Hebron region, south of Jerusalem, where an authentic local leader, Mustapha Dudeen, was already seeking to cooperate with Israel." The New York Times, however, kept its coverage focused on the urban mayors who were P.L.O. spokesmen. An article by correspondent Henry Kamm, "Pro-Israel West Bank Official Wounded by Bomb," (4/1, p. A3) gave few details of this significant story of truly moderate Arabs and their fate but focused instead on unrelated Middle Eastern diplomatic issues.

The New York Times' view of supposed "moderate" Arabs and alleged Israeli trouble-making was extended to the international sphere—to essential American foreign interests and to the American-Soviet conflict. Shipler reported (3/7, p. E4): "Bitter differences over Jerusalem have helped frustrate Washington's notions of bringing moderate Arabs into an anti-Soviet alliance with Israel." The onus for the frustration of Washington's goal, of course, must lie with Israel since the United States does not recognize Israel's claim to Jerusalem. Furthermore, the use of the word "moderate" here to describe highly immoderate, unstable countries served to obscure the situation. Shipler's statement also ignored the central and indisputable fact that the so-called "moderate" Arabs have repeatedly asserted that the major military threat in the area is Israel rather than the Soviet Union. No mention was made of the frequent and impolite Arab rebuffs of American requests for bases and/or cooperation aimed at fighting back any Soviet military aggression.

Biased coverage of Jewish-Arab relations *within* Israel was common in New York Times news stories during the time period under examination here. (One area—that of alleged unfair censorship of Arab newspapers—has already been described.) Subjective descriptions were readily used in news reports to the detriment of the Jews. For example, in an article attempting to show that the Bedouins in the Negev desert were being brutalized by the Jewish Israelis, a special governmental group (the "Green Patrol") formed to help oversee programs in this wilderness and whose members are akin to American park service rangers, was described as "a squad of tough young Israelis." (Shipler, 3/9, p. A2) It would have been better journalism to refrain from making such a characterization and just objectively present the facts concerning their actions and their work. Readers could then judge whether they were in fact "tough," and indeed whether they *should* have been.

The headline for this particular melodramatic news report by David Shipler was "Israelis Survive Storm over Bedouin Baby's Death." It tried to indicate an Israeli mistreatment of Bedouins which in this case resulted in the death of one sick infant. Several important factors were not dealt with in the story. For example, the physical condition of the baby's dozen brothers and sisters was not mentioned. Also omitted were *facts* concerning the origins and aims of these Bedouins: Did they originate in the Negev? Why had they *chosen* to live there under Israeli rule when there were (and are) alternatives? Ignored too was their general relationship to Israeli society: the efforts of the government to provide them with health care and education, and the generous housing offers Israel's Jewish citizens envy. Instead, Shipler began the news item with "The Israeli authorities involved in driving seminomadic Bedouins off their ancestral lands...." The Bedouins' roles as spies and large-scale smugglers of drugs and arms were not mentioned. The focus was on the unfortunate fate of one sick infant, in a manipulative attempt to create something from very little. Despite the sensational headline, it does not appear that there was, in fact, much of the proclaimed "storm," and it is no wonder that the "Israelis" managed to "survive" it, as the headline proclaimed. Shipler made the claim that "the Green Patrol has intensified a campaign of denigration of the Bedouin's culture and tradition." There was a photograph accompanying the piece which showed the father of the dead baby peacefully squatting and drinking some coffee in the traditional manner.

A few weeks later, a very long article by Shipler (4/4) starting on page one and taking up most of page sixteen—a rare occurrence in the New York Times—was a paean to Bedouin culture. Focusing on the Bedouins of the Sinai, it did maintain some balance by at least mentioning that when the area came under Israeli rule the Israelis made great efforts to provide education for the Bedouins, in contrast to the Egyptians when they had governed the territory. It even noted that the Bedouins engage in smuggling, but unfortunately presented this in a romantic light (e.g., there was an interview with a smuggler who writes poems about his way of life), ignoring both the deleterious effects of illegal drugs on Israel's young people as well as the civilian deaths caused by smuggled bombs and weapons. Once again, Arabs were portrayed as impotent, helpless people who are affected by others (mainly the Israelis) or by great social forces (for example, modernization), but who do nothing of their own volition, and do nothing which has any negative consequences for others: they are innocents. Incidentally, it could have been mentioned in these articles on the Bedouins that those living in northern Israel (who are generally ignored by the Times) are on relatively good terms with the Jews and have never had good relations with non-Bedouin Arabs. Many volunteer to serve in the Israeli army.

The Times' treatment of tension between Israelis and the Druze Arabs on the Golan Heights was also biased. It was stated in a news article (Shipler, 4/13, p. 2): "Long quiet and devoid of overt anti-Israeli activity, the Golan Heights region has grown tense since its annexation...." References were made elsewhere to the "Pro-Syrian Druzes" (Shipler, 3/24, pp. A1, A6) who began a long strike after the annexation.

Doubtless there were pro-Syrian Druze on the Heights. However, the focus should probably have been on the fact (mentioned only in passing) that a large percentage of these inhabitants had relatives in Syria, and that they feared reprisals against them for any overt gesture of cooperation with the Israelis' announced "extension of Israeli rule" to the Golan Heights. (One can be certain that they were aware of the Syrian army's destruction of one of its own cities, Hama, during this period, with the slaughter of at least twenty thousand of its civilian residents, many of whom did not support the government.) In addition, the Golan Heights has changed hands many times through history, and its inhabitants feared that an Israeli-Syrian bargain of "land for peace" might one day be made with the Golan, similar to that with the Sinai. Israel's stated policy did not preclude such an agreement, although it did seem unlikely. Under a renewal of Syrian rule, those who had agreed to cooperate with Israel—becoming citizens, serving in the army, etc., would face a bleak fate. The Druze on the Heights also knew well that although the area had been held by Israel since 1967, it was quite successfully—albeit temporarily—overrun by the Syrians in 1973.

Perhaps the most significant factor in the reluctance of these Druze to cooperate with an incorporation into Israel was the fear that they would lose the land (through purchase by the Israeli government) that they had seized when a large number of inhabitants fled during the 1967 war. This factor was never mentioned in the Times. Although pictured in the Times as yet another Israeli-oppressed Arab group, many of the inhabitants were in reality thriving squatters.

The treatment of this Israel-Druze conflict was done in such a biased manner by the major Western media that a Druze member of the Israeli parliament who was serving as an unofficial negotiator between the Israeli government and the Golan Druze came to the United States to publicly explain the actual situation. His visit was not reported by the Times. According to this parliamentarian, Zeidan Atashi, the three major fears concerning the Israeli rule expressed to him by the Golan Druze were the fear of being forced to accept Israeli citizenship, of serving in the Israeli army, and losing the land they held. (The *Jewish Press* of New York covered Atashi's visit adequately. See 4/16, p. 3.) He reported that citizenship was *not* being forced upon them, and that an involuntary draft would be illegal under Israeli laws concerning Druze since they are only conscripted when a Druze town council freely elects to have such a draft. The third great fear would be difficult to allay: all governments retain the right to expropriate and use land for the public good. Atashi noted that the whole affair was being exaggerated by the American media. There were only 9,000 Druze living on the Golan, compared to 45,000 Druze Israeli citizens within the borders established in 1948. Most of the latter opposed the strike by their brethren.

A large percentage of Druze elect to serve in the Israeli army and border police for many years. Traditionally a beleaguered minority in the Middle East, they did not fight alongside the other Arabs in the 1948 War of Independence and have enjoyed great freedom, prosperity and political power in the Jewish state. They dislike other Arab groups. Shipler's statement (4/13, p.2) that "Many Druze in Israel proper are drafted, and they often serve in the occupied West Bank, putting down demonstrations by Palestinian Arabs, with whom they have no affinity" did not give a clear, vivid picture of the situation. The danger of warfare between the Israeli Bedouins and Israeli Druze in northern Israel—a very significant story during this period—went unreported in the Times.

The Coverage of Clashes in the West Bank, Gaza, and Israel

There was gross distortion in the New York Times coverage of some violence which—rightly or wrongly—was in the spotlight of world attention during this time period: the clashes between Israelis and Palestinians in the West Bank and Gaza, and within the pre-1967 borders of Israel. In this story, the general portrayal of Arabs as the innocent victims of aggression was able to find a focus.

There were weeks of rioting; knifings; the throwing of rocks, pipes and burning torches at Israeli soldiers and civilians (as well as at Western tourists); and the menacing of outnumbered Israelis by Palestinian mobs. The violent aggressors committing these acts were labeled in the New York Times as "protestors" or "demonstrators," and their actions as "demonstrations" or "protests." (See, for example: Shipler, 3/24, pp. A1, A6; 3/25, p. 1; 3/29, pp. A1, A4; 3/31, p. A6.) These words connote an honest and earnest public display against an injustice. (See Webster's unabridged *New International Dictionary*.) In contrast, the same events were more accurately called "riots" and "clashes" in the *Sunday Times* of London (3/21, p. 1). In the New York Times, the precise actions of the Arabs were rarely described, although the riots were sometimes called "violent demonstrations" (Shipler, 3/25, pp. A1, A9; 3/31, p. A6). It is significant, however, that there were never "violent demonstrators." With the arrival in the Middle East of the Times correspondent, Henry Kamm, near the middle of the time period dealt with in this analysis, reporting on the riots improved slightly, although he too used the words "demonstrations," "demonstrators," and "protestors." (For example, see Kamm, 3/28, p. 9.) An Associated Press story printed in the Times on April 9th used the more appropriate term "clashes."

One article ("Special to the N.Y. Times," 4/17, p. 3) noted that the use of regular bullets by the Israeli army, rather than mere tear gas and rubber bullets, marked a very recent change. The army explained that the use of real bullets was necessitated by the threats to soldiers' lives. Statements that the soldiers' orders were to aim for the legs of the Palestinians was reported throughout these months.

Arab violence was rarely explicitly acknowledged, in contrast to the playing up of force used by the Israelis. It was also implied that the Israeli force was unwarranted. Thus, soon after the beginning of the riots, Shipler referred to "days of violence in the West Bank in which soldiers, firing into crowds of Palestinian demonstrators, killed 2 teen-age boys and wounded 16." (3/24, pp. A1, A6.) The next day he wrote (pp. 1, 9) that a "third Palestinian was killed in a demonstration." Note again the avoidance of attributing violence to the Arabs, and the use of the words "boys" and "demonstrators." (In a column dealing with the Golan Heights [4/5, p. A23], Anthony Lewis noted curtly: "Four Druze demonstrators have now been shot.")

As noted, Arab violence was consistently played down. One method of doing so mentioned earlier was to describe it in passive rather than active sentences. In addition, it was often portrayed as if it had been committed against inanimate objects rather than people. The example already given was in Shipler's article of 3/28, p. E3, which reported that six Palestinians had been "shot to death" by Israeli soldiers, while "one soldier died when his jeep was hit by a grenade."

The size and physical placement of the stories further distorted the truth. Unlike many of the previously-mentioned stories which appeared on page one, a *very* small article on page five ("Special to the N.Y. Times," 4/8) had the headline "Grenade Wounds a Nun in West Bank Town." Thus the headline stated that the brutal act was done by a grenade rather than by an Arab. The story noted that a grenade was thrown into a Greek Orthodox shrine on the West Bank town of Nablus after tourists went inside. Another very small article from the Associated Press two days later was also buried on page five: "Two Israeli Girls Hurt by Rocks in West Bank." It stated that "one girl, Brenda Kamm, suffered a fractured skull and other injuries when Arab demonstrators threw rocks at their bus." It noted that the sources for the story were Israeli military authorities and a spokesman for the Jewish settlement, Kiryat Arba. In yet another story considered low priority by the Times, Shipler noted in a page nine piece (3/25) that "A tourist bus was stoned and its headlights smashed." The Times could have made the shocking truth clear that innocent civilians were being attacked, and that the civilians were both Israelis and Western tourists.

Arab violence was explained and excused, and Israeli force criticized. The usual background picture described earlier of the alleged unfortunate Arab being forced to action out of a desperation caused by oppression was of course brought forward. The specific circumstances of each new event also provided material with which to criticize the Israelis.

Many Israeli soldiers were injured or killed in these numerous "demonstrations." An article by Shipler (3/26, pp. 1A, 4A) was headlined "Israeli Sergeant is Killed in Gaza in Grenade Attack," but only the first two sentences and one at the end concerned the murder of the Israeli. Thus there was almost no information about the killing or the soldier—no interviews with fellow soldiers, friends or family. It was not reported that this thirty-year-old man had a wife and three children. (In contrast, the "human interest" factor was common when the focus was on Arabs.) The story began: "An Israeli Army sergeant was killed and three other soldiers were wounded today, when a grenade was thrown into their jeep in occupied Gaza." It quickly shifted its focus, however. The Times noted that it was the first Israeli death, compared to six Palestinian deaths, in recent days. Again the usual picture was painted: "In the wide-spread demonstrations set off by Mr. Tawil's dismissal, Israeli soldiers, Jewish settlers and border police have fired into crowds of rock-throwing protesters, killing six. Most of the victims were teen-agers; a boy shot in the head Wednesday in the Gaza strip was 13, the *Jerusalem Post* reported today." The focus was also shifted from the killing of the Israeli by the photograph accompanying the story. It showed a smiling man in a nicely-tailored suit and had the caption "Bassam al-Shaka yesterday after he was removed from office."

The stabbing to death of a Druze Arab soldier in the Israeli army on the West Bank received little attention, despite the possibility here of an interesting "human interest" story as well as a story which could have revealed a good deal about the *actual* situation in this area of the Middle East. There was also no interest shown by the Times in the wounding of a female soldier by a hand grenade hurled by a Palestinian. The woman was riding in a van full of civilians in the Gaza strip when the grenade was thrown in. Thus, this was actually an attack on civilians, not even on military personnel. (The story was reported adequately in the New York-based *Jewish Press*.) It is telling that there was scant Times coverage when a Palestinian was blown up on the West Bank by an explosive device he was preparing.

Throughout these three months in early 1982, story after story told of an impending invasion of Lebanon which could be touched off by any occurrence. There was not much in the way of explanation of the causes which might make such an invasion necessary for the safety of Israel's citizens. The constant repetition created the image of a country always poised to invade its Arab neighbors, in much the same way it did not hesitate to brutalize the Palestinians under its control.

The application of a perverse double standard and the unjust castigation of the Israelis is made manifest when even comparable actions by Palestinians and Israelis were described differently. For example, Henry Kamm stated in a story (3/28, p. 9) that Israeli police "intimidated" Arab shopkeepers who wanted to close their stores as a show of protest, but he noted that there were "those [Arabs] who wanted to bring pressure on unwilling shopkeepers to join the strike." The actions of the Arab intimidators were dealt with gently: they do not "intimidate," they merely "want to bring pressure."

As noted in the previous section, the substitution of biased judgment for fact was common in Times news stories. A news report by Kamm (3/28, p. 9) referred to the "Government's harsh measures on the West Bank" as if this were a *fact*. The first line of the story was "The Israeli government last week enforced its hard line." On the same day, David Shipler (3/28, p. E3) presented as *fact* his opinion that the handling of the Arabs by the soldiers (who in truth were being assaulted) was "tough." Similarly, the headline in the Week in Review segment (p. E2) on the situation written by Barbara Slavin and Milt Freudenheim of the Times home office on April 4th was "Hanging Tough on West Bank and

Sinai." An objective outside observer might well have found the reactions of the government and the army *lenient*. In sharp contrast to this, there was little attention or analysis in the Times concerning the explicit public threat made by the Jordanian government during this period to kill the Palestinians on the West Bank who did not sever their connections with the moderate Village Leagues. There were, in fact, violent attacks on Arab moderates. (In November 1981 when Yusal al-Khalih of the Leagues had been ambushed and killed by two men, the P.L.O. claimed responsibility.) See the story by Kamm of one bomb attack on the head of a West Bank Village League. (4/1, p. A3)

The Times coverage was not *totally* lacking descriptions of Arab mob violence: "In the Gaza strip, Arab demonstrators in the town of Rafeh threw stones at troops, and soldiers were seen on Israeli television hurling stones back." (Shipler, 3/24, pp. A1, A6). This was an astoundingly mild reaction by a fully-equipped army to a violent provocation, and it was especially telling since this one was being accused of brutality. It is strange that the rather mild reaction of the soldiers was noted to have appeared on Israeli television. If Shipler meant to imply that Israel television was being used to present a distorted view of the army's activities, he was not being candid. In fact, the one state-run Israeli television station was strongly attacked by the government for being biased against it in its coverage of the West Bank clashes and of the army-Arab violence. The same article by Shipler rather delicately mentioned that "Stones were thrown [by Arabs] at pedestrians in the Old City of Jerusalem."

As mentioned, towards the middle of this three-month period in question the reporting on the clashes became slightly more balanced, in part due to the stories filed by Henry Kamm who had been sent to Israel temporarily to help cover the increased activity. The Times finally began to describe more fully the violent attacks by the Arabs, the moderate reactions of the Israeli soldiers and settlers, and the emotional feelings of the Jews when attacked. Thus one story (Shipler, 3/22, p. A3) reported that "the stone-throwing [at Jews in cars] infuriates settlers," and quoted one man as saying: "You can get killed. You're traveling at 50, 60 miles per hour, a rock comes, hits you in the face, you lose control of the car." This same man also pointed out that the settlers' general policy was to react to harassment by their Arab neighbors only after two such incidents. A story by Kamm (3/30, p. A13) noted that an Israeli on the West Bank "was stoned while driving on the Jerusalem-Hebron road. Injured, he retaliated by opening fire, wounding on of his attackers." The story was not given any prominence in the newspaper.

A story on April 17th ("Special to the N.Y. Times," p. 3) was subtitled, "13 Wounded While Assaulting Soldiers." Part of it read as follows:

> In the Sajiya quarter of Gaza, hundreds of Arab men wielding knives, stones, bottles and sticks tried to assault a detachment of troops, who fired tear gas and then shot into the crowd, the [army] spokesman said.
>
> In the town of Khan Yunis, the army spokesman continued, a group of Palestinian residents surrounded three or four soldiers, who first shot into the air and then at the legs of people in the crowd....
>
> In the Gaza beach refugee camp, about 500 people reportedly attacked a five-man patrol. The soldiers fired tear-gas cannisters and rubber bullets.
>
> [In the West Bank]... a crowd coming out of a mosque after Friday prayers attacked a small contingent of troops at a checkpoint, the spokesman said. They threw and rolled burning tires toward the soldiers, he reported, and the soldiers responded with gunfire, wounding three Arabs in the legs.

It was reported that an officer was asked why rubber bullets rather than live ammunition were not used in *all* situations, as before, and he replied that the special attachment necessary to fire rubber bullets made it take a dangerously long time to load and reload such bullets. There was no analagous questioning of rioters on the appropriateness of their weapons or tactics.

On April 15th (p. A7) Kamm described the violent actions of rioters:

"...a gasoline bomb was hurled at a military patrol..."

"In the town of Gaza, three Arabs were arrested after they assaulted an Israeli soldier and tried to wrest his weapon from him."

"Arabs were arrested on suspicion of overturning and smashing tombstones in a Jewish cemetery on the Mount of Olives in Jerusalem."

A day of Arab protest and riot within Israel focusing on the Israeli government's land policy—an annual event begun in the mid-1970's—took place at the same time as the West Bank and Gaza riots. Barbara Slavin and Milt Freudenheim tersely noted (4/4, p. E2) the "killing of six Arabs by Israeli troops in 1976 during protests against Government expropriation of Arab land in Galilee." This sentence, with the usual Times use of the words "killing," "protests," and "expropriation," was used to draw the typical, misleading picture of Israeli aggression against peaceful Arabs seeking justice. Henry Kamm stated (3/29, p. A5) that there had been "clashes" on that particular day in 1976, which did at least indicate that the Arabs may not have been merely passive prey. However, in another of Kamm's stories (3/31, p. A16) he referred to "the killing by security forces of six Arabs during protests against the Israeli expropriation of Arab-owned land in Galilee." In truth it was the *Arabs* who instigated the violence on that day in 1976. The *Daily News* (New York) noted in its story of March 31, 1982 (p. 6) that three Israeli police officers had been hurt in 1976 in the "violent protest" and "bloody riots." Although the expropriation of Arab land received attention in the Times, it was not noted that such expropriation is legal—as it is in other countries—and that *most* land in Israel is government-owned, i.e., "public land." The continuous and widespread illegal and immoral appropriation of public land by the Arabs in northern Israel—a grave national problem—was never mentioned.

127

Kamm's eye-witness account (3/31, p. A16) in the town hosting the major 1982 Land Day demonstration of ten thousand people reported: "Evidently determined to avoid clashes, the police and the army were not visible within miles of this town. The rally passed without incident...." Kamm also noted that a hand grenade had been thrown in an Arab terrorist attack in Jerusalem. On the very same page as Kamm's report was a story filed by David Shipler from Jerusalem about the generally quiet day on the West Bank. It contradicted Kamm's story when it reported: "While the Arab citizens of Israel proper clashed with the police...." Shipler was apparently committed to a particular view of events which was unaffected by the facts. One wonders why the editors assembling the paper in New York did not alter his news story so that it would not contradict Kamm's eye-witness report.

Despite the lack of a significant or eventful story here, the Times seemed committed to keeping Land Day in the public eye and presenting it in a particular light. Thus, there was a front-page photograph concerning the protests, and another one on page sixteen. The latter one was of the main demonstration, and showed a large number of shouting Arab protesters. Many were wearing keffiyas, cloth headwear rarely worn by Israeli Arabs, and using them to cover their faces. This style had become part of the image cultivated by Yasser Arafat and other P.L.O. terrorists, and it was thus a *potentially* telling photograph regarding the affinities of the demonstrators. However, the UPI photograph chosen for the front page was quite different. It showed three people: an Arab youth standing defiantly, a policeman aiming his rifle at him, and another policeman at his colleague's side with his hand on the other's shoulder, obviously urging restraint. The photographer had positioned himself behind the Arab, so the Times reader saw this situation from the point of view of the rioters, with the police rifle aimed at him or her. The caption read: "Violence is minor as Arabs Defy Israelis." This was not inaccurate. The rest of the caption in the early edition of the day's Times read: "Israeli policemen aim weapons at Arab youths who stoned their station." In the later edition this patently incorrect description of the scene was changed to note that one policeman's gun was trained on the Arab and the other policeman was physically and verbally urging control. The same picture was printed on page six of the *Daily News* (3/31), not page one, and the caption there showed that this paper's journalists were able to see from the very first that both policemen were not aiming their rifles. One must question how the erroneous Times caption came to be used in the first place, and why *this* photograph was chosen for the front page instead of the one on page sixteen which was more appropriate. The latter one was full of activity and emotion. Most importantly, it more accurately presented the central event of this news story.

In this, as in other instances, the Times seems to have been obsessed with Israelis aiming their guns at Arabs. Why was a photograph of the Arabs throwing stones at the policemen not shown? It is extraordinary that during these three months of stone-throwing, not *one* picture of these—or of any other Arab violence—appeared in the New York Times. The main demonstration Kamm witnessed and described was perhaps best shown in a photograph which appeared in the New York weekly, the *Jewish Press*. It showed a large number of protesters with clenched fists, and young men holding children aloft who were carrying P.L.O. flags.

The events related to the Times' front page picture were described by Kamm in his story on page sixteen:

> In the nearby town of Arabe, about 100 youths threw rocks at the police station. The police dispersed the crowd with teargas grenades. The police spokesman said the disorder had been set off by the appearance on the scene of a foreign television crew. By mid-afternoon Arabe was quiet.

It is quite probable that a good deal of the Arab activity on the West Bank during this entire period was encouraged by the very presence of the Western media, especially since its coverage of the events was so favorable to the rioters.

The 1982 Land Day demonstration in Israel was considered by many of its supporters to have been primarily a show of support for the West Bank and Gaza rioters. It was significant, therefore, that the major rally drew only 10,000 people. There are over 600,000 Arabs in Israel, most of whom live in the north within twenty miles of the demonstration site. The fact that relatively few of them came should have received a good deal of attention in the Times. Kamm did *briefly* note that 31 of the 54 local Arab councils in Israel refused to support the Land Day strike which had been called. Kamm stated that a large number of the groups which did support the strike were communist or communist-influenced, and that the leading role in the demonstration was played by the largely Arab, pro-Soviet, Israeli Communist Party. An in-depth analysis of these points was essential for an understanding of the situation which was receiving so much attention. It was never made, however. The focus of the Times coverage was elsewhere.

Propagandistic Photojournalism
and the Distorted Image

The use of photographs was an effective technique for the Times to present its distorted picture of events. The Land Day photos just described in the last chapter comprise a good example. So too does the previously mentioned picture of a well-dressed friendly-looking Bassam al-Shakr speaking on a telephone (4/2, p. A3.). This presented a favorable image (that of an American-style, white collar politician) of this dangerous political extremist. It appeared with the story headlined "Israeli Sergeant Killed in Gaza in Grenade Attack." As was also previously noted, the text of the story itself failed to deal adequately with the murder. The event mandated the headline, but it could not command the attention of the print and photo journalists.

The false view that the day-to-day life of Arabs in and near Israel is a dismal, oppressed existence was conveyed by the photographs appearing in the Times. For example, on April 6th (p. A2) there was a photograph of some pained-looking Arab children standing behind some barbed wire, looking as if they were in some sort of prison camp. If examined, however, it becomes quite clear that the photograph was staged. Any suspicion of its essential dishonesty is buttressed by the fact that when one looks closely, one can see several Arab men in the background watching the photography session and smiling.

Day after day the photographs of the clashes on the West Bank and Gaza showed only the Israeli response to Arab violence and pictured the Arabs only as victims. On the front page of the paper on March 25th was a photograph of an Israeli soldier leading away an Arab woman with the caption reading: "An Israeli soldier leads away an Arab protester in Ramallah, West Bank." Readers of the Times had no way of knowing that this photograph was actually a doctored version of the original UPI photo: the latter had been cropped at the bottom. The *Washington Post* of that day showed the full photograph on page twenty. Recognizable in the foreground of the complete photo was a burning, smoking tire. These burning tires were used as roadblocks by crowds of Arab rioters, and were sometimes rolled at soldiers at the same time torches, sticks and rocks were thrown. On aesthetic grounds alone, the original was a better photograph than that in the Times—it was clearer, better composed and more exciting. On purely journalistic criteria the original was much better since it showed what the scene of the riot actually looked like, and at least gave an indication of the Arab violence. The New York Times, however, was apparently not influenced much by these factors and did not give its readers the full picture.

The *Washington Post's* caption for the photograph was no more sound than that in the Times: "A Palestinian Girl is Led Away by an Israeli Soldier on the Sixth Day of West Bank Demonstrations." The flaming tire and the arrest would indicate to an objective observer that more than a mere "demonstration" took place, and the woman looks far too old to be called a "girl." The full photo was used in the Times' "Late City Edition" with this misleading remark added to the caption: "In foreground is a tire that caught fire...." There was no mention in either the Times or the *Washington Post* of what the "protester," as the Times called her, did to cause her to be arrested. It is interesting that the *Sunday Times* of London—overtly opposed to Israel's policies more than the New York Times—did not share the New York paper's aversion to showing or describing the violent actions of the Arabs. For example, on March 28th (p. 9) it printed a photograph (credited to Moshe Milner) with the caption: "Flames on the West Bank: Israeli soldiers shift a blazing oil drum after violent clashes at El Bireh."

The most common photographs concerning Israel that appeared in the New York Times during this period showed an Israeli soldier either arresting and leading away an Arab or committing some violent act against an Arab. Thus, on March 29th (p. A4) an Associated Press photograph showed a soldier grabbing a young Palestinian. Unlike most of the Times captions, however, this one did describe the violent provocation: "In Nablus, occupied West Bank, a Palestinian youth is seized by an

Israeli soldier after rocks were hurled at soldiers on patrol." On April 13th, there was a front-page photograph of helmeted soldiers and some young people with the caption: "An Israeli soldier firing tear gas at demonstrators in Jerusalem." It also noted that there was an Arab strike, which "... was called to protest an Israeli soldier's raid Sunday on the Temple Mount." As in other instances, there was no relevant front-page story and its placement thus seems wanton. Accompanying a news story on page three was an AP photograph of an Arab man holding up his hands to protect himself from an Israeli soldier menacing him with a club. The caption described it thusly: "An Israeli soldier raised a stick as he confronted a demonstrator yesterday in Nablus, in the Israeli-occupied West Bank. Protests were in reaction to an Israeli soldier's wild shooting Sunday on the Temple Mount." Thus Times readers were told of a "demonstrator" in a "protest" about something that sounds like a brutal Israeli act which warrants a protest. The violence presented in picture and word was all by Israeli soldiers. The *New York Post's* caption for the same photograph (4/13, p. 2) was: "Israeli soldier raises a stick against a Palestinian he caught throwing stones in a West Bank demonstration against a Jewish gunman's attack on a Moslem shrine." The latter caption is journalistically better than the one in the Times since it is more informative, more objective and more accurate. It notes the Arab's actions as well as the Israeli's, and its description of the attacker at the mosque as a "Jewish gunman" is much closer to the truth than the Times' pet term for him.

On April 17th (p. 3) a UPI photo in the Times showed several Israeli soldiers with an Arab man who bore a pitiful look on his face. The striking photo could easily evoke sympathy for the man, although this particular picture did offer an explanation of why he was being arrested: "Israeli soldiers removing an Arab youth from his home in Gaza. They said they were arresting him for throwing rocks during a demonstration." As usual, there was no photo of rock-throwing or other violence by Arabs. One is merely shown one frightened-looking civilian with several armed soldiers.

On April 18th (p. 3) there was a photograph of an Israeli tank in Gaza with the caption heading "Show of Force." There was no accompanying news story and no related news whatsoever—the rioting had ceased. Nevertheless, the Times apparently considered it important to keep the picture of Israeli military force before the eyes of its public. The photo caption also provided an opportunity to again remind its readers of the attack on Arabs at a Jerusalem mosque "by an Israeli soldier."

On April 22nd the New York Times printed its sole photograph in this entire three-month period of a violent attack on Israeli soldiers. In a remarkable action, it placed a huge photograph on the top of its front page which covered one-quarter of the page. The size of the photo and its placement signaled an extraordinary event in the history of this traditionally staid newspaper, and one would have assumed the photo to be of an event of truly mammoth proportions. It was not. The photograph showed *Jewish* civilians in Sinai who were opposed to Israel's final troop withdrawal on top of a building throwing objects at Israeli soldiers trying to get them down.

The Biased Coverage of Violence in Nearby Countries and against Americans

While the New York Times was focusing on the violence on the West Bank and in Gaza, there was little coverage of the violence occurring on a much greater scale between Arabs within fifty miles of Israel—in Lebanon and Syria—despite the fact that there were several Times correspondents in Beirut and Damascus. (There was also relatively little attention paid to the bloody Iraq-Iran war, a conflict with potentially great consequences for the region and for the United States.) In the case of Syria it was somewhat more excusable since there were restrictions on newsmen. For Lebanon, even the violent intimidation by the P.L.O. could not have accounted for the lack of significant information dispatched from there. In one news story the accusation of this laxity on the part of the Western press was noted. It was reported that Menachem Begin stated publicly that the Syrians had recently slain thousands of their own civilians in the city of Hama and destroyed dozens of mosques. In addition, the Syrians were guiltly of killing thousands of Lebanese Christians. Iraq, Begin said, was still fighting a war of aggression against Iran, and he tried to remind the world that in 1970 Jordan had not hesitated to use heavy artillery on Palestinian refugee camps to drive the P.L.O. out. (Thousands of Palestinians had been killed during "Black September.")

In February, March and April 1982 there were merely a few relatively minor news stories in the Times about the above mentioned attack by the Syrian army on the city of Hama, whose Muslim residents opposed the minority Alawite Muslim regime of President Assad. In an article sometime after this period, the Times reported that the city was largely in ruins from the shelling and that fifteen thousand civilians had been killed. Later estimates raised this to twenty thousand or more.

135

There was also far more bloodshed in Lebanon than in the West Bank or Gaza during this period, but *this* was not front page material in the Times, and the coverage was rather minimal. The most extensive treatment was presented in one article by John Kifner (4/16, p. A3) of the Times' Beirut office which noted that fighting in Beirut and south Lebanon between Lebanese Muslims and Palestinians had killed forty-two. (This was several times the number of fatalities which occurred in the Arab-Jewish clashes which was the major story in the Western media during these three months.) Kifner reported that the Lebanese Muslims were angry because the Palestinians had taken their land and because they attracted Israel's bombs. There was an AP photograph of a Palestinian girl whose father—a P.L.O. fighter—had been killed. Two days later a one paragraph AP story buried on page eight noted that in six days of fighting in Lebanon the death toll had reached 79, with 194 wounded. As for who was fighting whom and why, this report merely noted that "Rival Moslem militias battled...." A very short Reuters item on the same page noted that an American military attache had been shot by a sniper in Beirut. A rocket attack against the U.S. embassy there (Howe, 4/13, p. A6) was only mentioned in passing. (The failure of the Times to cover Arab attacks on American tourists in Jerusalem will be discussed later.) These stories would seem to have warranted more extensive treatment.

A rather small news article dealt with a significant situation in Lebanon which was related to the violence there ("Special to the New York Times," 4/5, p. A4). "Prominent delegates" from many countries, from the European Parliament, and from various organizations met with the Christians in Lebanon to call for the withdrawal of Syrian troops and the disarming of the P.L.O. Messages of support were sent by Senator Edward Kennedy, Congressman Jack Kemp, former French President Giscard d'Estaing, and other "prominent individuals." This article made the important point that the Christians in Lebanon comprised almost half of the total population.

When contrasted with the neglect of Arab violence, the Times' gratuitous preoccupation with Israeli counterattacks seems even more absurd and malicious. Israel was alleged to be brutish to Americans as well as to Arabs. A front page story by

Richard Halloran (3/25) of the Times' Washington bureau which focused on the subject of American military surveillance ships had as one of its subtitles: "Ship Attacked by Israel in 1967." It is difficult to see any journalistically valid reason for this subtitle, since the unfair, one-sided treatment of the subject—a tragic accident in the midst of the Six Day War which resulted in the deaths of many American sailors—was a very small part of the story.

Another news report ("Special to the N.Y. Times" 3/31, p. A15) which did not deal directly with policy ended with this statement: "Some State Department officials oppose allowing Israel to dictate policy towards friendly Arab countries, asserting that this polarizes the area." The Times was accepting the absurd charge and the absurd phrase which had been gaining currency among American government officials and among critics of Israel that Israel had in fact "dictated policy" or tried to. (Charges of Israeli control over Washington should certainly have ceased after that country's failure to stop the sale of AWACS to Saudi Arabia. However, being based on fantasies, the accusations were immune to such facts.) This attack was in strong contrast to the reference to "friendly Arab countries." No evidence of such "friendship" was provided. Indeed, it would have been impossible to do.

The Injudicious Use of Arab and Israeli Antigovernment Sources

New York Times reporters uncritically used the information and opinions provided by Arab and Israeli anti-government (anti-Begin) sources to present their negative picture of Israel. The reliance on such stories was injudicious, and their utilization in stories often propagandistic. Henry Kamm referred in a news story (4/22, p. A3) to the "Palestinian sources [for newsmen] here who gather information throughout the occupied territory." News reports *occasionally* noted when the sources were Palestinian (such as Shipler's story, 3/23, pp. A1, A7), but they *often* did so when the source was a spokesman for the army. (Usually, the stories were from an Arab perspective but of course were not identified as such.) Reports of an incident were sometimes given from both official Israeli sources and from Palestinian sources. This gave a false appearance of reportorial objectivity. Equating the two in this way gave the unidentified Palestinian sources a recognition and weight they may well not have deserved while derogating the official government statement from a person accountable for his remarks to the status of being merely another version. One example of this was in the very brief treatment ("Special to the N.Y. Times," 4/6, p. A3) about the finding of a dead Palestinian. It reported that an Israeli army official claimed that the dead man had accidentally blown himself up while preparing an explosive device, while "Palestinian sources quoted local Arab residents as contending that he had been killed by settlers." Some relatively simple investigation by the Times could have determined with some certainty which version was correct, and very possibly revealed some significant facts about the violent Arab activities on the West Bank. It could also have revealed something important about the relative reliability of Israeli and Palestinian sources. Such an investigation of trustworthiness—

essential to good coverage in the area—was apparently never made.

Many stories were one-sided, giving only the Arab version and perspective. (As noted, the general outlook of the reporters on the decades-old Jewish-Arab conflict seemed to coincide with that of the Palestinian Arabs.) One such report on the confrontations (Barbara Slavin and Milt Freudenheim, 4/4, p. E2) quoted Arab shopkeepers and West Bank mayors for their views, but neglected to give any Israeli opinions concerning the situation. Since it was not the expressed intention of this piece to give the Arab view, but rather objectively describe the situation, this was clearly an example of biased reporting.

Israel was also made to appear culpable through the use of damaging statements made by *unnamed* Israeli "officials." One was often told nothing about these "officials," even whether they held positions of some importance. This was done, for example, in the previously mentioned news article by David Shipler on censorship (3/30, p. A12). The content of the statements chosen for quotation would have made a very well-informed Times reader question the knowledge of this "official" on the subject. Since such statements by "officials" were often damaging to the Israeli position, the critical reader might have wondered about either the common sense or the political party affiliation of those quoted (that is, whether they opposed the government in power). The critical reader should have wondered how such "officials" were selected for quoting, and how such absurd statements were elicited. The use of such quotes should make one question the ability, judgment, objectivity and aims of the Times reporters.

One technique of the Times journalists for having others state what they themselves believed was to quote from the editorials of Israel's anti-government newspapers. Thus again, under the guise of "going to the sources," they quoted liberally from the *editorials* of the *Jerusalem Post*, an English-language organ which strongly supported the opposition Labor Party; *Haaretz*, a liberal, highbrow newspaper; and even *al-Hamish-mar*, the paper of a small, extremist, left-wing group. (One should note that *Haaretz* and the *Jerusalem Post* were able, to a large degree, to keep the opinions expressed in their editorial pages and columns separate from their objective news reporting. Although they often opposed the government's policies, it was difficult to detect this solely from their news stories.) It is significant that the readership of these newspapers was, and is, relatively small. To the discredit of the Times, the opinions expressed in the large circulation newspapers, *Maariv* and *Yediot Aharonot*, which were much more in tune with the general Israeli public opinion than the foregoing newspapers, were not reported. The pro-government daily *Hatzofeh*, geared primarily for the twenty percent of the population which is religious, was similarly ignored.

Opposition in Israel to the government's policies—real opposition and fabricated opposition—was focused on and played up, but popular support for the democratically elected government was ignored. Thus, David Shipler noted (3/23, pp. 1, A7) that the Begin government had been the object of increasing condemnation by "liberal-minded Israelis." On the subject of the West Bank he quoted from the *Jerusalem Post* to indicate that what he termed "extreme" statements of the Defense Minister, Ariel Sharon, had served to widen the gap between social groups. In the same story he also quoted from *Haaretz*. In another news story (3/28, p. E3) his source for a relevant quotation was *al-Hamishmar*, which he chose to describe as "socialist."

In a manipulative attempt to make Menachem Milson—the newly-appointed civilian governor of the West Bank and the architect of the new policies there—appear to be unreasonable, Shipler quoted a brief exchange between Milson and a news correspondent from Sweden. The journalist, Shipler noted, had been in a concentration camp, had been a foreign correspondent in Israel for several years, and had a son who was about to enter the Israeli army. The reader seems expected to interpret Milson's critical words to her in only the most simplistic way, and to assume the journalist's sagacity concerning Israel's security because of her background. Milson was, in fact, questioning her wisdom, although the newswoman's reply made it clear that (1) she did not understand this, (2) she believed her background made her beyond certain criticisms, and (3) she held that Milson was obviously unfair to her and out of touch with reality.

As stated, the New York Times reports from the Middle East generally gave the impression that there was a widespread and growing public disfavor in Israel with the government's policies, and much unwarranted attention was given to such sentiments. For example, Shipler wrote about protests by some Israelis concerning the treatment of the Bedouins in the Negev (3/9, p. A2), and in another story he stated that a public stir concerning the behavior of the army and the West Bank settlers was created (3/23, pp. A1, A27) in an incident on the West Bank which had been shown on Israeli television. Other Times correspondents did the same. Henry Kamm reported on March 28th (p. 9) that "In Tel Aviv, several thousand Israelis rallied after sundown ended the Sabbath to protest against the Government's harsh measures on the West Bank." (As noted before, the word "harsh" reflected a biased, subjective judgment, and should not have been used.) The next day Shipler mentioned (3/29, p. A4) that there were growing attacks on the government by Labor Party adherents and members of the Peace Now movement. The Times placed no stress where it should have been: on the unquestionable fact that Begin's West Bank policy was popular among the Israeli public (which had a good understanding of the matter). The *Sunday Times* of London reported on March 29th (p. 9) that Begin's new West Bank policy was approved of in Israeli public opinion polls.

New York Times journalists seemed to believe that they could perceive the true goals underlying the Israeli government's actions. This was despite the fact that the data necessary to support many of their assertions were absent. The accuracy of their glib judgments seems even more unlikely since the situation in the Middle East was extremely complex and fluid, as usual, and the Israeli government's policies seemed to be adjusting to the changing situation. Like other elements of the journalists' views of the past, present and future developments in the area, the alleged goals of the government were the same as those proclaimed by the Palestinians and by a few Israelis. The headline of David Shipler's "news and analysis" piece on March 27th (p. 4) was "Israel in the West Bank: The Goal Becomes Clearer." The supposed goal which Shipler was certain he could perceive was annexation. The next day the story by this pseudo-seer (p. E3) was headlined "The West Bank Occupation Now Resembles Annexation."

The Coverage of the Attack at the Mosque

The New York Times coverage of the killings at the Mosque of Omar (The Dome of the Rock) in Jerusalem and the rioting which immediately followed was very misleading. On April 12th it was the primary story of the day (Shipler, pp. 1, A12). The Times stressed that the culprit was an Israeli soldier, and the paper's headline read: "An Israeli Attacks Dome of the Rock, Killing at Least 2; Soldier at Moslem Shrine also Wounds 9 before Capture—Protests Injure Many." The first line of Shipler's story began: "An Israeli soldier with an automatic rifle...." No background on him was given in the story although it was stated that it was unclear at the time whether he was a reservist or a member of the regular army. (Almost all Israeli men serve in the reserves until the age of 55.) A sub-heading near the beginning of the story proclaimed: "Link to Extremists." This "link" to so-called "extremists" was merely the fact that some literature of the Kach movement had been found where he had been living. Past threats by the Kach movement to take over the Temple Mount were noted. The front page had a photograph of the attacker, and the caption referred to him as "A man identified as Alan Harry Goodman, formerly of Baltimore." On the inside pages were photographs of Arabs injured in the riots which followed the shootings.

The emphasis in other major newspapers was different from that in the Times, treating the culprit *primarily* as a maniac who had come from America, and focusing much attention on the rioting. Other newspapers were generally much more objective and accurate. The *Washington Post's* headline for that day (4/12) was "Two Killed in Mosque in Israel; Jerusalem Arabs Riot after Shooting by U.S.-Born Jew." There were photos of angry Arabs, the P.L.O. flag being held aloft, and an Arab injured by Israeli security forces. A photo caption referred to the assailant as the

143

"gunman." The story, by William Claiborne (a very strong critic of Israeli government policies) began: "An American-born Jewish gunman wearing an Israeli Army uniform and firing an M16 assault rifle...." The story reported that it appeared that the assailant had done a short stint in the army and was a reservist. (This was not true.) It stated that the United States State Department declared that the act was "obviously the work of a deranged individual."

The headline in the *New York Post* (4/12) was "Easter Sunday Mayhem." Featured on the front page was a photograph of an injured Arab and the explanation: "A wounded Arab is carried off by fellow Palestinians during the worst day of rioting in Israel's history following a shooting spree by a crazed American Jew." Inside the paper (pp. 2, 32, 33) were photographs of Goodman, of a woman who had been shot, and of an angry mob with a youth holding a P.L.O. flag aloft. The main story was written by a *New York Post* correspondent in Israel and entitled "Jerusalem Mayhem as Gunman Slays Two." Its lead sentence was "A crazed American-born Jew opened fire inside a sacred mosque...." It noted that he was wearing an Israeli army uniform and claimed that he had been called up to do reserve duty two weeks earlier. It added that "Police initially suspected that Goodman was a member of an extremist organization [the Kach movement] that is an offshoot of Rabbi Meir Kahane's Jewish Defense League. But officials later denied there was any involvement with the Jewish extremists."

The major *Daily News* story (4/12, pp. 2, 25), written from "combined dispatches," began with "An American-born Jew wearing an Israeli army uniform shot his way...." It said that he was apparently an army reservist. The news story provided background information on Goodman which showed that he was clearly mentally disturbed. There were photographs of an injured Arab, angry Arab crowds chanting, the P.L.O. flag being waved, and Alan Goodman.

The New York Times' identification and description of Goodman was generally erroneous, propagandistic and malicious. On April 13th, a day after its major story on the mosque attack, the Times had an article dealing with Goodman's background which indicated that he was not sane. As already shown, this highly significant information had been included in the main stories of the attack sent from Israel which had appeared in other newspapers the previous day, and the man's insanity was an essential and obvious element in their many subsequent stories. In the Times, however, his apparent insanity was almost entirely confined to this one article appearing a day after the major story.

In the days following the attack, the Times continued to refer to the assailant in the same terms it had in its first major story. Thus, a report from Israel on the following day ("Special to the N.Y. Times," 4/13, p. A3) referred to him *three times* in the first sentence as an "Israeli soldier," and gave the same identification two more times in the report. His name was mentioned once—in the seventh paragraph. A photo caption on page one also referred to "Israel soldiers" (*sic*). A Times Week in Review synopsis (Barbara Slavin and Milt Freudenheim, 4/18, p. E2) similarly referred to the shooting rampage by an "Israeli soldier." The primary designation in the news stories of Henry Kamm in Israel (4/15, p. A7) and Beirut correspondents John Kifner (4/15, p. A6) and Marvin Howe (4/14, p. 1) was "American-born Israeli soldier," although he was often simply referred to as "an Israeli soldier" ("Special to the N.Y. Times," 4/13, p. A3; Kamm, 4/17, p. 2). As already noted, the designations used by such newspapers as the *Washington Post*, the *Daily News* and the *New York Post* gave a very different (and more accurate) picture. The caption for an AP photograph which appeared in the New York Times (4/13, p. A3) referred to the assailant as an "Israeli soldier." The same photograph in the *New York Post* (4/13, p. 2) had the term "Jewish gunman" in its caption. An AP story the *New York Post* printed on the same page referred to Alan Harry Goodman, an "immigrant from the U.S.," and a UPI story described him solely as a "Gunman" in its title. Another news report in the *New York Post* referred to "American-Born Alan Harry Goodman."

The New York Times terminology was also incorporated into its coverage of the riots in the days following the assault. For example, one story ("Special to the N.Y. Times," 4/13, p. A3) began: "Violent protests erupted throughout the Israeli-occupied West Bank and Gaza Strip today over the rifle attack by an Israeli soldier on Moslems in the Dome of the Rock. Sixteen Arabs were reported shot by soldiers breaking up the demonstration." (See also "Special to the N.Y. Times," 4/17, p. 3 for a similar statement.)

The Times version of the events at the Dome of the Rock was inaccurate and incomplete. As with other stories, such things were never explicitly corrected in later days, and thus the facts did not appear in the Times even after their publication in other newspapers. In the main story on the attack by Shipler, he incorrectly asserted of the gunman: "In uniform, he had no trouble carrying his weapon through the two checkpoints leading to the [Temple] mount, where even handbags are usually searched for guns and explosives." In contrast, the *Washington Post* and other newspapers accurately reported in their first stories of the incident how Goodman had to shoot his way to the Mount, and that his first two victims were two police guards—one Arab, one Jewish.

In reaction to the shooting, Arabs began to crowd onto the Mount as well as elsewhere in Jerusalem and rioted. The Times reported that the Arabs waved sticks and shook their fists, and that "Stone-throwing youths injured at least 27 Israelis and foreigners on the Mount of Olives, and two of the injured were hospitalized." The *Washington Post* reported that the Israeli troops were called in "to disperse angry rock-throwing crowds" of Palestinians brandishing knives and clubs who filled the thirty-five acre Temple Mount. It noted that many Israeli police and troops, as well as foreign tourists, had been hurt by stones and had been sent to the hospital. It added that the Israeli news agency (ITIM) had reported that some of the tourists were Americans. The *Daily News* noted in the *first* paragraph of its report on this story that several of the tourists who were injured were Americans and that many other foreigners and Israelis were hurt. The *New York Post* also reported that American tourists were injured. As I have noted, the Times paid little attention to the Arab violence and described the injured tourists primarily as "foreigners."

The vocal enunciations of the rioting Arabs reported in the Times were much milder than those reported in other newspapers. The Times stated that the Arab mobs yelled what it termed "nationalist slogans": "Palestine is Arab," "Jews Out," and "God is Great." The *Washington Post* reported that the crowds chanted "P.L.O., P.L.O., Palestine is Arab," and "We will avenge with blood and spirit the [mosque's] honor." They vowed to "redeem in blood" the honor of the mosque. The *New York Post* correspondent reported that the rioters were screaming "God is Great" and "Death to the Jews."

A small incident which received some attention in the Times, and was apparently *supposed* to be telling, concerned the fact that when the Israeli troops were leaving at the end of the clashes one Israeli soldier threw a tear gas cannister near the mosque entrance, and that—according to the reporter—it was perfectly placed since a wind carried the tear gas directly into the mosque. In contrast, an action mentioned in the *New York Post* may have better characterized the general attitude and approach of the Israeli army: before entering the mosque to go after the gunman, the Israeli soldiers removed their boots out of consideration for Muslim tradition and sensitivity.

It has already been mentioned that indications that Goodman may well have been connected with the Kach movement were made in the Times. The early stories noted that those in this movement had made threats in the past, and that the Arabs believe there is a plan by the Israeli government to ban Muslims from this mosque on the Temple Mount. I should add that those in the Kach movement (the so-called "extremists") want the Great Jewish Temple—first erected by King Solomon on this spot—rebuilt, and are bitter about the fact that the Arabs constructed a mosque on this Jewish holy ground. They demand the right to pray on the site. The mosque was correctly identified in the Times as the third holiest place in Islam, after those in Mecca and Medina in Saudi Arabia. (Medina, or Yathrib, had been a Jewish city for five hundred years until the Jews were expelled by Mohammed.) The Times also reported that The Temple was destroyed by the Romans in 70 A.D., and that "There has been no Jewish presence on the mount since then, although it is one of the holiest places in Judaism." This and other statements concerning the Temple Mount were inaccurate, incomplete and misleading. The reason for the lack of a Jewish presence on the Mount should have been noted: Jews were forbidden to set foot on it by the successive conquerors of Jerusalem, who have primarily been Muslims. It is not "one of the holiest places in Judaism," but has been the only true Jewish holy place for thousands of years. The *Washington Post* correctly noted that it is the traditional site of the Holy of the Holies. Both the *Washington Post* and the *Daily News* reported that the Israeli government had placed the Temple Mount off limits to Jewish worshippers as a conciliatory gesture to the Arabs, who vehemently oppose their presence.

In all Times news stories during this period, in its maps and even in its Sunday travel section, the "Western Wall" of the Temple Mount was called the "Wailing Wall." (See, for example: Shipler, 3/17, p. A3; 4/12, pp. 1, A12; 4/11, pp. 1, 15, 19; "Special to the N.Y. Times," 4/13, p. A3.) This was the name given it in the past because Jews came there for almost two thousand years to bemoan the destruction of the Temple and the forced dispersion of the Jewish people, as well as to pray. After its repossession in the 1967 war, it was formally renamed the Western Wall since wailing was no longer relevant. It was insensitive and insulting to call it by its former name because of its associations, and the Times reporters should have known this and acted with some decency, especially those in the Jerusalem bureau (like Shipler) who have lived in Israel for years. The *Washington Post* called it the Western Wall in all of its stories and its maps. (See, for example, 4/12, pp. A1, A17.)

Two days after the attack at the mosque, the *Washington Post* noted that when Goodman was being led to court to be formally charged, he made a senseless attempt to escape. (See the photo caption.) The *New York Post* headlined its story of the day (4/13, p. 2) on the subject "Court Outburst by Temple Gunman." The New York Times story of the arraignment, "Israeli Arraigned in Mosque Raid" ("Special to the N.Y. Times," 4/14, p. A6), did not even mention his wild actions described in the *New York Post*. Unlike the *Washington Post* and other newspapers, it did not carry a photograph of his being brought to court by the police, that is, of his being brought to justice by the Israeli government. The story did report that police spokesmen stated that Goodman had been on leave from basic training when he carried out his attack, and that he had been in the army for only two weeks. However, this important story of the arraignment was relegated to page six of the Times and it was not noted in either the paper's detailed daily index or in its "News Summary" section of important items.

The other stories that day concerning Israel which *were* included in the index were: "Boy, 8 years old, Killed in Gaza Strip"; "Moslem Nations Denounce Israel at the U.N."; and "Brinkmanship Strategy on Peace with Egypt and War with P.L.O.," which was an analysis of Menachem Begin's policies by David Shipler.

A headline in the *New York Post* (4/13) used a quote by Alan Goodman in its story of the arraignment: "My Mosque Murder Spree was Act of Revenge against Arabs." It focused on the man and his stated motives. It indicated that he was insane, but that he did have a political ideology. The story began:

> A self-described "Zionist fanatic" told police here he joined the Israeli military reserves so he could get an automatic weapon and kill Arabs, the *Post* has learned. In a bizarre confession to Jerusalem police, American-born Alan Harry Goodman said he had decided "years ago" to "take revenge against Arabs for terrorist operations."

It goes on to report that he claimed to be taking vengeance for the March 1978 P.L.O. killing of 36 Israeli civilians and the wounding of 70 more when terrorists commandeered a bus in Israel. " 'The terrifying pictures of that massacre were chasing me,' the gunman said. 'I felt myself obligated to take vengeance.' "

In its many stories related to the Mosque incident and its aftermath, the Times mentioned several important items rather briefly which should have been reported in full and with some analysis. This would have revealed significant elements of Arab psychology as well as political policies which were of central importance to (1) the stories being covered, (2) the entire situation in the Middle East, and (3) American interests in the area. The Times quoted (4/13, p. A3, "Special to the N.Y. Times," "30 Injured in West Bank Violence") the wild claims of the Supreme Islamic Council that "it was absurd of the Prime Minister's [Begin's] office to describe the assailant as deranged because all regular soldiers were supposed to undergo physical examination. Moreover, the council contended the prisoner had not been alone. It said he had been covered during his attack by fire from many sides." The next

149

day ("Special to the N.Y. Times," 4/14, p. A6) the Times repeated the accusation of the Council that more than one person was involved in the shooting. Another story by its U.N. correspondent (Nossiter, 4/14, p. A11) indicated that King Hassan of Morocco said through his envoy at the UN Security Council that Israel bore responsibility for the Mosque attack, and accused Israel of 'passivity if not collusion' with 'Zionist-terrorist groups.' A piece in the Times' Week in Review section (Barbara Slavin and Milt Freudenheim, 4/12, p. E2) noted that the Arabs were trying to place the blame for the attack on Israel as a whole. It was never reported in the Times, or any other major American newspaper, that some Arab countries were broadcasting that the assailant was actually an American agent working for the Israeli government. It has already been noted that the first article on the Mosque attack reported the Arab belief that there is a plot by the Israeli government to take over the Muslim holy sites. (The fact is that the holy places have been left in the hands of Muslim officials, and such a belief is true paranoia.)

Coverage of the Impending Israeli Withdrawal from Sinai

During these same three months in 1982, the Times' treatment of Israeli fears concerning their return of the remaining part of Sinai to Egypt (in accordance with the Camp David agreements) tended to belittle the apprehensions of the Israelis concerning the real, tangible threat this posed to their security. The reluctance of many Israelis to give back Sinai was not usually attributed by the Times to their valid strategic concerns, but rather to religious impulses or to alleged psychological and near-spiritual elements embedded in the Israeli psyche. (This was in sharp contrast to the usual absence of any psychological analysis of the Arabs.) Thus Shipler claimed (4/1, p. A3) concerning the traumatic abandonment of the settlements in Sinai that for the Jews in Palestine and Israel "settlement has been a nearly-sacred precept since early in the century."

Related to this was the repeated minimization in the Times of the charges by Israel that Egypt was violating the recent treaty in the areas of Sinai already evacuated. One news story (Shipler, 4/6, pp. 1, A4) noted that Israel had "charged" that Egypt had allowed Bedouins to smuggle five hundred weapons through the area Egypt already controlled, and that Israel "claimed" to have intercepted them before they reached their proximate destination—Palestinians in Gaza. Concerning Egyptian troop violations, Shipler wrote that "they have been characterized by some officials as minor." It was not made clear whether these "officials" were Israeli, Egyptian, or American. He continued: "Some [alleged violations] apparently involve the deployment of units that provide the capability of rapid expansion into a wartime posture, Israelis say, and this is worrisome for officials in Jerusalem." The Egyptians, it was reported, agreed to withdraw the troops Israel "says" exceeded the allowable limit. Subsequent Times reports

151

clearly showed that the Egyptians had indeed exceeded these limits, but the significance of such transgressions was consistently minimized.

Another front-page Times story (Shipler, 4/14, pp. 1, A10) subjected Israelis and their leaders to psychoanalysis, and proclaimed Begin guilty of "Brinkmanship Strategy" in its headline because of his government's threat to not carry out the rest of the withdrawal agreement because of Egyptian violations. (It did at least mention that the Israelis "claimed to have captured guns, grenades and explosives in Gaza which had been brought from Egypt through the area of Sinai already returned to Egypt.") A story filed by Henry Tanner in Cairo the same day (p. A10) was headlined "Egypt Denies any Violations of Peace Accords with Israel." An article summarizing the developments before the final Israeli withdrawal (Shipler, 4/18, p. E2) attributed Israeli actions primarily to irresponsible guile: "Prime Minister Menachem Begin and his cabinet ministers led Israel and the rest of the world on a roller coaster of apprehension last week about the peace process with Egypt." He continued: "The rapid shift in Jerusalem's official mood appeared to be part manipulation, part authentic change." The very real and specific Egyptian violations of the treaty agreements to police the Sinai and adhere to certain numbers of troops equipped with specific arms were again minimized. It offered the incredible justification that "Egypt regards the limits as flexible." Shipler maintained that Egyptian President Mubarak's less-than-friendly actions and statements in recent weeks, which had caused great worry among Israelis, were made merely to please other Arab countries and were thus not significant. Back in March Shipler had stated: "For its part, Israel has shown little appreciation for Mr. Mubarak's political problems." (3/7, p. E4. In March [3/25, p. A2], the columnist Anthony Lewis, who was touring the Middle East, was permitted to file a "news" story from Egypt. It was a lengthy presentation of Mubarak's views.)

One of Henry Tanner's stories which complemented Shipler's April 18th article and was printed on the same page dealt with the Israeli "claims" of unwarranted Egyptian troop levels and Israel's repeated protests about the smuggling of arms into Gaza. This article was headlined "Why Egypt Regards the

Withdrawal as Overdue" and indicated that Egypt had no desire to confront or menace Israel. In one of the rare instances in the Times of analysis of the Arab psyche, Tanner focused on the supposed positive aspects of Egypt's concern for its "dignity" and "pride," and failed to discuss the bloody results of the neurotic Arab obsession with these matters.

Afterword: The Treatment of Israel in Times Editorials, Opinion Columns, and Op. Ed. Essays

The focus in this analysis has been on the New York Times' news stories, although a few words have been said about its opinion columns and editorials. Some brief comments should be added concerning these as well as the guest columns on the "Op. Ed." ("Opposite the Editorial") page. In general, these presented a view not very different from that in the news reports, and Times news stories were often referred to for evidence. The contributions of the staff columnist Anthony Lewis—which leaned heavily on the news stories of David Shipler—have received widespread criticism (in *Commentary* and *The New Republic*, for example) for their wild claims and gross inaccuracies, as well as for the unreliability of Lewis' sources. Although more leeway can be expected in such opinion pieces than straight news reports, some standards of evidence and fairness should be maintained.

Needless to say, the news stories and columns were generated and presented within a common social and intellectual context produced, in part, not only by the reporters and columnists, but the editors and the publisher.

The editor of the Op. Ed. page for several years, including this period, was Charlotte Curtis, a former society reporter. Curtis is the author of two books—one on Jacqueline Kennedy and the other on life among the "jet set." According to the Times, the purpose of the Op. Ed. page "is to give readers a broad range of opinion and analysis of current issues," and the Times' publisher Arthur Ochs Sulzberger stated publicly that "Charlotte Curtis has fulfilled that mission with great distinction." (4/15, p. C28.) The fact is, however, that the great preponderance of the opinion pieces by both the regular columnists as well as the guest writers during these months was strongly anti-Israeli.

155

J'accuse

by Norman Podhoretz

The war in Lebanon triggered an explosion of invective against Israel that in its fury and its reach was unprecedented in the public discourse of this country. In the past, unambiguously venomous attacks on Israel had been confined to marginal sectors of American political culture like the *Village Voice* and the *Nation* on the far Left and their counterparts in such publications of the far Right as the Liberty Lobby's *Spotlight*. Even when, as began happening with greater and greater frequency after the Six-Day War of 1967, Israel was attacked in more respectable quarters, care was often taken to mute the language or modulate the tone. Usually the attack would be delivered more in sorrow than in anger, and it would be accompanied by sweet protestations of sympathy. The writer would claim to be telling the Israelis harsh truths for their own good as a real friend should, on the evident assumption that he had a better idea than they did of how to insure their security, and even survival. In perhaps the most notable such piece, George W. Ball explained to the readers of *Foreign Affairs* "How to Save Israel in Spite of Herself." No matter that Ball warned the Israelis that unless they adopted policies they themselves considered too dangerous, he for one would recommend the adoption of other policies by the United States that would leave them naked unto their enemies; no matter that he thereby gave the Israelis a choice, as they saw it, between committing suicide and being murdered; he still represented himself as their loyal friend.

And so it was with a host of other commentators, including prominent columnists like Anthony Lewis of the *New York Times*, academic pundits like Stanly Hoffmann of Harvard, and former diplomatic functionaries like Harold Saunders. To others it might seem that their persistent hectoring of Israel was making a considerable contribution to the undermining of Israel's case for American support and thereby endangering Israel's very existence. Nevertheless, they would have all the world know that they yielded to no one in their commitment to the survival of Israel. Indeed, it was they, and not Israel's "uncritical" supporters, who were Israel's best friends in this country. As a matter of fact, they were even better friends to Israel than most Israelis themselves who, alas, were their "own worst enemies" (an idea which recently prompted Conor Cruise O'Brien, the former editor of the London *Observer*, to remark: "Well, I suppose Israelis may be their own worst enemies, but if they are, they have had to overcome some pretty stiff competition for that coveted title").

This kind of thing by no means disappeared from the public prints with the Israeli move into Lebanon. In the thick file of clippings I have before me there are many expressions of "anguish" and "sadness" over the damage Israel was doing to its "image" and to its "good name." In a fairly typical effusion, Alfred Friendly wrote in the *Washington Post* (of which he was formerly the managing editor):

> Perhaps it was expecting more than was possible—that Israel should remain the country with a conscience, a home for honor, a treasury for the values of mind and soul. At any rate, it is so no longer but merely a nation like any other, its unique splendor lost...its slaughters are on a par with...Trujillo's Dominican Republic or Papa Doc's Haiti. Still absent are the jackboots, the shoulder boards, and the bemedalled chests, but one can see them, figuratively, on the minister of defense. No doubt Israel is still an interesting country. But not for the reasons, the happy reasons, that made it such for me.

In addition to lamenting Israel's loss of moral stature as a result of Lebanon, these great friends of Israel condemned the resort to "unselective and disproportionate violence" (Anthony

Lewis) on the ground that it "cannot serve the spirit of Israel, or its true security."

But the sympathetic protestations of this particular species of friend—including even Lewis, perhaps the most unctuous of them all—became more perfunctory and more mechanical in the weeks after the war began. One got the feeling that they were offered mainly for the record or to fend off criticism. And in any case, the preponderant emphasis was no longer on the putative damage Israel was doing to itself by its wicked or stupid policies. The focus was unmistakably on the evils Israel was committing against others, as in this passage from a column by Richard Cohen in the *Washington Post*:

> Maybe the ultimate tragedy of the seemingly
> nonstop war in the Middle East is that Israel
> has adopted the morality of its hostile neigh-
> bors. Now it bombs cities, killing combatants
> and non-combatants alike—men as well as
> women, women as well as children, Palestini-
> ans as well as Lebanese.

Israel's "true friends," then, were liberated by Lebanon to say much more straightforwardly and in more intemperate terms than before what they had all along felt: that Israeli intransi-gence and/or aggressiveness and/or expansionism are the main (and for some, the only) source of the Arab-Israeli conflict and therefore the main (or only) obstacle to a peaceful resolution of that conflict.

Even if this were all, it would have increased the volume and intensity of the attacks on Israel to an unprecedented level. But what made matters much worse was the proportionate escalation and increasing respectability of the attacks from quarters that had never pretended to friendly concern with Israel.

To be sure, apologists for the PLO who had always been ugly about Israel—Edward Said, Alexander Cockburn, and Nicholas von Hoffman, to mention three prominent names—had been getting a more and more deferential hearing in recent years. Books by Said like *The Question of Palestine* had been widely and sympathetically reviewed in the very media he indiscriminately denounces for being anti-Arab; Cockburn, whose weekly pieces in the *Village Voice* have set a new standard of gutter journalism in this country (and not merely in dealing with Israel), has been rewarded with regular columns in *Harper's* and the *Wall Street Journal* (where in exchange for access to a respectable middle-class audience he watches his literary manners); and von Hoffman, who is only slightly less scurrilous than Cockburn, has also found a hospitable welcome in *Harper's* and a host of other mainstream periodicals both here and abroad (not to mention the television networks). Writing to a British audience in the London *Spectator* (for which he does a regular column), von Hoffman exulted openly about this change:

> Where before it was difficult to print or say something that was critical of Israeli policies and practices, the barriers are now coming down. Some writers used to believe—rightly or wrongly—that to expound a Palestinian point of view was to risk blacklisting. Now many have become emboldened....

But if they were becoming "emboldened" before Lebanon, their tongues now lost all restraint. Von Hoffman himself is a case in point, having been emboldened in another piece in the *Spectator* to compare Lebanon to Lidice and the Israelis to the Nazis: "Incident by incident, atrocity by atrocity, Americans are coming to see the Israel government as pounding the Star of David into a swastika."

Whether von Hoffman published these words in the United States, I do not know, but by his own account he could easily have found an outlet. "Where once, among the daily press, only the *Boston Globe* could be counted on to print other points of view as a matter of consistent policy... now other voices are becoming somewhat more audible."

Somewhat? According to one estimate, of the first 19 pieces on the war in Lebanon to appear on the *New York Times* Op-Ed page, 17 were hostile to Israel and only two (one of them by me) were sympathetic. I have not made a statistical survey of the *Washington Post* Op-Ed page, but my impression is that the balance there was roughly the same. In short, not only did the kind of virulent pieces formerly confined to the *Village Voice* and other yellow journals of the Left and Right increase in number and intensity; such pieces now also began appearing regularly in reputable papers and magazines.

Thus no sooner had the Israelis set foot in Lebanon than Edward Said was to be found on the Op-Ed page of the *New York Times* declaring Sidon and Tyre had been "laid waste, their civilian inhabitants killed or made destitute by Israeli carpet bombing," and accusing Israel of pursuing "an apocalyptic logic of exterminism." The comparison of Israel with the Nazis here was less brazen than in von Hoffman's piece, but William Pfaff more than made up for it in the *International Herald Tribune*: "Hitler's work goes on," he began, and concluded with the prediction that Hitler might soon "find rest in Hell" through "the knowledge that the Jews themselves, in Israel, have finally... accepted his own way of looking at things." The famous spy novelist John le Carré was imported from England by the *Boston Globe* to deliver himself of similar sentiments:

> Too many Israelis, in their claustrophobia, have persuaded themselves that every Palestinian man and woman and child is by definition a military target, and that Israel will not be safe until the pack of them are swept away. It is the most savage irony that Begin and his generals cannot see how close they are to inflicting upon another people the disgraceful criteria once inflicted upon themselves.

Finally, the syndicated cartoonist Oliphant, like Cockburn in the *Wall Street Journal*, portrayed besieged west Beirut as another Warsaw ghetto, with the PLO in the role of the Jews and the Israelis in the role of the Nazis.

Many other writers were also "emboldened" by Lebanon, but not quite enough to compare the Israelis with the Nazis. Alfred Friendly, in the passage quoted above, only compared them to Trujillo and Duvalier. Hodding Carter, in the *Wall Street Journal*, invoked Sparta (though his use of language like "Several Lebanese towns have been pulverized by the tactics of total war [and] tens of thousands of Lebanese have been killed or injured since the blitzkrieg was launched" suggested that Sparta was not really the state he had in mind). And Joseph C. Harsch, in the *Christian Science Monitor*, brought up Communist Vietnam: "Vietnam is imperial. It dominate[s] its neighbors Laos and Cambodia. In that same sense Israel is now the dominant power in its own area." Extending this ingenious comparison, Harsch wrote:

> Israel's major weapons come from the U.S. Israel's economy is sustained by subsidies from the U.S..... It depends on Washington, just as Vietnam depends for major arms and for economic survival on Moscow. Neither Israel nor Vietnam could dominate their neighborhoods if the support of their major patrons were withdrawn.

But the prize for the most startling comparison of all goes to Mary McGrory of the *Washington Post*, who was reminded of the dropping of atomic bombs on Hiroshima and Nagasaki. More startling still, Miss McGrory said that in her opinion what the Israelis were doing in Lebanon was worse. Addressing Begin directly she wrote:

> You were trying to save your own troops. We understand that. We are, after all, the country that dropped atomic bombs on Hiroshima and Nagasaki.... But grant us that we were up against a mighty, if weakened, war machine and a totally mobilized nation. You were punishing a wretched country that reluctantly shelters factions, which, while hostile to you, could not wipe you off the face of the earth, however much they might want to.

What are we to make of words and images like these? How are we to explain them? How are we to understand what they portend?

There are well-wishers of Israel, among them a number of Jews, who recoil in horror from the idea that the Israelis are no better than Nazis, but who believe that Israel under Menachem Begin and Ariel Sharon has brought all this violent abuse on itself. Even though the degree of condemnation is excessive, say these anxious well-wishers, the Israelis have only themselves to blame for besmirching their "good name." Yet I would suggest that the beginning of wisdom in thinking about this issue is to recognize that the vilification of Israel is the phenomenon to be addressed, and not the Israeli behavior that supposedly provoked it. I say "supposedly" because when a reaction is as wildly disproportionate to an event as this one was, it is clearly being fed by sources other than the event itself.

But what am I or anyone else to say to those for whom there is nothing obvious about the assertion that in this particular case the reaction was disproportionate? From such people one is tempted to turn away in disgust. Yet difficult as it may be to entertain, even for as long as it takes to refute it, the loathsome idea that Israel is to the Palestinians as the Nazis were to the Jews, the world evidently still needs to be reminded of the differences.

To begin with, then, the Nazis set out to murder every Jew on the face of the earth, and wherever they had the power to do so, they systematically pursued this objective. Is this what the Israelis have tried to do to the Palestinians? If so, they have gone about it in a most peculiar way.

In Germany under the Nazis, the Jews were first stripped of their civil and political rights and then sent to concentration camps where virtually all of them were put to death. For more than thirty-five years, by contrast, Palestinian Arabs living in the state of Israel have enjoyed Israeli citizenship and along with it a degree of civil and political liberty, not to mention prosperity, unknown to Arabs living in any country under Arab sovereignty.

For fifteen years, moreover, about a million Palestinians on the West Bank and Gaza have been in the power of Israel under military occupation. Have squads of gunman been dispatched to shoot them down in the fashion of the *Einsatzgruppen* who murdered an approximately equal number of Jews in those parts of the Soviet Union occupied by the Nazis? Have the West Bank Palestinians been rounded up and deported to concentration camps in preparation for being gassed, as happened to some three million Jews living in other countries occupied by Nazi Germany? The Nazis in less than six years managed to kill more than five million Jews in occupied territory. How many Palestinian Arabs

163

have been killed by the Israelis in fifteen years? A hundred? And if even that many, has a single civilian been killed as a matter of policy? Again, the fact is that the Palestinians living even under Israeli military occupation, and even since the recent political offensive against PLO influence on the West Bank, have enjoyed a greater degree of civil and political liberty than any of their brother Arabs living anywhere else *except* in Israel as Israeli citizens.

It is or ought to be obvious, then, that any comparison between the way Israel has treated the Palestinians and the way the Nazis dealt with the Jews is from a rational perspective, let alone morally, disproportionate to a monstrous degree. Anyone who makes such a comparison cannot possibly be responding to the facts of the case and must be driven by some other impulse.

But what about the comparisons of Israel with Sparta, or Haiti, or Communist Vietnam? Are they any the less disproportionate? If so, it is only because nothing could match the intellectual and moral excess of equating Jews with Nazis. Still, these comparisons are sufficiently outlandish in their own right.

Sparta, to start with the least repellent of them, was a police state so dedicated to war and so singlemindedly devoted to the martial values that any male child deemed unfit to become a soldier was taken to the mountains and abandoned to his death. Israel is a democracy with an army made up largely of civilian reservists to whom nothing is more distasteful than going to war and to whom peace is the highest value. As for Haiti or the Dominican Republic under Trujillo, they have so little in common with Israel in any respect that bringing their names into the discussion can only be seen as an effort to sneak by with the absurd charge that Israel is no longer a democratic country.

Apparently, though, not even this charge was too absurd to surface openly in the public prints. Thus, Douglas S. Crow, Professor of Religion, no less, at Columbia University, wrote in a letter to the *New York Times* of Israel's "posturing as a bastion of democracy." But if Israel, where all citizens, including Arabs, have the right to vote and where all individuals and parties, including the Communists, enjoy a full range of liberties—speech, press, assembly, and so on—is not a bastion of democracy, where shall such a bastion be found?

The same point can be made of the analogy with Communist Vietnam, where there is even greater repression than in Trujillo's Dominican Republic and perhaps even greater economic misery than in Haiti. To compare Israel—which can indeed be described as a bastion of democracy—with what is by all accounts one of the most Stalinist regimes in the entire Communist world, is a sufficiently gross travesty. But is the comparison Joseph C. Harsch makes between the behavior of the two states toward their respective neighbors any more justifiable?

Both, says Mr. Harsch, are "imperial" states using military forces to dominate the countries of the region. That this is an apt characterization of Communist Vietnam very few will nowadays contest. Two years after signing a peace treaty with South Vietnam, the Communist regime of the North invaded and conquered the South. Not content with that, Vietnam proceeded to invade Cambodia where it installed another puppet regime, while keeping some 40,000 troops in Laos to insure its domination over the Communist regime there. Nor could Vietnam nor Cambodia nor Laos pose any threat to Hanoi.

If we now ask what this set of relationships has in common with the relations between Israel and its neighbors, the answer can only be: nothing whatever. One grows weary of reciting the facts of the Arab-Israeli conflict over and over again. But the controversy generated by Lebanon demonstrates that far from being tiresomely familiar, they are still unknown by some and forgotten or deliberately ignored by others for whom they are politically inconvenient.

In 1947, then, the Unites Nations adopted a partition plan for Palestine, dividing it into a Jewish state and a Palestinian one. The Jews accepted the plan; the Arabs rejected it. The form this rejection took was a war against the new Jewish state of Israel launched by the armies of five neighboring Arab states, with the aid and encouragement of all the others. Israel successfully fended off this assault and begged its neighbors to make peace with it. But they all refused, rededicating themselves instead to the elimination of any trace of a sovereign Jewish state from the region.

Living in consequence under siege, with a coalition of nineteen nations pledged to its destruction, Israel maneuvered as best it could. In 1956, it joined forces with the British and the French in an attack on Egypt with left the Israelis in control of a stretch of the Sinai desert. But in response to American pressure, all three parties soon withdrew, and Israel in particular returned the Sinai to Egypt (without any *quid pro quo*). So much for the first instance of Israeli "expansionism" or "imperialism" and the only one to which these epithets have so much as a remotely plausible claim.

The next episode occurred in 1967, when Egypt took a series of actions clearly spelling an intention to resort once again to military force whose explicit objective was—as its then leader, Nasser, put it—"the destruction of Israel." After waiting for about two weeks while the United States and others worked unsuccessfully to avert a war in which they might be "wiped off the map" (Nasser's language again) if the Arabs struck the first blow, the Israelis launched a preemptive attack. Six days later, thanks to a brilliant campaign, they found themselves in possession of territory formerly belonging to or occupied by Egypt (the Sinai), Syria (the Golan Heights), and Jordan (the West Bank).

To the Arabs and their apologists, this was another instance of expansionism and imperialism. But since virtually no one doubts that Nasser provoked the 1967 war or believes that there would have been a war at all if not for his closing of the Straits of Tiran (among other actions he took), how can it be regarded as an imperialistic operation by Israel? In any case, Israel begged King Hussein of Jordan to stay out of the war once it started, and if he had agreed, the Israelis would not have ended the war in control of the West Bank.

Even so, Israel once again, as it had been doing since the day of its birth, asked only for recognition and face-to-face negotiations with its Arab neighbors. Such negotiations would have resulted in the return of occupied territories with whatever minor boundary adjustments security might dictate. Yet once again, as they had from the beginning, the Arab states refused, responding this time with the famous three No's of Khartoum: No recognition. No negotiation. No peace.

Finally, seven years later and after yet another war—this one unambiguously started by Egypt in a surprise attack—Anwar Sadat (Nasser's successor) called what had been universally regarded in the Arab world as Israel's "bluff" by offering recognition and face-to-face negotiations. Almost overnight, Israel responded by agreeing to return every inch of Egyptian territory and then honored the agreement. So much for imperialism.

Now comes Lebanon. To show that Israel is behaving toward Lebanon as Vietnam has behaved toward Cambodia, Joseph C. Harsch writes:

> Israel has now decreed that there must be no more "foreign" military forces in Lebanon. That means that Israel wants all Palestinian and Syrian armed units out of Lebanon, leaving Lebanon in the hands of elements which would be sympathetic to Israel and to its interests.

There are so many astonishing features in these two sentences that one hardly knows where to begin. In the first place, why the quotation marks around the word foreign? Is Harsch trying to suggest that the "Palestinian and Syrian armed units" are indigenous or native to Lebanon? In the second place, what is illegitimate about Israel's desire to leave Lebanon "in the hands of elements which would be sympathetic to Israel and its interests"? In view of the fact that those "elements" would be the Lebanese people themselves, there can be nothing wrong in leaving Lebanon in their hands; and in view of the fact that before Lebanon was taken over by the PLO and the Syrians it was sufficiently "sympathetic to Israel and its interests" to live peacefully alongside Israel, a more accurate way of putting the case would be to say that Israel hopes to free Lebanon from the domination of foreign forces who have turned an unwilling Lebanon into a battlefield of their war against Israel.

But of course putting it that way would defeat the purpose of portraying Israel as an imperialistic power imposing its will upon a helpless neighbor. And it would also show the falsity of describing the war as an invasion of Lebanon. Yes, the Israelis did invade Lebanon in the sense of sending military forces across the Lebanese border. But if we are looking for analogies, a better one than any fished up in recent weeks would be the invasion of

France by allied troops in World War II. The purpose was not to conquer France but to liberate it from its German conquerors, just as the purpose of the Israelis in 1982 was to liberate Lebanon from the PLO.

Harsch and many of his colleagues may not know this, but the Lebanese people do. In spite of the sufferings inflicted upon them by the war, and in spite of the fact that they have no love for Israel, they have greeted the Israelis as liberators. Representative Charles Wilson, a Texas Democrat who is so far from being reflexively pro-Israel that he voted for the AWACS sale and intends to vote for the Jordanian arms sales, testified after a visit to Lebanon in July to

> the universal enthusiasm with which the Lebanese welcomed the Israeli army.... I mean it's almost like a liberating army.... It was astonishing. I expected this, somewhat, from the Christian population. But I didn't expect if from the Muslim population.... And in talking to a group of people, some of whom had lost relatives, they said it was awful. But they said that all in all, to be free of the PLO it was worth it.

One can see why. According to a news story by David K. Shipler in the *New York Times*, the PLO, whose "major tool of persuasion was the gun," ruled over a large part of Lebanon, terrifying and terrorizing the local populace, Christian and Muslim alike. It took over land and houses, it confiscated automobiles, it stole at will from the shops, and anyone who complained was likely to be shot. Operating as a state within a state, the PLO humiliated local Lebanese officials and displaced them with its own police and "people's committees."

On top of all this, writes Shipler, the PLO "brought mercenaries in from Bangladesh, Sri Lanka, Pakistan, and North African countries. By all accounts the outsiders were crude, undisciplined thugs." And then there were the killings. "Before the PLO," one Lebanese woman told Shipler, "we used to be pro-Palestian.... [But] when we saw the Palestinians were killing us and threatening us and having barricades and shooting innocent people, then came the hatred."

Rowland Evans and Robert Novak, whose column has always been notorious for its pro-Arab bias, arrived at the same assessment: "Once incorruptible, its extraordinary success in accumulating arms and money... had made the PLO itself an occupying power... permeated by thugs and adventurers."

If this disposes of the idea that a Vietnam-like Israel was imposing its imperial will upon Lebanon, it does not dispose of the charge that the war in Lebanon was imperialistic in a different sense—that Israel's purpose, as Anthony Lewis (among many others) charges, was "to exterminate Palestinian nationalism" in preparation for annexing the West Bank.

Here again, before taking up the substance, one is forced to begin by pointing to the form in which the charge is expressed. By using the word "exterminate"—a word which is inescapably associated with what the Nazis did to the Jews—Lewis contrives to evoke the comparison while covering himself by designating "Palestinian nationalism" rather than the Palestinian people as the victim. But even in this form the charge is an outlandish misrepresentation. For the *maximum* objective of the Begin government is to establish Israeli sovereignty in the West Bank while allowing to the Palestinians living there a degree of control over their own civil and political affairs far greater—once more the point must be stressed—than they have ever enjoyed in the past, or than Arabs enjoy in any country under Arab sovereignty. This is "to exterminate Palestinian nationalism"?

And even this—to repeat, Begin's *maximum* objective—is subject by Begin's own commitment to negotiation. That is, in signing the Camp David agreement, Begin has obligated the state of Israel to settle the question of sovereignty after five years by negotiations among all the interested parties, including the West Bank Palestinians. This means that whether Begin and Sharon like it or not, they or their successors might well find themselves turning over the West Bank to Jordan or to a new Palestinian leadership willing, unlike the PLO, to live in peace both with Israel and Jordan.

It is precisely the hope of encouraging such a leadership to emerge that lies behind the two-sided strategy of destroying the

PLO as a military force in Lebanon and as a political force on the West Bank. I urge anyone who doubts this to read "How to Make Peace with the Palestinians" by Menahem Milson (*Commentary*, May 1981). In that article Milson said that Israeli policy on the West Bank had in the past inadvertently led to the strengthening of the PLO's influence there. He therefore advocated a new policy aimed at weakening the PLO so that the "silenced majority"— which in his judgment wished to live in peace with Israel—could make itself heard. The end result was to be a demand by the Palestinians on the West Bank that King Hussein repudiate the PLO as "the sole representative of the Palestinian people" and resume his old role of the spokesman.

After reading that article, Begin and Sharon appointed Milson (then a professor of Arabic literature at the Hebrew University) to the post of civil administrator of the West Bank, from which position he has been putting the policy outlined in the article into practice. The PLO and its apologists have naturally done everything in their power to sabotage and discredit Milson. But the political war against the PLO was proceeding on the West Bank as the military campaign against the PLO in Lebanon was being launched.

No one can say what the eventual disposition of the West Bank will be. What one can say with complete assurance, however, is that so long as the only alternative to Israeli occupation is a Palestinian state ruled over by radical forces pledged to the destruction of Israel, then no Israeli government—no matter who might be its prime minister—will be permitted by Israeli public opinion to withdraw. But one can also say, though with less assurance, that if an alternative should present itself, then no Israeli government, including one headed by Ariel Sharon, would be permitted by Israeli public opinion to absorb the West Bank.

Israelis have different reasons for wanting to rid themselves of the West Bank. Some fear the effects of continued occupation on the character of Israel as a democratic society; others fear the effects on the character of Israel as a Jewish state of adding so many Arabs to its demographic mix; still others are convinced that continued occupation is a formula for continued war.

But whatever their motives, many or (as I read Israeli public opinion) most Israelis would favor a withdrawal from the West

Bank provided they were reasonably confident that the successor regime would be willing to live in peace with a neighboring Jewish state (and provided also, probably, that Jews who wished to go on living in Judea and Samaria would have the same right to do so as Arabs have in Israel). Elimination of the radical rejectionist Palestinians—whether or not they call themselves the PLO—is a precondition for any such resolution of the Palestinian problem. Consequently, if Begin and Sharon succeed in their objective of destroying the PLO, they may well make it impossibly difficult for Israel to annex or absorb the West Bank—not because of pressures coming from Washington but because of pressures coming from within Israel itself.

All this, however, is for the future. Returning to the present and to the war in Lebanon, we still have to face the charge that Israel was waging a wanton and indiscriminate campaign against defenseless civilians.

In the early days of the war, words like "holocaust" and even "genocide" freely circulated in the media, along with horrendous estimates of the number of civilians killed or rendered homeless by Israeli arms. At first it was said that 10,000 people had been "slaughtered" in southern Lebanon and 600,000 turned into refugees. But no sooner had these figures been imprinted on the public mind than it was revealed that the *total* population of the area in question at 510,000—almost 100,000 fewer than were supposedly driven out of their homes. Israel claimed that there were 20,000 refugees and perhaps 2,000 casualties, of whom more than half were only wounded. Correspondents and other visitors to Lebanon soon confirmed that the original figures were "extreme exaggerations" (Shipler), while casting evenhanded doubt on the much lower Israeli figures. Even though "discussions with local officials and residents of the cities tend to reinforce the Israeli estimates of casualties there," wrote Shipler, "the Israeli figures exclude a lot."

Thus arose what came to be called "the numbers game." But the damage to Israel had already been done. In any case, what did it matter, asked Mary McGrory, what the exact figures were? Whatever the precise number, "it is already too many." In her open letter to Begin, she asked:

Does Israel's security have to be purchased by the slaughter of innocents?... We have been seeing every night pictures of wounded babies and old men. We read about people standing outside devastated apartment buildings, wearing masks against the stench of corpses, waiting to go in to claim their dead. They were a threat to you? Yes, we know, your planes dropped leaflets before they dropped the bombs. But why did you have to bomb their cities at all? People in apartment buildings may be PLO sympathizers or even devoted adherents of Yasir Arafat. But they were unarmed civilians.

Indeed they were, but Miss McGrory's letter might better have been directed to Arafat than to Begin. For (in Shipler's words):

The huge sums of money the PLO received from Saudi Arabia and other Arab countries seem to have been spent primarily on weapons and ammunition, which were placed strategically in densely populated civilian areas in the hope that this would either deter Israeli attacks or exact a price from Israel in world opinion for killing civilians. Towns and camps were turned into vast armories as crates of ammunition were stacked in underground shelters and antiaircraft guns were emplaced in schoolyards, among apartment houses, next to churches and hospitals. The remains could be seen soon after the fighting, and Palestinians and Lebanese can still point out the sites.

This strategy of hiding behind the civilians was entirely natural for the terrorist organization whose greatest exploits in the past invariably involved hijackings and the killing of innocent bystanders. Having held airplanes and buildings hostage, the

PLO—as the American Lebanese League declared in a newspaper advertisement—was now holding much of Lebanon itself hostage, and especially west Beirut. Who, the League asked, gave "the PLO authority to insist that Lebanese civilians die with them?" Certainly not the Lebanese civilians themselves.

It is also important to note that under international law (specifically Article 28 of the Geneva Convention of 1948), "the presence of a protected person may not be used to render certain points or areas immune from military operations," and the responsibility for civilian casualties or damage rests on the party, in this case the PLO, who thus uses protected persons or areas. What the other side, in this instance Israel, is required to do is exactly the kind of thing Miss McGrory derides in her reference to the dropping of leaflets: that is, warn the civilians so that they have a chance to leave the area or otherwise protect themselves.

While scrupulously observing this requirement, the Israelis also took other steps to minimize civilian casualties, some of which led to an increase in their own casualties. This is why Miss McGrory's citation of the bombing of Hiroshima and Nagasaki is so bizarre. As it happens, I myself agree with her in thinking that the United States was justified in that action (because the result was to shorten the war and to save many more lives than were lost in the two raids). But the whole point of the bombing of Hiroshima and Nagasaki was to wreak indiscriminate damage which would terrorize the Japanese into surrendering. The Israelis were doing almost exactly the opposite in Lebanon. Their strikes were so careful and discriminating that whole areas of southern Lebanon were left untouched. If they really had been carpet bombing, both the levels of destruction and the number of casualties would have been far greater.

That a left-wing liberal like Mary McGrory should be driven into comparing Israel's military tactics in Lebanon with the dropping of the atom bomb on Hiroshima and Nagasaki is demented enough. But that she should go on to defend the use of the atom bomb by the United States (which in any other context she would surely condemn) in order to score an invidious point against Israel is a measure of how far her animus extends. It literally knows no bounds.

173

Obviously a reaction like this can no more have been provoked by the facts of Israel's behavior than the comparisons of Israel with Nazi Germany. Nor can the relatively milder denunciations of Israel as comparable to Sparta or Haiti or Vietnam be taken as a rational response to what Israel has done. What then can explain them?

In thinking about this question while reading through dozens of vitriolic attacks on Israel, I have resisted the answer that nevertheless leaps irresistibly into the mind. This answer, of course, is that we are dealing here with an eruption of anti-Semitism. I have resisted because I believe that loose or promiscuous use of the term anti-Semitism can only rob it of force and meaning (which is what has happened to the term "racism"). In my judgment, therefore, it should be invoked only when the case for doing so is clear and precise. When that condition is met, however, I also believe that one has a duty to call the offending idea by its proper name.

Not everyone agrees, not even Meg Greenfield, who in *Newsweek* happily endorses "plain talk about Israel" and who as editor of the *Washington Post* editorial page has certainly done a lot of plain talking herself. Miss Greenfield sees it as a "good thing" that the "resentful, frustrated, expedient silences" Americans have maintained over Israel have now been "interrupted by outraged, emotional condemnation of what Israel is doing." Some of this, she acknowledges, is excessive: "The comparison [of the Israeli invasion] to Nazi policy, for instance, has been as disproportionate in its way as the military violence it complains of." But the rest is understandable, and is anyway not to be confused with being anti-Israel or anti-Semitic. Indeed these very accusations have intensified the pent-up resentments which are now exploding into what Miss Greenfield calls "no-holds-barred attacks on the Israeli action."

In other words, though we are to have "plain talk about Israel," and though such talk is healthy when directed against Israel, we are not to have equally plain talk about the attacks on Israel. To say that such "no-holds-barred attacks on Israel" are anti-Israel is unhealthy, and to say that they are anti-Semitic is even worse.

George W. Ball also rules out any use of the term anti-Semitism:

> I long ago made it a practice not to answer any
> letter questioning my position on Middle East
> problems that contains the assertion or impli-
> cation that I have said or written anything
> anti-Semitic. That accusation, in my view, is a
> denial—I might even say an evasion—of ra-
> tional argument.

Yet when he goes on to explain why it is absurd to accuse him
of anti-Semitism, he brings forth so shallow a conception of what
the term means that it can only be described as historically
illiterate. Anti-Semitism, according to Ball, is the dislike of Jews;
it is therefore a sufficient refutation to point out that some of his
best friends are Jewish, and that all his life he has admired the
Jews for their contribution to the arts, to intellectual life, and to
liberal political causes.

That a man of George Ball's experience and education should
regard this as an adequate account of anti-Semitism reveals an
astonishing blind spot. But this blindness is an advantage,
enabling Ball to accuse American Jews of dual loyalty—a classic
anti-Semitic canard that also surfaced in the debate over the
AWACS—and then indignantly and self-righteously to deny that
this makes him an anti-Semite.

Unlike Ball, Conor Cruise O'Brien, who has a habit of
speaking plainly on all subjects, does believe that some critics of
Israel are "motivated by some kind of anti-Semitic feeling, possibly unconscious." In some instances, he concedes, it may be that
what is at work is "genuine compassion for suffering Arabs,
expressing itself in terms of a generous hyperbole." But in most
others "there are indications to the contrary." These indications
include the absence of any concern for the civilian casualties in
the war between Iraq and Iran, and the silence that greeted the
killing of an estimated 20,000 Sunni Muslims recently by President Assad of Syria in the city of Hama. (To O'Brien's examples
may be added the indifference to the 100,000 people killed in
internecine strife in Lebanon since 1975 on the part of virtually
all those who have wept over the civilian casualties in Lebanon
since the Israelis went in.) O'Brien suggests, however, that a term
other than anti-Semitic is needed because "the people in question

are...extravagantly *philo*-Semitic these days, in their feelings for the Arabic-speaking branch of the Semitic linguistic family." He proposes "anti-Jewism," and he offers a test by which it can be detected in the discussion of Israel: "If your interlocutor can't keep Hitler out of the conversation,...feverishly turning Jews into Nazis and Arabs into Jews—why then, I think, you may well be talking to an anti-Jewist."

The trouble is that the term "anti-Jewist" cannot be applied to those like George Ball who are loud in their protestations of friendship for the Jewish people, and who might even agree that comparing the Israelis with the Nazis deserves to be called anti-Semitic.

Let me therefore propose that we retain the historically sanctioned term "anti-Semitism" and let me outline a more general criterion for identifying it than the one O'Brien suggests. Historically anti-Semitism has taken the form of labeling certain vices and failings as specifically Jewish when they are, in fact, common to all humanity: Jews are greedy, Jews are tricky, Jews are ambitious, Jews are clannish—as though Jews were uniquely or disproportionately guilty of all those sins. Correlatively, Jews are condemned when they claim or exercise the right to do things that all other people are accorded an unchallengeable right to do.

As applied to the Jewish state, this tradition has been transmuted into the double standard by which Israel is invariably judged. The most egregious illustration is the UN resolution condemning Zionism as a form of racism. According to the thinking of this resolution, all other people are entitled to national self-determination, but when the Jews exercise this right, they are committing the crimes of racism and imperialism. Similarly, all other nations have a right to insure the security of their borders; when Israel exercises this right, it is committing the crime of aggression. So too, only Israel of all the states in the world is required to prove that its very existence—not merely its interests or the security of its borders, but its very existence—is in immediate peril before it can justify the resort to force. For example, whereas the possibility of a future threat to its borders was (rightly in my opinion) deemed a sufficient justification by the United States under John F. Kennedy to go to the brink of nuclear war in the Cuban missile crisis of 1962, the immense caches of arms discovered in PLO dumps in southern Lebanon have not persuaded many of the very people who participated in or applauded Kennedy's decision that the Israelis were at least equally justified in taking action against the PLO in Lebanon.

Criticisms of Israel based on a double standard deserve to be called anti-Semitic. Conversely, criticisms of Israel based on universally applied principles and tempered by a sense of balance in the distribution of blame cannot and should not be stigmatized as anti-Semitic, however mistaken or dangerous to Israel one might consider them to be. A good example can be found in the editorials published in the *New York Times* on Lebanon. Unlike the consistently superb editorials on Lebanon in the *Wall Street Journal*, the ones in the *Times* have been harsh on Israel, they have often been unfair, and they have pointed toward policies that would jeopardize Israel's security. But they have not been guided by the usual double standard, and therefore cannot and should not be stigmatized as anti-Semitic.

Criticisms of Israel that *are* informed by a double standard on the other hand, deserve to be called anti-Semitic even when they are mouthed by Jews or, for that matter, Israelis. That being Jewish or possessing Israeli citizenship guarantees immunity from anti-Semitic ideas may seem a plausible proposition, but it is not, alas, borne out by experience. Like all other human beings, Jews are influenced by the currents of thought around them; and like all other minority groups, they often come to see themselves through the eyes of an unsympathetic or hostile majority. Jews are of course the majority in Israel, but the state itself is isolated among the nations, and subjected to a constant barrage of moral abuse aimed at its delegitimation. This seems finally to be taking the inevitable psychological toll in the appearance among Israelis of the term "fascist" in talking about their own society, when by any universal standard it is among the two or three countries in the world least deserving of this epithet.

To be sure, very few Israelis have reached the point of blaming the Arab-Israeli conflict largely on Israel or Menachem Begin or Ariel Sharon. But a number of American Jews have been adding their own special note to the whining chorus of anti-Israel columnists, State Department Arabists, and corporate sycophants of Saudi Arabia which has grown more raucous over

Lebanon than ever before. The misleading impression has been created that these "dissenters" reveal a serious split within the American Jewish community over Israel. In fact, however, with a few notable exceptions they represent the same minority of roughly 10 or 15 percent which has all along either opposed Israel (because as socialists they considered Zionism a form of reactionary bourgeois nationalism for other reasons), or else came to support Israel grudgingly and only on condition that it comport itself in accordance with their political ideas. It is these people who have lately been congratulating themselves on their courage in "speaking out" against Israel. A few of them—those who live and work within the Jewish community—are actually dissenting. But most of the rest live in milieux like the university or work in professions like journalism in which defending Israel takes far more courage than attacking it.

Not only do these people invoke a double standard in judging Israel: they proudly proclaim that they do. "Yes, there is a double standard. From its birth Israel asked to be judged as a light among the nations." These words come from one of the endless series of columns Anthony Lewis has written on the war in Lebanon. Lewis is Jewish, and even though he makes no public point of it, I single him out here because his thinking is typical of the way Jewish "dissenters" who have been signing ads and giving interviews see not only the war in Lebanon but the Arab-Israeli conflict as a whole.

Thus while he usually pays his rhetorical respects to the Arab refusal to recognize Israel, Lewis's emphasis is always on the sins of Israel, whether real or imaginary.* And while piously proclaiming his great friendship for Israel, he harasses it relentlessly and obsessively, justifying himself in this by hiding behind the political opposition in Israel or behind Zionist heroes of the past like Justice Brandeis. (Others use the Bible for these purposes, humbly comparing themselves to the prophets of old: "[The] biblical tradition of criticism and dissent should now guide public practice," two young Jewish academics declared on the Op-Ed page of the *Times*. "Jeremiah's polemics indicate that a government's foreign and security policies, as well as societal inequity and immorality, are grounds for legitimate dissent.")

But is it true that "From its birth Israel asked to be judged as a light among the nations," or even as the socialist paradise dreamed of by so many of Israel's Jewish "friends" on the Left? No doubt there have been Zionist enthusiasts who indulged in such rhetoric, but it is a historical travesty to claim that this was the animating idea behind the Jewish state. If perfection had been the requirement, it would have been tantamount to saying that an imperfect Israel had no right to exist; and since imperfection in human beings is unavoidable, Israel would have been sentencing itself to an early death from the day of its birth.

In any event, the opposite is more nearly true: that the purpose of Israel was to *normalize* the Jewish people, not to perfect them. The Jewish state was to create not a utopia but a refuge from persecution and a haven of security in which Jews who chose or were forced to settle there could live a peaceful and normal life. Thanks to the refusal of the Arab world to agree to this, the Jews of Israel have instead had to live in a constant state of siege. It would have been fully understandable if under those conditions Israel had become a garrison state or a military dictatorship. Yet no such development occurred. Founded as a democracy, it has remained a democracy, a particularly vital variant of the species—the only one in the Middle East and one of the few on the face of the earth.

In reminding ourselves of that enormous and wondrous fact, we come to the greatest irony of this entire debate. Although Israel is no more required than any other state to justify its existence through what Anthony Lewis or anyone else, myself included, considers good behavior; and although elementary fairness dictates that Israel not be condemned for doing things that all other nations are permitted to do as a matter of course; even so, even judged by the higher standard that Lewis and his ilk demand, the truth is that Israel *has* become a light unto the nations.

Thus, in remaining a free democratic society while surrounded by enemies and forced to devote an enormous share of its resources to defense, Israel has demonstrated that external threats do not necessarily justify the repression of internal liberties. For casting this light, in whose glare the majority of the nations of the world stand exposed, Israel not surprisingly wins no friends at the UN.

If its persistence in democratic ways under the most unpromising circumstances has helped win Israel the enmity of the Third World, the fierceness of its will to live is what has made it a scandal and a reproach to its fellow democracies in the Western world. For in the glare of *that* light, the current political complexion of the Western democracies takes on a sickly, sallow, even decadent look. We in the West confront in the Soviet Union a deadly enemy sworn to our destruction, just as Israel does in the Arab world. But whereas the Israelis have faced the reality of their peril and have willingly borne the sacrifices essential to coping with it, we in the West have increasingly fallen into the habit of denial, and we have shown ourselves reluctant to do what the survival of our civilization requires. We tell ourselves that the danger comes from our own misunderstanding and misperception; we castigate ourselves for being the main cause of the conflict; we urge unilateral actions upon ourselves in the hope of appeasing the enemy.

It is a rough rule of thumb that the more deeply this complex of attitudes is rooted in an individual or a group or a nation, the more hostility it will feel toward Israel. I readily admit that other factors also come into play. Anxiety over oil or business connections in the Arab world often turn people against Israel who might otherwise admire it precisely for setting the kind of example of realism and courage they would wish the West to follow. Secretary of Defense Caspar Weinberger is perhaps one such case and there are others scattered through the Defense Department, and State Department and the White House. There are also so-called hardliners where the Soviet Union is concerned (Evans and Novak come to mind) who have always believed that a tilt away from Israel and a more "evenhanded" policy in the Middle East is necessary if we are to contain the spread of Soviet power and influence in that region. This idea dies so hard that it may even survive the tremendous blow it has suffered in Lebanon.

On the other side, one can find many American Jews and liberal politicians concerned about Jewish support who back Israel even though in most other situations they tend to sympathize with forces comparable to the PLO (such as the guerrillas in

El Salvador) and even though they are great believers in the idea that all disputes can and should be settled through negotiation.

Even allowing for these complications, however, one can still say that the more committed to appeasement of the Soviet Union a given party is, the more it opposes "military solutions to political problems," and the more hostile it will be to Israel. Thus the West European governments—the very governments which are so eager to prop up the Soviet economy, to ignore Afghanistan and Poland, and to ratify Soviet military superiority in Europe through arms-control negotiations—are far less friendly to Israel than is the American government. And within the United States itself, the people who are most sympathetic to the European point of view on the issue of the Soviet threat are among those least friendly to Israel.

These are the same Americans who also tend to pride themselves on having learned "the lessons of Vietnam"—lessons which, as Terry Krieger points out in a brilliant piece in the *Washington Times*, Israel has dramatically refuted. For Israel has shown that military force is sometimes necessary; that the use of military force may also be beneficial; and that a Soviet client, "whether it be a guerrilla force or a terrorist organization," can be defeated by an American ally. This, Krieger thinks, is why such people have turned on Israel with vitriolic fury: "Those Americans who have denounced Israel's invasion of Lebanon eventually may forgive Israel for defending itself, but they may never forgive Israel for illuminating our own confusion and cowardice."

Again Anthony Lewis offers himself as a good illustration. Indeed, the terms in which he has denounced Israel's invasion of Lebanon are strongly reminiscent of the hysterical abuse he used to heap on the United States in Vietnam. This being so, it is worth remembering that Lewis called the Christmas 1972 bombing of Hanoi—in which by the estimate of the North Vietnamese themselves no more than 1,600 were killed—"The most terrible destruction in the history of man" and a "crime against humanity." It is worth recalling too that only days before the Khmer Rouge Communists would stake a claim to precisely that description by turning their own country into the Auschwitz of Asia, Lewis greeted their imminent seizure of power with the question: "What future possibility could be more terrible than the reality of what is happening to Cambodia now?" Yet with that record of political sagacity and moral sensitivity behind him, Lewis has the effrontery to instruct Israel on how to insure its security, and he has the shamelessness to pronounce moral judgment upon the things Israel does to protect itself from the kind of fate at the hands of the Arabs that has been visited by the Communists upon South Vietnam and Cambodia.

The Bible tells us that God commanded the ancient Israelites to "choose life," and it also suggests to us that for a nation, the choice of life often involves choosing the sacrifices and horrors of war. The people of contemporary Israel are still guided by that commandment and its accompanying demands. This is why Israel is a light unto other peoples who have come to believe that nothing is worth fighting or dying for.

But there is more. In the past, anti-Semitism has been a barometer of the health of democratic societies, rising in times of social or national despair, falling in periods of self-confidence. It is the same today with attitudes toward Israel. Hostility toward Israel is a sure sign of failing faith in and support for the virtues and values of Western civilization in general and of American in particular. How else are we to interpret a political position that, in a conflict between a democracy and its anti-democratic enemies, is so dead set against the democratic side?

Even on the narrower issue of American interests, George Ball, Anthony Lewis, and those who share their perspective are so driven by their animus against Israel as to think that (in Lewis's astonishing words) "Looking at the wreckage in Lebanon, the only people who can smile are the radicals and the Russians." Yet consider: Israel, an American ally, and armed with American weapons, has defeated the Syrians and the PLO, both of them tied to and armed by America's enemy, the Soviet Union. Are the Russians insane that this should cause them to smile? The military power of the PLO, representing the forces of radicalism and anti-Americanism in the Middle East, has been crushed; and (unless Ball and the others, who are so desperate to save it, should work their will) its power to terrorize and intimidate may also be destroyed, leaving the way open for such forces of moderation as may exist in the Arab world to come forward. How should this make the radicals smile and the United States weep? Egypt, America's best friend in the Arab world, has been strengthened and the policy of accommodation it has pursued toward Israel has been vindicated in comparison with the rejectionist policies of Syria and the PLO. Can this be good for the Russians and damaging to American interests?

George Ball says that it can be and that it is. But this is so palpably absurd that it cannot be taken as the considered judgment of an informed and objective mind. Therefore if it is proper to indict anyone in this debate for bias and insufficient concern for American interests, it is Ball who should be put in the dock and not the Jewish defenders of Israel against whom he himself has been pleased to file this very indictment.

In the broadside from which I have borrowed the title of this essay, Emile Zola charged that the persecutors of Dreyfus were using anti-Semitism as a screen for their reactionary political designs. I charge here that the anti-Semitic attacks on Israel which have erupted in recent weeks are also a cover. They are a cover for a loss of American nerve. They are a cover for acquiescence in terrorism. They are a cover for the appeasement of totalitarianism. And I accuse all those who have joined in these attacks not merely of anti-Semitism but of the broader sin of faithlessness to the interests of the United States and indeed to the values of Western civilization as a whole.

* For an example of the latter, see Ruth R. Wisse's discussion in "The Delegitimation of Israel," in the July 1982 *Commentary*. The case in point was a false allegation of censorship against the Israeli authorities on the West Bank, combined with complete silence about the repression of free speech on the East Bank—that is, in Jordan.

The War in Lebanon

by Frank Gervasi

An old adage has it that truth is the first casualty of war. The maxim was abundantly confirmed by Western journalists last summer during Israel's war against the Palestine Liberation Organization in Lebanon. The opportunity for fair, balanced reporting was unique; correspondents of both the print and electronic media could cover the fighting from both sides simultaneously. Unfortunately, however, the overall results were more often misleading than illuminating and, on the whole, considerably less than objective.

There were notable exceptions, of course. Much of the coverage, however, especially when it originated from Beirut while that city remained the "capital" of the PLO's virtual state within a state in Lebanon, was remarkable mainly for its distortions of the truth. From the moment the Israeli incursion began on the morning of June 6 until the horrendous mid-September massacre of Moslem Palestinians by Lebanese Christian militiamen, egregiously distorted accounts flooded the public in print and over the air. Indeed, not since Hitler and Goebbels perfected the technique of The Big Lie back in the 1930s was truth more blatantly violated for evil ends than during the bloody summer of 1982. Historically, those who would destroy a people first destroy its good name. Throughout most of the fighting in Lebanon, particularly in the early stages, media seemed intent upon destroying Israel's credibility and its image as a stalwart democracy. Veracity often gave way to mendacity.

"Every man has a right to his opinion," the late Bernard Baruch once said, "but no man has a right to be wrong in his facts." And the facts about Israel's incursion, code-named Operation

Peace for Galilee, were often twisted or ignored altogether by foreign correspondents under pressure to produce sensational stories to sell newspapers or to boost TV news ratings.

Media in general, but television in particular, tended to depict the Israelis as brutal invaders bent less upon victory over their longtime PLO tormentors than on the extermination of Palestinian Arabs as a people, naturally with resultant deadly consequences to whatever Lebanese civilians who happened to be in the way. In many correspondents' accounts, the Israelis emerged as the villainous conquerors of a foreign Arab land while Yassir Arafat's terrorists—almost invariably identified as "freedom fighters" or "guerrillas"—were characterized as heroic defenders of a righteous cause.

The world was made to see Israel's military action as a gratuitous onslaught on a small, defenseless Lebanon whose sole guilt lay in having given shelter to the "resistance movement" of Palestinian Arabs seeking fulfillment of "legitimate rights." In some dispatches obscene comparisons were made between the Israelis' campaign against the PLO and the Nazi Holocaust.

Television's Role

The chief offender, however, was television. Rarely did the electronic media bother to explain that the PLO's strongholds, for instance, were purposely located in or near civilian centers, thus rendering civilian casualties inevitable. *All* the major American networks, furthermore, showed Israeli tanks and artillery rolling past the ruins of Tyre, Sidon and Damour—cities which already had been heavily damaged by the PLO—creating the impression that what the viewers were seeing was the result of Israeli military action. Little attempt was made by anchormen or commentators to explain that the battered homes, churches and shattered public buildings so dramatically portrayed in full color on TV screens were at least as much the result of previous PLO depredations as they were the consequence of Israeli combat action.

Seldom, moreover, were TV viewers told that the places shown had served as redoubts for PLO troops and were therefore logical targets for Israeli bombs or shells. Nor were TV watches informed that before every assault on population centers the

186

Israeli Air Force dropped leaflets urging the inhabitants to flee to safety. The drops were almost invariably followed by loudspeaker announcements from Israeli sound equipment warning civilians of impending danger and providing explicit information—in Arabic—about safe escape routes to nearby beaches or mountains.

The Israeli army actually sustained greater casualties because of its efforts to spare civilians, but this fact never emerged in TV broadcasts. Instead, TV audiences were told that Israel was "carpet bombing" the cities, town and villages of southern Lebanon, and "slaughtering" the civilian population as part of a systematic policy of "decimation" against Palestinian Arabs. Incredibly, one wire reporter (Helen Thomas, of UPI) went so far as to compare the Israeli action in Lebanon to the Soviet invasion of Afghanistan. By and large, however, when compared with TV coverage, the print media at least strove for fairness and evenhandedness.

The Big Ad Lie

Meanwhile, pro-PLO elements in the USA were quick to seize the occasion for a propaganda holiday of flagrant misinformation and *dis*information. Full-page advertisements appeared in such leading newspapers as *The New York Times* deploring the "wholesale killing and destruction" in Lebanon, using statistics manufactured by the PLO itself and released through the International Red Cross. The first full-page ad (June 20, 1982) claimed that the "Death and Devastation" wrought by the Israelis in Lebanon had caused "40,000 killed and wounded" and made "700,000 homeless."

The advertisement was signed by some 200 or more or less prominent intellectuals—Gentile and Jewish—professors, clergymen, politicians and writers. The signers were headed by Senator James Abourezk, whose anti-Israel bias is well and widely known, the Berrigan Brothers, Congressman Paul McCloskey, and Noam Chomsky, who according to George F. Will (*Newsweek*, August 2) has collaborated with a French author in claiming the Holocaust of Hitler's time never happened. Few of the signers, if any, qualified as objective students of the Arab-Israeli struggle in the Middle East. But the damage they did to

Israel's image as a free, progressive democracy—the only such society in the whole of North Africa and Southwest Asia—proved almost irreparable. Accompanying as it did the twisted accounts provided by TV—and by some newspapers and newsmagazines—the advertisement provided a distorted but enduring perception of Israel's war in Lebanon.

As a veteran correspondent who has known war—oftener than not at combat level—since the late 1930s, I strongly suspected that the figures cited in the pro-PLO ads, in some reporters' dispatches and in many TV broadcasts were either gross exaggerations or outright lies manufactured by the able propagandists of the PLO. Given the nature and speed of the Israeli advance, it was inconceivable that there had been "40,000 killed and wounded." By the third week in June, the Israeli military operation, although considerably more than "police action," was still substantially less than a full-scale war, and had moved so quickly that Israeli forces were already at the gates of Beirut.

At the time, the Israelis' own dead numbered fewer than 200. Clearly, there could not have been such serious fighting as to have caused 40,000 dead—or even 10,000, as was subsequently claimed by Beirut—on the other side. Otherwise, by the time the sensational ads appeared, the TV screens would have been filled with piles of corpses and with images of hospitals overflowing with wounded.

Moreover, since the entire population of southern Lebanon in the area of Israel's military operations—south of Beirut and west of the Bekaa Valley—was known to comprise only 510,000 inhabitants, it was hardly possible that 700,000 had been made homeless. But the figures were widely accepted even by Secretary of Defense Caspar Weinberger. Furthermore, much of the territory involved is made up of Christian and Shia Moslem towns and villages friendly to the oncoming Israeli forces, in which no fighting occurred. By no stretch of the imagination, therefore, could the population in the limited areas of actual combat have equaled the 700,000 figure of homeless refugees citied by the ad in question.

Lebanon at First Hand
As a longtime Middle East watcher, I was determined to see for myself what was really happening in the area, and made two

trips to Israel and Lebanon. The first, on behalf of Network News, a Washington-based feature service, spanned five weeks from June 22 through July. The second, undertaken under the auspices of the Center for International Security, covered the period from mid-August to September 5.

Arriving in Lebanon during the third week of the hostilities, I visited the entire southern region from the border to East Beirut, which by then was securely in Israeli hands. Like Martin Peretz, of *The New Republic*, I found that much of what I had read in the newspapers and newsmagazines—and even more of what I had seen and heard on television—was "simply not true." Worse, it grievously damaged the reputation of America's only trustworthy ally in the region, indeed, in the whole of what is commonly called the Arab World, which is neither wholly "Arab" nor even an approximation of a "world."

I found no signs of "carpet bombing" by the Israeli Air Force (IAF), certainly nothing comparable to what I had seen as a correspondent in Sicily, northern Italy and southern France during the Allied advances in those areas in World War II. Nowhere did the IAF do to Lebanese population centers what the Allied air forces did to Anzio, Cassino, or Naples back in the 1940s. On the contrary, the visible evidence pointed to extreme care on the part of the IAF in its choice of targets, even along the coastal battlefields in and around Tyre and Sidon where the worst fighting occurred in the Israelis' drive toward Beirut.

Mosques, for instance, were meticulously spared, as were hospitals and schools unless anti-aircraft guns were mounted on their rooftops by the PLO (as they often were), or the buildings were known to have become depositories for PLO munitions or to have been converted into training schools for PLO terrorists.

Meanwhile, Israeli ground forces took all possible precautions against needlessly tearing up tobacco fields, vineyards, banana plantations, orchards and olive groves. In fact, there were no indications anywhere of wanton Israeli destruction. This is not to say there was no damage to homes and public buildings. Wherever advancing Israeli tanks or troops were fired upon from schools, hospitals and other buildings in highly concentrated residential areas, the Israelis fired back, causing unavoidable civilian casualties. It may fairly be said, however, that the Israeli armed forces took extraordinary care to minimize civilian casualties and were largely successful.

By mid-July, I had canvassed hospitals in the coastal cities where there had been heavy fighting. In Tyre, local Lebanese officials said that their city had suffered 56 dead and 96 wounded, only 20 of whom were still hospitalized when I visited the place. In populous Sidon, there were, by official count, 265 dead and about 1,000 wounded, of whom some 300 did not require hospitalization. But what of Palestinian Arab "civilian" casualties in or near the southern fields of battle?

Before the start of the siege of Beirut (incidentally, it was never a "siege" in the strictest military sense of the word, for the besiegers periodically allowed the besieged to receive food, water and medical supplies, denying them only gasoline and munitions), the heaviest civilian casualties occurred in the so-called "camps" of the Palestinian Arab refugees. I visited two, one at Ein el-Hilwe, near Sidon, and the other at Rashediye, on the outskirts of Tyre. The "camps" were really typical Arab towns with squat one-story row houses solidly constructed of reinforced concrete around small patios or gardens. Both refugee communities were badly damaged, the IAF having hit at least one house in every three or four. Nearly every one of the demolished homes, however, was erected over, or adjacent to, deep underground bunkers which usually had served as storehouses for PLO weapons and ammunition. Casualties in the two camps, according to the local *muktahrs*, totalled between 1,000 and 1,200—far too many from a humanitarian point of view, but far fewer than PLO propagandists would have the world believe.

At predominantly Christian Nabatiyeh, inland from the potted and rutted north-south coastal highway which, by the way, was already heavy with the southbound traffic of refugees returning from Beirut and other points to the north and west of the battle zone, town authorities told me that they had sustained 10 dead and 15 wounded during the fighting between Israeli troops and retreating elements of the PLO. And in Nabatiyeh, in mid-July, life was already returning to normal. Cafes and hotels had reopened and were crowded with well-dressed young men taking their ease over elaborate meals, sucking on their water-pipes, playing the imported Bally-made slot machines in the lobbies, and ogling the comely, fashionably-attired young women who paraded the main street in two's and three's in the late afternoon sunshine.

Driving southward over winding, narrow mountain roads I saw town after town, village after village, untouched by war. Like Nabatiyeh, Jezzine, a lovely mountain resort town, was also crowded with Lebanese refugees from Beirut and the Syrian-occupied Bekaa Valley. Here, too, there were few signs that war had passed.

Indeed, what I saw in an intensive tour of the battlefields and rear areas was not an Israeli war of conquest but a war of liberation. The Lebanese, Moslems as well as Christians, showered the advancing Israelis with rice and flowers, the traditional gifts of welcome, and thanked them for having removed the oppressive presence of the PLO whose brutal occupation had made life miserable for the inhabitants.

On each of five one- and two-day visits to the war zone, I talked with Lebanese doctors, lawyers, merchants, municipal officials and individuals chosen at random in Tyre, Sidon, and the northern outskirts of Damour, East Beirut and finally, West Beirut itself. Many spoke English or French, hence I did not require the services of my Arabic-speaking Israeli escort officers, and could converse freely with the persons I interviewed. Moslem and Christian Lebanese alike expressed themselves happy to be free at last of the PLO's interference in their daily lives. Some Christian Lebanese even rebuked the Israelis for not having come sooner. More significantly, perhaps, they could not understand why their plight was not known to the outside world. This complaint, after investigation, proved to be well-founded.

The Seven-Year Rape

Beginning in 1975, the PLO ruled over the Lebanese population through coercion, intimidation and force of arms. In the absence of any semblance of law and order, life and property were in constant danger. The people were in fact hostages of the PLO. This intolerable state of affairs was not unknown to the many foreign journalists, diplomats and businessmen stationed in Beirut. Yet, there was no public outcry abroad, not even after the situation was graphically described by Suleiman Franjieh,

Lebanon's president in the mid-1970s, in his farewell radio address to the nation on September 19, 1976. As reported by the Associated Press, the retiring president said, in part:

"They (the Palestinian Arabs) came to us as guests. We awarded them every possible hospitality but eventually they turned into savage wolves. They sought to kill their hosts and become masters of Lebanon. Indeed, our guests have already sabotaged Lebanon's executive, legislative and judicial authorities, as well as the nation's regular army...."

The following month, Ambassador Edouard Ghorra, Lebanon's Permanent Representative to the United Nations, was even more explicit about what was happening to his country. In a speech to the U.N. General Assembly on October 14, 1976, Ambassador Ghorra protested that PLO groups had "increased the influx of arms into Lebanon, and transformed most—if not all—of the refugee camps into military bastions where common-law criminals fleeing from Lebanese justice found shelter and protection."

"Those camps," Ambassador Ghorra said, "became in fact centers for the training of mercenaries sent there and financed by other Arab states. Palestinian Arab elements belonging to various organizations resorted to kidnapping Lebanese—and sometimes foreigners—holding them prisoners, questioning them, torturing them, sometimes killing them. They committed all sorts of crimes in Lebanon. They smuggled goods and went so far as to demand 'protection money.' It is difficult to enumerate all the illegal activities committed by those Palestinian elements...."

But the world at large remained unmoved, although Dr. Wilson Salim, a distinguished Lebanese Christian physician, observed—in a pamphlet published in London in the early spring of 1982—that the PLO was shelling the homes of Lebanese day and night, mining their roads and causing much loss of life. "Many women and children have been killed," Dr. Salim wrote, adding that since the entry of the PLO in Lebanon, "we Lebanese have had little respite. Many of our people, for whom the constant tension became unendurable, have fled the country in fear of their lives...."

For the most part, however, the Lebanese people remained silent during the years of the PLO occupation out of fear of reprisals. Freed from restraint after the Israeli incursion, Father John Nasser, a Maronite priest from Aishiya, told reporter Aaron Dolev, of *Ma'ariv*, what the PLO did to his village:

"A thousand armed terrorists attacked Aishiya in force. They burst into the houses and dragged out the villagers, the members in all of about 100 families. They crowded most of them into my church, and locked us in. About 65 villagers remained outside. After about an hour had passed, those of us in the church heard shooting, burst after burst of machine gun fire. We were kept in the church for two days while the attackers ransacked and pillaged the town. When the raiders left, we found the bodies of the 65—all friends and relatives—lying dead in pools of dried blood. And Aishiya was no exception. Our beloved, unhappy Lebanon is full of Aishiyas...."

But the slaughter of innocents by the PLO was seldom publicized abroad. The PLO was understandably reluctant to allow Beirut-based reporters to witness what it was doing in the countryside. There were no TV cameras at Aishiya, nor were TV crews invited to record the PLO's massacre of civilians at Christian Damour in 1975-1976, or the Syrian shelling of Tel Zatar where the victims were not Lebanese but Palestinian Arabs.

From time to time word of the horrendous events taking place in Lebanon did filter through to the West. There was heavy fighting between the PLO and its Christian and Shi'ite Moslem opponents in 1978. Radio Beirut claimed that during that year alone some 60,000 Lebanese were killed. In a rare glimpse into what was happening, *Time* reported that 400,000 Christians had fled from PLO terror in the Lebanese capital and that some 35,000 homes had been destroyed.

In 1979, Nicholas Tatro, of the Associated Press—one of the more fearless correspondents based in Beirut—wrote that 990 persons had been killed in the city. The following year Tatro, quoting police figures, wrote that 2,183 Lebanese were killed and 6,815 wounded in fighting between PLO "troops" and Lebanese forces. The Lebanese newspaper *A'Liwa'a* reported in April 1981, that in that month alone some 200 civilians were killed and 1,500 wounded by PLO and Syrian terrorists.

However, there was still no audible public outcry in the West. No full-page newspaper ads appeared in New York, Chicago and Los Angeles denouncing the activities of Yassir Arafat's organization and calling for a halt to the slaughter. The United Nations sat on its hands and while the PLO and its Syrian allies remained above criticism, the story of what was happening to once free, independent and prosperous Lebanon remained untold. With the country's liberation from PLO domination, a brief reconstruction is now possible, and is essential to an understanding of the objectives and accomplishments, as well as the shortcomings, of Israel's Operation Peace for Galilee.

Background to Chaos

The PLO's first major base was Jordan, from whose territory it launched attacks against Israel. In 1970, when King Hussein realized that the terrorist organization seriously threatened his own regime, he sent his well-armed Arab Legion to crush the PLO, killing thousands of Arafat's followers and expelling the rest in an episode that entered Palestinian Arab history as "Black September."

Then as now, however, the Arab states were reluctant to grant the PLO sanctuary, and Arafat sought and found refuge for his forces in Lebanon. They brought with them the involvement in Lebanese affairs of those countries—Saudi Arabia and Syria, among others—which sponsor several of the PLO's eight main groupings.

Actually, the PLO had started creating bases in Lebanon in 1968, and by the Cairo agreement of the following year the country was pressured by the late Gamal Abdul Nasser, then Egypt's president, to allow the PLO what was tantamount to extra-territorial rights to run the Palestinian Arab refugee camps. Along with extra-territoriality went freedom to conduct terrorist activities against Israel.

The armed presence of the PLO in Lebanon grew through the 1970s, as did the PLO's harassment of the Christian population and attacks on Israeli civilians in Galilee and everywhere else. The PLO brought under its control certain areas, including such ancient Christian towns as Damour, from which thousands of inhabitants were driven out and slaughtered.

Lebanese efforts to curb the PLO were prevented by Syrian intervention, leading to a 1973 arrangement whereby the PLO was given even greater freedom of action. By 1975, the PLO was in effect a state-within-a-state with its headquarters in West Beirut. It interfered with the internal affairs of the country, defied the weak central government, made alliances with some of Lebanon's leftist internal forces, and exacerbated the ongoing feuds between the Christians and those Sunni Moslem groups which had allied themselves with the PLO. Lebanese Christians and foreigners were frequently stopped at gunpoint by PLO activities for body searches and examination of identity cards. In short, by 1975, Lebanon virtually belonged to Arafat and his terrorists.

In time, Israeli retaliation against attacks emanating from PLO bases in southern Lebanon led to the migration of some 300,000 Shi'ite Moslems from the south to Beirut, where tensions were further heightened between them and the PLO. Meanwhile, the PLO expanded its control over new areas of Lebanon including nearly the whole of the south and Beirut, the Bekaa Valley and the north. Internal disorders increased accordingly. Bank robberies, letter bombs, kidnappings, confiscations of private property and assassinations became almost daily occurrences. The Shi'ites added to the mounting chaos by creating their own paramilitary organization, the Free Fighters Front, to defend themselves against left-wing Sunni Moslem groups allied to the PLO.

The attempted assassination in 1975 of Pierre Gemayel—founder (in 1936) of the Maronite Christian Phalange and father of the recently murdered Bashir—precipitated major retaliatory action against the PLO. The fighting between Arafat's forces and the Phalange escalated into what came to be known in news dispatches out of Beirut and elsewhere as the Lebanese "civil war" but was really the PLO's war to subdue all of Lebanon. During the struggle the Lebanese civilian death toll rose to 100,000, some 50,000 children were orphaned, and Lebanese in the tens of thousands were made homeless.

It may fairly be said, therefore, that the PLO was the main catalyst of the internal warfare that erupted in Lebanon in the spring of 1975. Meanwhile, the PLO entrenched itself among the population of southern Lebanon, cultivating ties with local leftist Moslems, training and arming their various private militias and gaining their support and trust. Gradually, segments of the Moslem community began looking upon the PLO as an ally whose aim was the concentration of all authority in Lebanon in PLO-Moslem hands. This eventually disrupted the delicate balance among the country's many ethnic and religious groups—Maronites, Greek Orthodox, Greek Catholics, Druze, and Shi'ite and Sunni Moslems—upon which the existence of the Lebanese government depended. The violent clashes of April 1975 between Christian and Moslem elements resulted in 18 months of bloody confrontations during which the central authority of the Lebanese government disintegrated.

The Extent of Syrian Aggression

Ever since Lebanon achieved independence in 1943, the various regimes which have ruled in Damascus have never concealed their desire to annex the country, always considering it really part of "Greater Syria." No Syrian government has ever accepted the reality of Lebanese sovereignty nor established diplomatic relations with Beirut. The Lebanese crisis of 1975-1976 gave Syria's Ba'athist leader, Hafez Assad, an opportunity to advance a long-standing Syrian ambition to extend its hegemony over its neighbor.

In June, 1976, Syria sent regular units of its army into Lebanon in the guise of a "peace-keeping mission" legitimized later, in October, when an Arab Summit Conference created an "Arab Deterrent Force" in Lebanon based on the several thousand Syrian troops already there. At first, Syria intervened on behalf of the besieged Christian community against leftist Moslem-PLO forces, and occupied much of Lebanon. When it became clear to Damascus, however, that the Christians opposed Syrian domination and were determined to resist it, Syria started coordinating its military efforts with those of the PLO and turned against the Christians.

In 1978, Syrian forces unleashed a violent offensive against the Christians in East Beirut, causing thousands of civilian casualties and destroying entire neighborhoods. The action was roundly condemned in London by *The Economist*, in its issue of October 7, 1978, as "sociological warfare: ...the application of military power against civilians to achieve non-military objectives...to cause as much disruption and suffering as possible by shattering the structure of organized social life...."

Between December 1980 and June 1981, the Syrians held the large Christian town of Zahle under siege, subjecting it to repeated shellings which killed thousands and wounded many more. Meanwhile, the Syrians stationed large numbers of troops in the Bekka Valley where they also introduced powerful Soviet-made, latest model SAM surface-to-air missile batteries giving Damascus virtual control of all of southern Lebanon and that part of northern Israel known as the Galilee.

The so-called "civil war" ended with Syria firmly entrenched in Lebanon, policing a substantial portion of the country in what was tantamount to a Syrian quasi-hegemony over its neighbor which Israel could not tolerate. During the years since 1973, the Syrians had moved from initial animosity toward the PLO, to rapprochement and, following the conclusion of the Egyptian-Israel Peace Treaty under the terms of the Camp David accords, to open alliance.

As of early June, 1982, Lebanon as a viable political structure had ceased to exist. In its place there existed only individual fiefdoms with about 100 different political groupings and at least 40 private armies. Beirut itself was divided into two zones, a predominantly Moslem West and a preponderantly Christian East. North of Beirut there emerged a Christian enclave based on Jouniyeh. The area further north was held by Sunni Moslems backed by the Syrians. In the south the area close to the Israeli border was controlled by Major Sa'ad Haddad, the Roman Catholic commander of a 2,000-man militia armed and supplied by the Israelis. Although Haddad's force was composed mainly of Christians, it also contained substantial numbers of anti-PLO Shi'ites. In 1979, Major Haddad, a former officer in the Lebanese army, proclaimed an Independent Free Lebanon in a strip of land adjacent to the Israeli frontier about eight miles wide.

Following Israel's limited police action into southern Lebanon in March, 1978, planned to root out terrorist bases, the United Nations Interim Force in Lebanon was formed to assist in restoring peace in the area. But the UNIFIL territory soon was heavily infiltrated by PLO terrorists who established therein several bases from which attacks were launched on 23 Israeli towns and villages in Galilee.

It seems fair to state at this point that little of the background outlined above found its way into the dispatches of the correspondents of the print media covering Israel's Operation Peace for Galilee last summer, and even less in the segments aired by the TV networks.

Reporting from Lebanon before the Israeli incursion often took the form of black comedy rather than realistic appraisal of the confessional and personal factors involved. Throughout the "civil war" period that preceded the Israeli military action, the conflict was usually oversimplified as merely a struggle between a Christian Right and a Moslem Left. The Israeli military campaign against the PLO that began June 6 was similarly treated in simplistic terms as an outright "aggression" and was generally characterized as "expansionist," and even "imperialistic."

Meanwhile in that international community euphemistically known as the United Nations, hardly a voice was raised in condemnation of Syria's and the PLO's encroachment in Lebanon. From the beginning of Lebanon's nightmare in 1975 until June, 1982 neither the General Assembly nor the Security Council passed a single resolution dealing with the enormous tragedy that was being enacted under the eyes of numerous foreign observers. Both bodies, however, rarely missed an opportunity to condemn Israel for a multitude of mostly imaginary sins, going so far at one point as to equate Zionism with racism.

Yet, much of the responsibility for the Lebanese tragedy was attributable to the United Nations, which committed a historic blunder on November 13, 1974, when it illegally allowed Yassir Arafat to appear on the podium of the General Assembly to expound his widely publicized "real solution" to the "Palestinian problem"—a solution that would have merely "liberated" Israel from Israel. Overnight, the U.N. turned the arch-terrorist into an internationally recognized figure.

198

Crowned with a propaganda victory and clothed in his newly-won worldwide prestige, Arafat returned to Beirut as though to his own capital and unleased his armed gangs. Four months later, in the early spring of 1975, Lebanon was swept into the bloody whirlwind erroneously called a "civil war." Thereafter, the world never again saw the true face of the PLO. But in Lebanon, I met many Lebanese who recognized the PLO and its Syrian allies for what they really were and denounced them as murderers, rapists and thieves capable of almost unimaginable cruelties.

Atrocities Abounding

One of my many informants was Dr. Khalil Torbey, a distinguished Lebanese surgeon with degrees from Harvard Medical School and Boston's Massachusetts General Hospital. A portly gentleman in his early 50s, Dr. Torbey minced no words in describing his experiences during his country's torment under PLO-Syrian domination.

Torbey confirmed that since 1975 approximately 100,000 people were massacred by Arafat's minions and their Syrian partners. Many of the victims, he said, were not Christians but Moslems. Their deaths were callously used in a studied effort to make the world believe that what was happening in Lebanon was not a PLO takeover of the country but a "civil war" between its own main religious groups.

As a physician, Dr. Torbey was frequently called upon to attend to victims of PLO torture sessions which were usually conducted at the terrorists' "detention center" at Armoun, a village in the mountains east of Beirut.

"I know of cases," Dr. Torbey said, "of people being thrown into acid tanks and reduced to unrecognizable masses of porous bone. Many young girls came to me for abortions after being raped by PLO gangsters. Very often, mine was the only car circulating the perilous streets of West Beirut after dark to help some unfortunate victim or other of PLO or Syrian violence. I treated persons with arms severed by shelling, and men whose testicles had been crushed by torturers.

"I saw men—live men, mind you—dragged through the streets from fast-moving cars to which they were tied by their feet. All this, I am certain, was motivated in the early years by a desire to create the impression that a civil war was going on.

"In time, the Lebanese had nothing with which to defend themselves and no one to help them so that it was easy for the terrorists to take over homes, shops, garages, apartment houses—anything they wanted. Our children were growing up in terror and our people, robbed of their homes and belongings, were reduced to living like Bedouins, moving from place to place, seeking refuge from the terror. The lucky ones were received by friends or relatives in the hills and mountains to the north or south. The less fortunate lived like hunted animals."

Dr. Torbey himself was one of the victims of the technique employed by the PLO and its Syrian allies for the appropriation of property suitable to their purposes. Early in 1979, Dr. Torbey had nearly completed construction of what he described as "one of the largest medical facilities in the world, comparable to the Mayo Clinic" on ground close to the so-called Green Line that divided Beirut into a preponderantly Moslem western sector and a predominantly Christian eastern portion. Later that year, the Syrians attacked the Torbey Medical Center, drove out the defending forces of the enfeebled Lebanese Army, and took the place over as their main headquarters.

Another of my informants was Frederick El-Murr, a 54-year-old civil engineer and prominent Lebanese industrialist. Like Dr. Torbey, Mr. El-Murr was convinced that what had happened in Lebanon from 1975 onward, following Arafat's triumphal return from the United Nations, was not a "civil war, as the press hastened to characterize it, but a conquest of my country by the PLO and the Syrians."

"The terrorists," Mr. El-Murr added, "virtually destroyed with artillery and Katyusha rocket fire such Christian cities as Damour and Tyre, and badly damaged mostly Moslem Sidon. In West Beirut, hardly a building remains untouched. In 1978, the apartment building in which we lived in East Beirut was hit by PLO rockets 16 times.

"And we have seen mutilations and rape. I know a worker in my factory whose mother was raped by PLO terrorists. A favorite method of ridding themselves of political opponents was to tie the feet of the male victims to separate cars speeding off in opposite directions. One such incident was witnessed by my 17-year-old daughter, Nada."

Intimidating the Press

The outrages described by Dr. Torbey and Mr. El-Murr were comparable only to those perpetrated by the Nazis during World War II with refinements harking back to the Dark Ages. How did what both called "an organized gang of criminals" manage to impose a reign of terror and silence on a population of hundreds of thousands for more than seven years?

A partial answer was provided by Mr. El-Murr who said that the PLO had "plenty of money" with which to "persuade" Lebanese editors and journalists to write favorably about the PLO's so-called "revolution" or to remain silent. One editor whom the PLO could not "buy," Mr. El-Murr said, was his friend Salim El-Lawzi, owner of the independent Lebanese Arabic weekly, *El Hawadess.* Exactly how El-Lawzi was "silenced" I learned from other sources: Moslem newspapermen who preferred to remain anonymous.

El-Lawzi was a Lebanese patriot from one of the wealthiest Moslem families in West Beirut and, above all, a courageous journalist. He began warning his countrymen against the Palestinian terrorist organizations back in the early 1970s, when he saw that their ultimate goal was the creation in Lebanon of a state-within-a-state. Threats against his person started in the summer of 1975 by means of letters, telephone calls, and visits by

PLO hooligans to his weekly's editorial offices located near the PLO-controlled neighborhood known as Burj al-Barajne. El-Lawzi ignored the warnings until two explosive charges went off one night in the building that housed the weekly's presses, editorial rooms and administrative offices. The entire building collapsed. El-Lawzi moved to London where he revived his paper and continued his anti-PLO editorial policy. He stayed away from Beirut for three years but the desire to visit members of his family whom he had left behind got the better of him.

After obtaining a "safe-conduct" from his friend, the then Prime Minister Salim al-Hus, El-Lawzi landed at Beirut Airport in July 1978. A few days earlier, the latest issue of his paper had appeared in the Lebanese capital with a blistering attack on those Arab oil countries which, the paper said, were buying insurance from PLO terror within their own borders by financing the sojourn of the "gangs of murderers and thieves" in Lebanon. The journalist, who was 54 years old at the time, remained with his family for three days.

At the end of his visit, El-Lawzi headed for the airport by automobile. His car was stopped at a Syrian Army roadblock, where a group of armed men from the pro-Syrian terrorist organization known as As-Saiqa dragged him out. They did not harm the driver, who was later suspected of having cooperated with the kidnappers, but El-Lawzi was taken to the notorious PLO mountain village of Armoun. There, the victim was held for three days in the torture chambers. The fingers of his hands were cut off joint by joint. He was subsequently dismembered and his remains turned up scattered about the village. Horrifying photographs of El-Lawzi's mutilated body spread terror throughout the capital's journalistic colony.

Edouard Saab, editor-in-chief of the French language Beirut daily *L'Orient Le Jour* was 46 years old when he fell victim to an armed attack while crossing the Green Line in his automobile in the course of his daily trip from his newspaper's offices in West Beirut and his home in East Beirut. Saab, who also served as correspondent for the great Paris daily, *Le Monde*, had been systematically criticizing PLO terrorist tactics since September, 1970, calling repeatedly for liquidation of Fatahland along the Israeli border, and urging the Lebanese government to break

202

relations with those Arab countries which were pouring hundreds of millions of petrodollars into the coffers of the PLO. Saab was murdered at one of the many roadblocks maintained by the PLO. A terrorist fired a round into the journalist's head. Oddly enough an American friend—the Beirut stringer for an American newsweekly who was sitting beside him—was unharmed.

Over the years, the PLO terrorized into conformity, submission or silence the entire Lebanese press community, using arson, sabotage, assassination and bribery to gain its ends. On April 1, 1975, an explosion destroyed the offices of the weekly *Al Jamhoud* and killed a number of the building's occupants. The following month, similar explosions occurred in the editorial rooms of *Al Mouhared* and the printing plant called *Abi Sadar* which printed several of Beirut's many daily and weekly journals. PLO threats to blow up the offices of *Al Moustagbal* in August of that same year caused the paper's editorial and administrative staffs to move to Paris as a group.

In July 1980, Riyad Taha, president of the Beirut Publishers' Union, was shot to death in an ambush. In November, explosions destroyed the buildings of *A-Safir* and *Al-Liwa's*, both important dailies. By the end of the year, nearly all of Beirut's 36 once flourishing daily and weekly newspapers had been bullied into acquiescence or silence.

In the meantime, according to Edouard George, a former senior editor of *L'Orient Le Jour*, PLO terrorists killed a number of foreign correspondents based in Beirut. Among them Mr. George listed Sean Toolan, a correspondent for ABC-TV; Robert Pfeffer, who represented West Germany's *Der Spiegel* and Italy's *Unita*, official organ of the Italian Communist Party; two Italian journalists, Tony Italo and Graziella di Falco; Jean Lougeau, who represented an independent French TV network; and Mark Tryn, of the "Free Belgium" broadcasting station.

Knowledgeable Lebanese newsmen, able to speak freely after the Israelis had expelled Arafat and his trigger-happy followers from Beirut last summer, said that most of the capital's press corps—national and foreign—entered into a "conspiracy of silence" during the long occupation by the "the Palestinian Mafia." The journalists tended to divide their colleagues into roughly four categories:

A large number, of whatever political persuasion, were truly sympathetic to the PLO and the leftists.

Another group simply sold out to the PLO, receiving bribes proportionate to their importance or influence, and rewarding their paymasters with sympathetic articles about "the Palestinian struggle."

A third group, fewer in number than the "sellouts," went underground. Its members emerged now and then to try to publish the truth but seldom succeeded. They met stubborn resistance from publishers and editors-in-chief who had been bribed or terrified into silence. Most simply gave up journalism and went into other less frustrating and less dangerous activities.

A last group, perhaps the largest, constituted what my informants called "The Order of the Silent Ones"—composed of Lebanese and foreign correspondents who did not have to be bribed, but were merely frightened out of their wits by a constant stream of threatening letters and telephone calls and, from time to time, severe beatings or assassinations.

It was not unusual for Lebanon's journalistic opponents of terrorist activities to find on their doorsteps human limbs in plastic containers with warnings that unless they toed the mark editorially they too would "wind up wrapped in plastic." Small wonder, perhaps, that in this atmosphere even some staunch Western correspondents became extremely wary of incurring the wrath of the PLO, and saw more merit in "the cause" than it deserved.

Despite the harassment, however, responsible Lebanese journalists compiled what they called "An Album of Terrorist Atrocities." Published clandestinely in 1978, the document was quickly suppressed within Lebanon, and never saw the light of day abroad. Thus the outside world remained in ignorance of the true nature of the PLO, and utterly unaware of Arafat's preparations for eventual *jihad* against Israel.

By the end of 1981 the PLO, with Syrian help, had virtually conquered Lebanon but the full story never surfaced in the dispatches and broadcasts emanating from Beirut. There were no articles in the Western press—certainly not under a Beirut dateline—about how the PLO was (1) amassing huge stores of highly sophisticated weapons; (2) converting its guerrilla gangs into a close approximation of a conventional army of some 18,000 men fully equipped with artillery, armor and "hi-tech" electronic communications gadgets; (3) recruiting and training more than 2,000 mercenaries from a score of Arab (and non-Arab) nations for service in "the cause"; (4) honeycombing West Beirut and adjacent refugee camps with miles of deep underground tunnels and bunkers; and (5) placing batteries of artillery in civilian centers, thereby creating for itself a human shield.

Meanwhile, however, there was no lack of material in Western media—printed and visual—critical of Israel's every move to ensure her security in a hostile world. Much of the criticism was directed at Prime Minster Begin personally as an inflexible and fanatic nationalist whom the media openly disliked despite the fact that he had made peace with Israel's most populous and militarily most powerful enemy, Egypt, and remained steadfastly pro-American.

The View From Beit Agron

In February, 1982, the persistent anti-Israel bias detectable in the Western news media's reporting and commentary of the Arab-Israeli conflict prompted Ze'ev Chafets, then director of Israel's Government Press Office, to charge that even such eminent journals as *The Washington Post* and *The New York Times*—as well as such important electronic media as ABC-TV and the BBC—followed a "double standard" in their coverage. With one eye constantly on the implications of Arab terrorism, they took for granted and abused the freedom allowed them in Israel's open society, Chafets said.

Interviewed in his office in Beit Agron, the press headquarters in Jerusalem, Chafets, a bearded mild-mannered 34-year-old American who emigrated to Israel in 1967, explicitly charged that terror prevented critical reporting on the activities of the PLO and Syria in Lebanon. He cited as an example an ABC program entitled "Under the Israeli Thumb: Life on the West Bank" which was broadcast on February 4 as part of the network's weekly "20/20" show. Chafets described the segment dealing with Israel as one of the "most malicious, distorted and one-sided programs (about Israel) shown on any American network in recent years," purposely made and transmitted in order to "pander to Arab terror."

Chafets was certain that the program had a causal, not accidental, connection with the murder of ABC reporter Sean Toolan in July 1981, and that by putting it on the air the network hoped to remain free of further harassment from the PLO. The network's reply was predictable. In New York, Roone Arledge, President of ABC News, dismissed the allegations as "utter nonsense."

I could NOT agree with Mr. Arledge. I saw the "20/20" broadcast in question, and having visited the West Bank in 1967, when the Israelis occupied it, and revisited it many times since, I can bear witness to the steady improvement made over the years in the economic and social conditions of the area's Palestinian Arab inhabitants. It seemed to me that ABC set out to prove that the Palestinian Arabs were, as the segment's title itself implied, suffering under the heel of the Israeli Army. In this, ABC succeeded admirably. Totally ignored by ABC reporter Tom Jarriel were the advances made since 1967 in West Bank agriculture, industry, education, housing and public health.

A point by point rebuttal of the ABC story has no place in this report, but a few observations might not be amiss. Far from having "stamped out" the Arab inhabitants' "cultural identity"— as ABC charged—four universities and three schools for advanced vocational studies have been established in a region where no such institutions existed while the West Bank was under the rule of Hashemite King Hussein. Utterly false, also, was the broadcast's contention that under Israeli administration the West Bank's rate of infant mortality has been rising. Actually, it has been declining sharply from 33.6 per 1,000 births in 1968 to a recent (1980) 28.3. ABC's "Under the Israeli Thumb" not only distorted truth, it compounded falsehoods into anti-Israel propaganda. It is a masterpiece of tendentious antipathy.

In fairness to ABC, however, what I saw of the network's coverage of Israel's war against the PLO in Lebanon before I left for the war zone June 22 seemed eminently balanced and objective. All the networks had a busy weekend June 4-6 with the shooting of Israeli Ambassador Shlomo Argov in London, the rain of PLO rockets and artillery fire on the towns and villages of northern Galilee, the Israeli bombing of PLO targets in Beirut and, finally, the massive movement of Israeli troops and armor across the Lebanese frontier.

Among all the misinformation about the war, one network, ABC, deserves recognition for some of its coverage. I recall anchorman Frank Reynolds' effort to put the incursion into historical perspective by remarking that "terrorism has led to tragedy" in a memorable broadcast which, if memory serves, included a piece from Bill Seamans in Israel showing the damage the PLO's rockets and shells had wreaked in Galilee, intercut with segments depicting the Argov shooting and the Israeli raid on the Beirut sports stadium, a PLO training site for guerrillas and an ammunition storage point. Some days later, ABC emphasized that the Israeli raid was aimed at eliminating "PLO bases in Lebanon" and Seamans was back on the air with a piece on how Beaufort Castle, which had fallen to the Israelis in bitter fighting, had been used by the PLO to direct rocket and artillery fire into Israeli population centers in Galilee.

In his criticism of media coverage of Israel, Chafets also alleged that late last year the Marxist-oriented PLO splinter group known as the People's Front for the Liberation of Palestine (PFLP) abducted five Western correspondents in Lebanon, held them "for 24 hours" and "threatened to kill them." One of the five, Chafets said was "a *New York Times* reporter, and the other was a *Washington Post* man." A condition for their release, Chafets charged, was that their respective papers not mention their abduction "and the papers complied."

A member of the *Times*' Foreign Desk in New York had a somewhat different version of the "abduction." Actually, he said, not one but two *Times* correspondents were involved—William Farrell and John Kifner, both veteran Middle East hands. They were not "abducted" but were merely held for a few hours after they were stopped at a PLO checkpoint late one night while the reporters were on their way by car to investigate a tip on what they had been led to believe might be a major news story—one big enough to risk violating the PLO's curfew.

It is true, however, that the incident remained unreported for nine months. In response to Chafets' allegations of a "coverup," the *Times* indicated that what happened to its reporters had not been deemed newsworthy. The paper subsequently published a frank piece by Kifner relating the perils of reporting from the Lebanese capital—meaning the Beirut *before* Israel launched is Operation Peace for Galilee.

"To work here as a journalist," Kifner wrote, "is to carry fear with you as faithfully as your notebook. It is the constant knowledge that there is nothing you can do to protect yourself and that nothing has ever happened to an assassin. In this atmosphere, a journalist must often weigh when, how and sometimes even whether to record a story. In the Middle East, facts are always somewhat elusive. But there is a pervasive belief among the Beirut press corps that the correspondents should be extremely wary of incurring the wrath of the Syrian regime...."

The Washington Post, after pondering Chafets' charges, admitted that its Beirut correspondent. Jonathan Randal, had in fact been arrested, but added that so seasoned a newsman—a veteran of wars and revolutions—could hardly be expected to take account of so minor an incident as captivity by the PLO.

Chafets further charged that other representatives of major Western media had fallen afoul of the PLO and the Syrians, and had tried to cover up the incidents. He cited a gun attack on Berndt Debusemann, Reuters bureau chief in Beirut, who was first threatened by a pro-Syrian PLO faction which disapproved of his reporting on Syrian activities in Lebanon, then was shot in the stomach while walking home from work. Reuters played down the incident.

Even the mighty BBC, Chafets indicated, could be intimidated. The British network's Beirut correspondent, Tim Llewellyn, saw the shooting of Debusemann from the window of his office and after reporting the episode his life was threatened by pro-Syrian PLO elements. Llewellyn was rushed to safety in Cyprus, but the BBC omitted to mention the city from which he was reporting and, contrary to custom, did not replace him with a staff man in Beirut.

To what extent American reporters based in Beirut yielded to the terror tactics of the PLO or the persuasiveness of Madmoud Labadi, Arafat's spokesman in the Lebanese capital—a charmer who always carried a pistol in his belt—is difficult to gauge by anything less than an exhaustive survey of media coverage.

However, the mounds of clippings from *The New York Times* that awaited me on my return from the war zone early in September reflected a fair amount of even-handedness *in the news columns*. On the *Times'* Op-Ed page, Anthony Lewis and others, among them former Undersecretary of State George Ball—a prominent exponent of the notion that practically every conflict stems from Israel's "failure" to solve the "Palestinian problem"—seemed determined to savage Israel in every printed line. However, William Safire was usually also there to do the counter-punching. I leave it to others to plumb the dark depths of the anti-Israel animus of Messrs. Lewis and Ball.

Since Arafat's expulsion from Beirut, there have been a number of analyses of American media treatment of the Israeli military operation in Lebanon. One, prepared by the American Jewish Committee, reported that press coverage, in sharp contrast to television, indicated considerably more balance than the Israeli Press Office claimed. According to the AJC's analysis, the reporting was "by and large even-handed, although consistent condemnation of particular Israeli actions produced an overall impression of pervasive censure."

Surveyed by the AJC's researchers were editorials, columns, political cartoons and letters to the editor dealing with the events in Lebanon from June 22 to August 26. Of the 167 editorials examined, the report said, 49 (29%) were clearly antagonistic, 35 (21%) were preponderantly supportive and uncritical of Israel's actions, and most of the remaining 83 were "relatively balanced."

A majority of the editorials and columns reviewed, the AJC report asserted, focused attention on three issues: (1) the urgent need to remedy the plight of the Palestinian Arab refugees; (2) the civilian casualties; and (3) Israel's offensive use of American arms in apparent violation of existing agreements.

The results were reflective of the obsession of all Western journalists with the problem of the Palestinian Arab refugees and the parallel preoccupation with Israel as the major source of turmoil in the Middle East. It has become a journalistic cliché that virtually every conflict in the Middle East is due to Israel's "failure" to resolve the "Palestinian problem." Rarely was it mentioned that if the Arabs had accepted the United Nations partition plan of 1947, the Palestinian Arabs would have had a state west of the Jordan or that a Palestinian Arab state already exists east of the river, but is called Jordan (it was once called by its true name, Transjordan). As Professor Edward Alexander put it in an article in the September-October issue of the British magazine, *Encounter*, "Israel has become the moral playground for the journalism of the world, a gymnasium in which they do ethical calisthenics designed to revitalize muscles that have grown flabby from disuse during their assignments in other countries."

The widespread focus on resolution of the Palestinian dilemma, the AJC report concluded, was "a clear harbinger of future accelerated pressure on Israel to cooperate. It was equally evident that as Israel's chief ally and supplier of (military and economic) aid, the United States was perceived as the key agent in future negotiations."

A predominantly negative view of Israel, the AJC analysis found, was produced by the cartoons appearing in the American press. Out of 81 cartoons examined, nearly half (35) were clearly hostile. Of the latter, the vast majority dealt with civilian casualties and destruction in Lebanon.

Letters to the editor, on the other hand, the AJC said, were about evenly divided between those generally supportive of Israel (76) and those which were hostile (74). Only a very few letter writers (20) exhibited what could be called a "balanced" viewpoint.

A New Low In European Coverage

A distinctly anti-Israel bias seemed to me far more evident in the reporting by European journalists than in the work of American newspapermen. While abroad, I read with some regularity the London *Times* and the *Observer*, the Manchester *Guardian*, Paris' *Le Monde* and Milan's *Corriere della Sera*. The contrast in journalistic approach was perceptible: American correspondents tended to consider themselves simply recorders of what they saw but their European counterparts were much given to making political statements.

The European reporters appeared to be striving to make amends for their various countries' past colonial domination of native peoples by upholding the aspirations of the downtrodden

210

populations of the Third World. In the Middle East, this means support for anyone attacked by Israel, especially the Palestinian Arabs. In the dispatches of the Europeans—with the notable exception of the pieces in the London *Observer* by Connor Cruise O'Brien—Israel invariably emerged as a morally repressive force, a threat to world peace which somehow had to be restrained. Arafat's men, on the other hand, were never "terrorists" but "guerrilla fighters," the Syrian occupying army in Lebanon was nearly always a "Syrian peacekeeping force" and Palestinian Arabs were simply "Palestinians," although historically a Palestinian nation has never existed.

Similarly, Saudi Arabia, which has consistently advocated Holy War against Israel, has bank-rolled the PLO to the tune of hundreds of millions of petrodollars ($450 million in 1981) and is without doubt the world's most racist state, rarely appeared in print as anything but "moderate." The epithet was frequently also applied to King Hussein's Jordan, whose "moderation" has consisted in having frustrated every effort since 1967 to achieve a negotiated settlement in the Arab-Israeli dispute, and in persistently refusing to talk with the Israelis about the future of the so-called West Bank.

Newspapers of record like the *New York Times*—unlike the newsweeklies which throughout the war strove for dramatic effect as vigorously as television—made sporadic efforts to bring the conflict into historical perspective. Notable was a piece by David Shipler, of the *Times*, datelined Sidon, July 25, 1982, relating how Lebanese Christians and Moslems welcomed the Israelis as liberators of their country from the yoke of the PLO. Shipler described graphically what the Lebanese had suffered during the years of terrorist occupation, and inferentially justified the Israeli incursion.

But such articles were the exception rather than the rule. The words "holocaust" and "genocide" appeared often enough in most Western reporting to suggest a persistently anti-Israeli, indeed, sometimes even anti-Semitic bias that was echoed by Western leaders who should have known better but whose judgments were blurred by cowardice in the face of the ever-present threat of a curtailment in Arab oil supplies, petrodollar flows or— who knows?—fear of PLO terrorism. Generous coverage was accorded every outburst of Francois Mitterand, Andreas Papandreou, Bruno Kreisky and other leftists in high places who alleged that the Israelis were doing to the Palestinians what the Nazis had done to the Jews.

Inaccurate and imbalanced reporting obviously can have a critical impact not only on public perceptions but also on government attitudes and polices. A case in point was the shocked reaction of President Reagan, August 2, to a photograph distributed by United Press International and prominently published by, among others, the prestigious *Washington Post*. The photo showed a 7-month-old Lebanese baby girl swathed in bandages from head to foot. The caption that accompanied the picture said the child had lost both arms and had been severely burned in the "accidental bombing" of an apartment house in East Beirut by the Israeli Air Force. Outraged, President Reagan put in a personal telephone call to Premier Begin urging him to suspend the Israeli bombing of PLO targets in West Beirut, using the word "holocaust" in the ensuing exchange.

Israeli authorities challenged the report, made a thorough investigation, and on August 22 released a photo of the same child after treatment. The infant had *not* lost both arms, and had suffered no burns and only slight injuries to the wrists. Moreover, the baby, it turned out, was not hurt by an Israeli bomb but by a shell from a PLO battery in West Beirut. The UPI confirmed that the original caption was inaccurate and expressed regret. But whereas the original photo was splashed everywhere, the corrected version barely made the inside pages (*The New York Times* printed it on page 14).

Generally speaking, press coverage could be faulted for its omissions at least as much as for its distortions, half-truths and downright lies. There was little reporting, if any, on such subjects as: (1) the significance of the vast quantities of arms found by the Israelis in PLO bunkers and tunnels; (2) the rapidity with which the Lebanese were able to resume normal life as they returned to their homes in the liberated areas; (3) the benefits that accrued to Lebanon itself and to Western influence in the Middle East as a result of the Israeli military action; (4) the realities of the PLO as an instrument of international terrorism which was revealed in the tons of documents captured by the Israelis; and (5) the extent of Israeli help in the relief and rehabilitation of the Lebanese population, including the sizeable Palestinian Arab minority.

As Through a Tube, Darkly

But the print media, with whatever its faults, was a model of diligence and accuracy compared with the visual medium. I personally believe television is capable of great journalism. But its handling of history's first complete "TV dinner war," outclassing even Vietnam, left much to be desired in terms of fairness, balance and truthful presentation of the unfolding drama of the summer of 1982, possibly because since the days of Edward R. Murrow, television journalism has increasingly become more Show Biz than journalism.

It may be true that "a picture is worth a thousand words." It is equally true, however, that a picture can tell a thousand lies. After watching TV at home for a fortnight before flying off to the war zone, I was sure, for instance, that Tyre and Sidon had been destroyed, and most of the their inhabitants killed. That was the impression produced by the highly seductive use of the TV cameras, the file footage (often undated) and the highly misleading labeling of the material shown. As I have indicated earlier, I was surprised to find both cities not nearly as badly damaged as the TV images had indicated, and to learn that civilian casualties had been minimal because the inhabitants of those towns had heeded Israeli warnings to evacuate or take adequate cover.

Television gives viewers a startling image of what is happening, when, where and to whom, but falls far short of making clear that what they are seeing is not the totality of truth, or of adequately explaining *why* the event is taking place. The total truth is not merely the 30 seconds or so of an image, but of the succession of the many, many 30-second images which preceded the event and which will follow it. Yet the picture, whatever it may be, tells the audience that what the camera has recorded is undeniable fact, absolute truth. By aiming their cameras on selected destroyed buildings in Sidon, for example, without showing the untouched neighboring structures in the vicinity or in the same street, the electronic journalists dramatically exaggerated the degree of devastation, thus deliberately failing to project a balanced scene.

The man who holds the camera, whatever his qualifications as a journalist, determines what is conveyed to millions of viewers in his home country and, often, throughout the world. He not only purveys a picture but he, and/or his director or producer, also determines what the scene shall be. By moving his camera to the left or right, up of down, he can project a totally different reality. He holds in his hands the instrument of a tremendous truth or an enormous lie. By training their cameras on the stark rubble and bloody civilian casualties, the television reporters transformed the reality of Israel's most judicious and selective use of military might into the distorted image of a brutal aggressor.

By not showing viewers PLO katyushas firing rockets and PLO artillery raining shells at civilians in East Beirut, and the agony and casualties such attacks cause, and by rarely explaining how the PLO used civilians as shields, the knights of the Electronic Cyclops failed to give viewers a balanced picture of the fighting. The conclusion is irresistible that friendship for the PLO and rage against Israel prompted much of the lopsided television coverage, and motivated the UPI misrepresentation of the notorious photograph of the "wounded child" that so moved President Reagan.

Nearly every day of the long semi-siege of Beirut through July and August, TV photographed Arafat with babies in his arms outside the entrance of one of his several bunkers in West Beirut. But I recall no single instance of a TV reporter asking him any pointed questions about his own responsibility for the carnage, or about the PLO's right to use the Lebanese capital's civilian population as hostages to his political maneuverings. There can be no doubt that favorable coverage by the media, particularly television, encouraged Arafat and the PLO to stay on in Beirut day after day, every one of which cost lives on both sides.

At the risk of being accused of "selective criticism" of TV coverage, one of the most tendentious broadcasts of the entire summer came from John Chancellor, of NBC, normally a serious, almost school-teacherish figure on his network's nightly news program. It happened during the torrid, early stages of the final battle for Beirut.

Earlier, on June 16, Chancellor had commented on "the growing feeling that Israel has turned into a warrior state," using "far more force that is necessary," and questioning Israel's "legitimate security problems in Lebanon." At the time, he was speaking from New York. Later, during the first few days of August, he was in Beirut, and on August 2 aired one of the most provocative commentaries of the entire war. Speaking while silhouetted against a smoking Beirut skyline, he said:

> What will stick in the mind about yesterday's savage Israeli attack on Beirut is its size and scope. This is one of the world's big cities. The area under attack is the length of Manhattan island below Central Park. Five hundred thousand people live here. One in a hundred is a PLO fighter. And it went on for such a long time—before dawn until five in the afternoon. Systematic, sophisticated warfare. The Israeli planes just never stopped coming. For an entire day, Beirut rocked and swayed to the rhythm of the Israeli attack. The Israelis say they were going after military targets with precision. There was also the strench of terror all across the city.... Nothing like it has ever happened in this part of the world. I kept thinking yesterday of the bombing of Madrid during the Spanish Civil War. What in the world is going on? Israel's security problem on its border is fifty miles to the south. What's an Israeli army doing here in Beirut? The answer is that we are now dealing with an imperial Israel which is solving its problems in someone else's country, world opinion be damned. Nobody knows how the battle of Beirut is going to end. But we do know one thing. The Israel we saw here yesterday is not the Israel we have seen in the past.

Chancellor asked many questions, good questions, maybe, but he was supposed to answer them, not merely pose them. He

215

was trying hard to be Ernest Hemingway but succeeded only in being an earnest schoolmaster who had forgotten past lessons. The Israel that Chancellor described had undergone a sudden puzzling transformation into a "savage" and "imperial" state, but what puzzled me most was why Chancellor "kept thinking of the bombing of Madrid during the Spanish Civil War." Was he there at the time? The year of the bombing of Madrid by the Junkers 52s of Hitler's burgeoning *Luftwaffe* was 1936, when John was 12 or 13 years old.

Chancellor's editorializing was no worse, however, than Tom Brokaw's reference on August 4 to "what's left of Beirut" as though the entire city had been *demolished.* Despite the audible and visible bombing of West Beirut's PLO positions, this was definitely a gross exaggeration. In any case, Chancellor redeemed himself somewhat later by a thoughtful commentary from a Palestinian refugee camp wherein he observed that, although Israel bore "some of the blame" for those homeless people, it had been the Arab countries which had refused them refuge. The wretched Palestinian Arabs were "useful" he said because they helped the Arabs make "Israel look bad."

On the whole, and again with some exceptions, television tended to equate the performance of the Israeli forces in Lebanon with that of the hordes of Attilla, Tamerlane and Hitler. Despite the denials of the networks' various presidents, the conclusion seems inescapable that television coverage was heavily biased against Israel. It uncritically and consistently inflated casualty figures, dwelt unduly on atrocities, and overstressed the fact of Israeli censorship which was not nearly as total as contemporaneous British censorship during the Falklands campaign. The thrust of the reporting of the new breed of electronic journalists was to depict Israel as the guilty party. The Palestinian Arabs have suffered at the hands of others, most notably Jordan's Hussein, whose Arab Legion killed an estimated 10,000 or more of Arafat's PLO "fighters" in 1970's Black September, but TV never trumpeted that particular outrage, or the Syrian slaughter at Hama in which tens of thousands died.

Television was invariably late, furthermore, in correcting mistakes whenever it was caught in error. Not until October, on an ABC *Viewpoint* program discussing media reliability, did the network's chief European correspondent, the personable Peter Jennings, acknowledge, for instance, that he himself was surprised when he visited Tyre and Sidon to find how exaggerated the earlier reports of wholesale destruction had been.

One of television's own stars, the erudite Bill Moyers, came closer than any critic or commentator to defining the shortcomings of the medium in the piece he did on Dan Rather's CBS *Evening News* show on August 23, when the long-delayed departure of the PLO forces from West Beirut got under way, machineguns blazing in air. It was a masterful summary of the situation up to that moment and worth quoting in full. Mr. Moyers:

> Watching scenes of the Beirut evacuation this weekend, I was struck by how it is possible for the cameras to magnify a lie. These Palestinian troops left town as if they'd just won a great victory. Arafat, they praised as a conquering hero. In fact, they are leaving town in defeat. And in fact, Arafat led them to this cul-de-sac where they made their last stand behind the skirts of women and among the playgrounds of children. The only victory they won was to give General Sharon an excuse for total war and so to bring upon Israel the condemnation of world opinion and to many Jews, a tormented conscience. But the world was condemning Israel even before Beirut, and will for time to come. And the anguish of Jews at the suffering caused by their own war machine comes from the bitter experience of having learned that those who die by the sword must live by the sword. Carnage, indeed, and no one's hand too clean. But it could have been otherwise if Arafat and his allies accepted the reality of Israel, if they had not established within Lebanon a terrorist state sworn to Israel's destruction, and if Arab governments had not found it useful to nurture the PLO in the bloody illusion that Israel

217

can one day be pushed into the sea. Argue as you might about the events leading up to the establishment of Israel. Weep as you must for the Palestinian refugees. But a fact is a fact, and Israel is a fact. Yet, the guerrillas leaving Beirut this week are vowing to fight on until victory. Well, there will be no peace in the Middle East until the Arabs stop asking their young men to die for a lie.

The Massacres: Who Was to Blame?

The departure of Arafat and most of his forces was policed— "observed" might be a more accurate word—by a small contingent of American, French and Italian troops. The terrorists gone, the American quit the international force soon after, two weeks before their scheduled time. Something approximating a vacuum was created by September 1, when Begin, aware that the PLO quite probably had left at least 2,000 armed men among the population of West Beirut, ordered the Israeli army to enter that portion of the city.

The decision had a tragic aftermath in mid-September when Lebanese Christian militiamen entered the Shatila and Sabra camps of Palestinian Arab refugees and massacred several hundred men, women and children. The episode was a climactic agony and moral trauma for all men and women of good will, deeply felt by Israel and by people everywhere. That the mass murders took place after the Israeli Army had entered West Beirut and virtually under the noses of Israeli military personnel sent shock waves throughout Israel where an outraged, democratic people immediately demanded an accounting from Premier Begin and Defense Minister Ariel Sharon.

Sharon's insistence that Israeli commanders had stressed to the leaders of the Lebanese Christian militia that their military action was to be solely against the many terrorists still hidden in West Beirut, not against civilians, failed to abate the Israelis' sense of dismay and guilt. Instead, it provoked massive demonstrations in Israel itself against the Begin-Sharon government for apparently having disregarded the possibility of a continuation of the feudal Moslem-Christian cycle of vengeance that had tormented Lebanon for decades. Only a week before the massacre, Christian President-elect Bashir Gemayel and more than a score of his followers were blown literally to bits by a mysterious explosion in their Phalangist party headquarters. It was foreseeable, or it should have been, that the Christians, who had lost not hundreds but tens of thousands of their men, women and children over the years of PLO occupation, would seek revenge. The Christians' "pogrom" against the Palestinian Arabs, rather than Israeli failure to foresee or deter it, was a *cause celebre* that cried out for a proper moral response.

A moral response did not come from the Vatican, certainly. Arafat, who had caused the murder of tens of thousands of Christians in Lebanon—and of hundreds of Jews in Israel and elsewhere—was received by Pope John-Paul II and was photographed with the peripatetic Pontiff of that Holy Roman Church which has not seen fit to recognize Israel's existence by exchanging diplomatic representation.

Meanwhile, the Soviet reaction to the tragedy at Shatila and Sabra was an official statement, issued by Tass, accusing Israeli troops of carrying out the massacre. Not one Arab witness of the killings had seen even a single Israeli soldier in the camps. Actually, there were reports that Israeli troops had fired upon Christian militiamen in an eleventh-hour attempt to end the blood-letting when the truth finally dawned on the Israeli commanders. But Moscow made no mention of the fact that Christian militiamen had entered the camps to wreak bloody vengeance on Palestinian Arabs. Tass villified Israel alone and concluded by making the predictable comparison of the Israeli "atrocity" to the Nazi massacres at Babi Yar outside Kiev during World War II.

This time, Western journalism backed away from such comparisons, but it did rival the Soviets in the venom, even distortion, that moved Premier Begin to cry "Goyim kill goyim, and the Jews get the blame." In democratic Italy, political leaders from far Left to the neo-Fascist Right heaped vituperation on Israel. A statement from the office of Prime Minister Spadolini in Rome distorted the truth almost as effectively as the Soviets had done: "The Italian government expresses herewith the strongest condemnation and the most indignant censure for the bloody actions perpetrated or at least concurred in by the Israeli Army."

Even China joined the chorus. In Peking, the *People's Daily* echoed Moscow, its ideological enemy, in describing the murders at Shatila and Sabra as Israeli crimes. Israel, and only Israel, was once more at the center of calumny, and the Jew once again cast in the role of the genocidal Nazi.

Also disturbing was an NBC newscast immediately following the Beirut massacre wherein a PLO spokesman claimed that Israeli soldiers actually had killed thousands of innocent persons in the two camp hospitals. NBC's newscasters never challenged the PLO representative's statement or asked him for proof of his allegations; they merely looked properly somber and nodded as though assenting to his outrageous fabrications. To the best of my knowledge, the false information was never retracted or corrected.

Prime Minister Begin, truth be told, did not help matters by refusing at first to institute a thorough independent investigation of the tragic episode. The impression abroad was that he only relented after some 400,000 Israelis took to the streets of Tel Aviv to demand an inquiry.

The fact remains, however, that when Christians murdered Moslems for having slaughtered Christians, the world immediately began denouncing the Jews who were at the very worst only indirectly responsible for what happened. Many Jews, at home and abroad, blamed Israel's leaders for their blindness to the possibility of Christian revenge in Lebanon. But is the rest of the world totally blameless? Would the massacres have occurred, for instance, if the U.S. Marines of the international force that "policed" the PLO's departure remained in place instead of going home two weeks earlier than had been agreed upon?

To this day, incidentally, the real killers have not been found. No serious investigation of the incidents has been mounted by President Amin Gemayel, Bashir's brother and successor. Nor have the Western media pursued the story with the intensity with which they slammed Israel during the fighting in Lebanon.

TV News Credibility

Israel was the darling of Western journalism while it remained the underdog of Middle East politics. It only started having trouble with the media when, to paraphrase the late Golda

Meir, Israel refused to die so that the world could speak well of it. This process continued in the wake of the quasi-disastrous Yom Kippur war, when Israel, out of sheer necessity, became a formidable military power fully capable of defending the country and its people, and of pursuing peace on its own terms rather than those dictated by the PLO and its masters in the Kremlin.

Outrages continue in Lebanon among the diverse ethnic and religious groupings as well as by the remaining PLO and Syrian occupation forces. Yet this is simply the world's "business as usual," not containing the same interest for the electronic media. Rather, what was of interest in 1982 was the Israeli (read "Jewish") rain of destruction on the PLO, especially if this could be capsulated as Israeli destruction per se. How facile to switch "dog" and "underdog" to suit picture-board fads, while relegating PLO and Syrian massacres over a period of seven years to "never-ever land." How easy to overlook Israel's remarkably pinpointed bombing and shelling of PLO facilities—better sustained targeting in urban areas than that displayed by any other military in modern times—when images of screaming women can have more media shock value.

The true horror is when dog bites man, not vice versa, yet this is not news. It surely doesn't play as well in America's living rooms and Nielsen ratings. The electronic media's rewriting of history in the Lebanese summer of 1982, when one small long-suffering country was finally liberated from radical and Soviet control (without, by the way, the loss of a single American life), is a warning to us all that "1984" and "News-speak" may not be far off. Let the American viewer beware, especially when it is the public credibility of a U.S. ally which is at stake.

Sabra and Shatilla—Now (1985) and Then (1982)

by *The Committee on Media Accountability*

In September 1982, Christian militiamen entered the Sabra and Shatilla refugee camps in West Beirut and killed over 300 Palestinians, some of them women and children. Three years later, in May of 1985, Shiite militiamen attacked those same camps and killed over 500 Palestinians, including women and children and hospital patients. The circumstances surrounding both massacres were conspicuously similar. First, both massacres took place at the same place and had roughly the same number of victims. Second, the victims in both massacres were Palestinians—civilians and PLO fighters. Third, in both cases reporters were kept out until the killings were over, and they had to rely on the testimony of survivors with no independent verification. In both cases, the killers were local Lebanese militiamen—Christians in 1982, Shiites in 1985.

In spite of those similarities, the 1982 massacre became the biggest news story of that year, while the 1985 massacre passed almost unnoticed by the American public. The most apparent reason was an inordinate discrepancy in the way the American press presented both events.

A review of the *New York Times* coverage of both massacres reveals the shortcomings of that coverage.

VICTIMS: Despite claims by the *Times* and other media that a large civilian massacre had occurred at the two camps in 1982, evidence was available all along which tended to contradict both the reported numbers and character of the killings. Our research

223

indicates that on July 23, 1982, just weeks before the killings, UPI reported that the two refugee camps were "almost empty, except for guerillas." On February 11, 1984, the *Washington Post* issued a two-inch, page-two retraction of a previous story concerning the identity of the victims at Sabra and Shatilla in 1982, conceding that "most of the dead were adult males." This account was published almost a year and a half after the fact, following many months during which the *Post*—and others—circulated precisely the opposite information.

DENSITY OF COVERAGE: In 1982, the intense *Times* coverage of the killings at the camps reached 15 stories in a single day (9-20-82). There were more than 80 stories in one week alone, and a total of 131 stories in the three months following the massacre. In 1985, on the other hand, 15 was the *total* coverage of the killing of over 500 in and around those same camps. There were far fewer stories in 1985 than in 1982, and they were much shorter (223 column-inches, compared to 3,641 in 1982).

LANGUAGE: The disparity between the *Times'* coverage in 1982 and 1985 is particularly striking in terms of the language used to describe each killing—in news stories and editorials alike. In 1982, the *Times* used the word "massacre" 49 times in headlines alone to describe the killings at the camps. In 1985, on the other hand, though citing doctors' reports of "many civilian casualties" (5-25—27-85), "wounded Palestinians... pulled from hospitals and shot" (5-27-85), and "Shiite Moslem militiamen butchering Palestinians in those same camps" (editorial, 5-28-85), the *Times* did not use the term "massacre" even once. Instead, *Times* headlines employed terms like "fighting," "clashes," "battles," or "intramural violence," which conjured the image of a struggle between essentially equal forces. Ironically, even in 1985 the *Times* continued to reserve the term "massacre" only for the 1982 killings, as stories out of a total of 15 recalled the earlier bloodshed. Phrases such as "massacre by Phalangists," and "massacred by Israeli-backed Christian Phalangist militiamen" (5-21-85) were applied to the events of 1982.

EDITORIALS: In 1982, a *Times* editorial described the events at Sabra and Chatilla as "horror and shame," "barbarity in Beirut," "blood bath," and "mass slaughter of Palestinians whom Israel had undertaken to protect"—all in just one editorial three days after the killings (9-21-82). There were no less than three *Times* editorials on Sabra and Shatilla in the eight days following the 1982 massacre. A fourth editorial, concerning El Salvador and having nothing to do with Lebanon, nevertheless carried the headline reminder: "Echoes of Beirut." In 1985, only one editorial dealt with the killing of Palestinians at the camps by the Shiite militias, but even this one opened with a reminder of "Christian militiamen slaughtering Palestinians in 1982" while "Israel's occupying army was held responsible, even by Israelis." Although ostensibly prompted by the 1985 killings, that one editorial, titled "The Heartbreak of Lebanon," devoted only two and one-half lines to the current slaughter. The rest of the editorial was taken up with a general historical review of "those ghastly divisions ... inherent in Lebanon's origins."

BROADER COVERAGE: In 1982, community and world reactions to the killings in Beirut received prominent coverage in the *Times*: "Reagan Horrified" (9-19-82), "Soviet Calls Killings in Beirut Heinous Crime" (9-20-82), "Major Jewish Paper in Britain Urges Begin to Quit" (9-24-82), "Mourning, Anger, Moral Outrage (in Israel)" (9-26-82), "Egyptians Bitter over Beirut Killings Have Second Thoughts about Israel" (9-29-82). Such items were totally missing from the *Times* coverage in 1985. While a *Times* editorial accused the world of "shrugging" at the "butchering of Palestinians," one might wonder how much of that seeming world apathy was due to the *Times'* failure to report the news with the same intensity as the previous massacre.

ASSIGNING RESPONSIBILITY: While the *Times* acknowledged that the Syrians were Lebanon's "protectors" during the 1985 killings, it relieved them of any responsibility: "though the Syrians remain, they are plainly not in command." The *Times* failed to explain why the Syrian "protectors" in 1985 were not responsible for the killings that took place under their protection, but the Israelis and the Americans, who were in Lebanon in 1982, were.

ASSIGNING BLAME: In 1982 (before, but especially after, the Sabra and Shatilla killings), the *Times* constantly and pointedly described particular Christian militia leaders as "war lord" or "butcher of Beirut." In 1985, although briefly noting in an editorial that it was Nabih Berri and his Amal militiamen who had been "slaughtering Palestinians in recent weeks," the *Times* nevertheless represented Berri as a "moderate." Even the fact that he was holding American hostages, in collusion with their terrorist kidnappers, had no effect on this.

The *Times* attitude toward the two massacres was also reflected in the way its star columnist, Anthony Lewis, covered them. In one of two columns he wrote about the 1982 killings, titled "Averting Their Eyes," Lewis lectured Menachem Begin about "Jewish values," about "closing his eyes to evil," and about Israel's responsibility for the "mass killings" at the camps. However, Lewis had no such advice for Nabih Berri in 1985 during the weeks Berri's Amal militiamen were killing over 500 Palestinians. On 6-20-85, while Amal was holding American hostages, Lewis described Berri as "a moderate (who) must worry about falling behind the fervor of his people." This column made no mention of the killings at the camps.

The data below indicates the "packaging" of these news stories in three major American newspapers:

New York Times

	1982	1985
Number of victims	over 300	over 500
Duration of killing	3 days	5 weeks
Coverage: Number of stories	139	15
Coverage: News column-inches	3,641	223
Page-one news stories	33	8
Number of times "Massacre" used in headlines	49	0
Number of editorials	4	1
Number of op. ed. articles	6	0
Number of syndicated columns	12	3

Washington Post

	1982	**1985**
Number of victims	over 300	over 500
Duration of killing	3 days	5 weeks
Coverage: Number of stories	103	15
Coverage: News column-inches	2,778	331
Page-one news stories	40	6
Number of times "Massacre" used in headlines	33	1
Number of editorials	11	2
Number of op. ed. articles	11	4
Number of syndicated columns	15	1

Los Angeles Times

	1982	**1985**
Number of victims	over 300	over 500
Duration of killing	3 days	5 weeks
Coverage: Number of stories	117	14
Coverage: News column-inches	2,307	288
Page-one news stories	56	4
Number of times "Massacre" used in headlines	40	1
Number of editorials	5	2
Number of op. ed. articles	16	0
Number of syndicated columns	3	0

The "Holocaust Analogy" and the Media: The Lebanon War and Today

by Frederick Krantz

Much has been written about American media failings, ranging from simple error and uncritical credulity to partisan anti-Israel "analysis," in reporting the Lebanon War of 1982. But while attention was also drawn to the use of imprecise historical analogies, above all to America's experience in Vietnam, little has been said about media use of the "Holocaust analogy." This analogy worked to delegitimate Israel's limited military action and, by extension, its moral standing as a state and a legatee of the Holocaust itself. Not psychological denial of the Holocaust but appropriation of its moral capital sanctioned condemnation of Israel as a *Jewish* state. This clear break with earlier media attitudes toward Israel is of major consequence for the current crisis in Israel's territories.

The Vietnam analogy, applied to the 1982 war, rekindled negative memories and associations among the largely Left-liberal media, and reinforced opposition to American involvement in Lebanon. But the Holocaust analogy, once invoked, elicited different, deeper, less conscious, and implicitly anti-Semitic images and resonances. It fostered a series of role-reversals in which Israelis, as "bad" Jews wreaking a "holocaust" on innocent Arab and PLO victims, negated Israel's moral standing. By emptying the Holocaust of its specifically Jewish content, use of the analogy legitimated—implicitly, and in some cases explicitly—hoary old anti-Jewish themes that had long marked Soviet and Arab propaganda, and the reflections of this propaganda in West European media of the Right and the Left.

The Holocaust role-reversals were prefigured in media handling of the Christian-Muslim conflict within Lebanon itself. Where one might have expected some sympathy on the part of the American media for the beleaguered Christian minority, one found it instead actively and consistently championing the Muslim majority. The complex Lebanese civil war was presented as a simple Christian-versus-Muslim conflict, with justice on the side of the Muslims struggling for Parliamentary representation adequate to their numbers. American media sympathy for the Muslims was extravagant; the internal divisions within both groups, Muslim and Christian, were ignored. So too were divisive roles in the struggle of the PLO (which had built up its own terrorist state-within-a-state in Lebanon since the 1970's) and of Syria (which alternately supported both Christian and Muslim groupings in its "divide and conquer" policy toward Lebanon). Further, the Muslims were represented as a homogenized whole, comprehensibly "Western," while the Christians, also monolithic, were "feudal" and "bloodthirsty," that is, stereotypically "Arab." However feudal both of these groupings actually still were, the Muslims' self-proclaimed "progressive" or "socialist" labels were taken literally, while the Christians, in an echo of the Phalangist group's party-label, became homogeneously "fascist."

Significantly, media opposition to American involvement turned not only on the Vietnam analogy—fear of inextricable involvement in another morass—but also on the fact that, by reinforcing an Israeli-imposed peace, the U.S. would be favoring the wrong side, the Christians. Subsequent events have shown how simplistic, and dishonest, the media's good guys-vs.-bad guys morality play really was, and how terribly divided both the Muslims and the Christians really were, and are. They have also validated the role of both the PLO and the Syrians and, now, of the Iranian-directed Hizbollah, or Party of God, in perpetuating Lebanon's agony. At the time, journalists and commentators, blinded by their partisan views, never asked what might become of the Lebanese Christians should the Muslim "majority" triumph in their "just" struggle, just as they failed to note either initial Shi'ite sympathy for Israel (especially in the south, where the PLO was hated), or the striking phenomenon of the Jewish state alone protecting a Christian Arab minority.

Media sympathy for the Muslims was mirrored in media idealization of the PLO. Neither PLO irredentism (its Covenant calls for the liberation of *all* "Palestine," with no Jew whose family came to the area after 1880 to be admitted into the vaunted "secular, democratic state" which would replace Israel), nor the PLO's bloody terrorist history, within and without Lebanon, before and after 1982, was analyzed. If Israel was the media heavy, Arafat and the PLO—"underdogs" benefiting from both the Vietnam analogy and Left-liberal media idealization—were its heroes. Edward Alexander's characterization of the NBC News' sustained line on the PLO as "idealistic freedom-fighters longing for a land and a state of their own," characterized much of the other network and print media reporting. *Newsweek*, recounting the Palestinian Arabs' loss of their "green paradise" and their "dream ... of returning home," explained away their terrorism as stemming from "the surpassing sense of grievance and injustice" due to Israeli "expansionism" and its goal, "to do away" with the Palestinian Arabs. Arafat himself, responding during the siege of Beirut to an interviewer's hopeful question about possible positive changes in American public opinion toward the PLO, replied, "We hope so. I began to touch it through the mass media.... I began to touch it."

Media sympathy for the Lebanese Muslims and the PLO, a compound of ignorance, ideological bias, and repertorial response to editorial/network policy signals, exhibited another, more complex dimension. If Israel was presented as a (non-Jewish) Goliath, the PLO became a (Jewish) David. This inversion reflected long-standing PLO propaganda directed at the West (but not, in Arabic, at the East). The scattered Palestinian Arabs are a "diaspora"; they seek (the reference is to the 1917 Balfour Declaration) a "homeland," the PLO's constitution is a "Covenant," and its Chairman, Arafat, is a gun-toting analogue to Chaim Weizmann, representing his homeless people to the world. In short, Palestinian Arabs, often termed the most intelligent, capable, enterprising Arabs, are "Jews," victims of a now-powerful people who, once powerless and wandering and persecuted like themselves, have robbed them of their legitimate rights and land.

The Palestinian Arabs-as-persecuted-Jews inversion, however, did not transform the Israelis into Arabs; rather they became "bad" Jews, or Germans, Fascists, *Nazis*. The Palestinian Red Crescent's estimate of *600,000* civilian casualties in the first days of the war (one-third Lebanon's population), consciously echoing the Holocaust's 6,000,000, was uncritically broadcast by the media. Use of the term "refugee camps" to describe long-settled Palestinian Arab areas, where homes and hospitals functioned as armed PLO bases, evoked images of World War II displaced persons, that is, of Jews. Reporters and commentators likened Israel variously to a "Middle Eastern Prussia" out to rule subject Arabs by "blood and iron," to the Fascist camp in the Spanish Civil War, to Germans waging a "Blitzkrieg" on helpless civilians, upon whom they were imposing "the disgraceful criteria once inflicted upon themselves." An NBC News commentator saw in the war Israel's "final military solution" of the Palestinian Arab problem, while *The New York Times'* Anthony Lewis flatly asserted that Israel was seeking to "exterminate" Palestinian Arab nationalism. In one of the many cartoons with Holocaust themes, the *San Francisco Chronicle* showed an ugly Begin staring at the date "9/17/82"—a reference to the Sabra and Shatila massacres—tattooed on his forearm.

One of the most disturbing aspects of the American advent of the term "Judeo-Nazi" imagery was its mirroring, for the first time, of longstanding Soviet and Arab themes. There, explicitly anti-Semitic caricatures of Israel present it as a Nazi-like state allied to U.S.-dominated "world capital" and imperialism. Not stopping short at extermination, Israel brutally exploits Third World Arabs and Palestinians in its lust for territorial expansion and even world-domination (The "Protocols of the Elders of Zion" are alive and well in Soviet anti-Zionist calumny).

Similar anti-Semitic distortions have marked much of the West European media, both Left and Right, since at least 1967, and reached fever pitch during the Lebanon war. But what Robert Wistrich has termed the "demonization of Israel" was a new and unaccustomed phenomenon in mainline American reporting and commentary. The American Nicholas von Hoffman, writing for the *Spectator*, compared Lebanon to the Nazi massacre at Lidice, writing that "Americans are coming to see the Israeli government as pointing the Star of David into a swastika." *Newsweek* discerned Israel's goal as "to do away" with the Palestinian Arabs, and William Pfaff in the *International Herald Tribune* (published jointly by *The New York Times* and *The Washington Post*) averred that "Hitler's work goes on," carried out now "by the Jews themselves." Even local papers got in on the act, with the *Asbury Park Press* (published in a Jewish resort area in New Jersey) running a cartoon showing skeletal concentration-camp survivors peering over barbed-wire carrying the sign "Auschwitz," and captioned "Wasn't it Begin who condemned others for standing by while a slaughter took place?"

In contrast with Soviet and Arab propaganda, however, the American media's "Lebanon-as-Holocaust" imagery bore a peculiarly moralizing, liberal stamp. The functional consequence of its role-reversal, in which Israelis first became Jews, then Germans, fascists, and Nazis, was two-fold: the delegitimation of Israel and, by extension, of the North American Jewish support for Israel. Media attention focused on divisions within the Jewish community over the war, divisions themselves at least in part the product of the initial distorted, condemnatory coverage itself. At the same time, media handling of the PLO, of Sabra and Shatila (almost universally presented as Israel's direct responsibility), and of the "siege" of Beirut also reflected and reinforced the Holocaust reversal. The presumed "slaughter of innocents" was a consequence of what NBC News' Roger Mudd termed Israel's obdurate "eye for an eye, tooth for a tooth" mentality. Israelis-as-Jews killed and maimed children (an echo of old blood-libels?), while Arafat, portrayed as prepared for martyrdom, was repeatedly pictured kissing babies. Well-fed PLO guerrillas, negotiating the fine points of their U.N.-assured extrication from commandeered highrises, were likened—one of the more offensive media analogies—to the ill-armed, starving, and doomed Jewish fighters of the Warsaw ghetto. And the PLO's forced eviction from Beirut became a media event: AK47s and machine-guns blazing, defeat was masked as victory in a festive celebration of Palestinian Arab "resistance."

The unaccountably naive and remarkably idealized handling of the PLO was the reverse side of the moral disenfranchisement worked on Israel, which seemed to lose its "Western" status in the course of much of the coverage. Formerly a valiant little democracy, a Middle Eastern outpost of the "Judeo-Christian heritage," Israel was now (as a cleverly-inverted *Time* cover had earlier announced) "Beyond the Pale." Fascist-and Nazi-like Israelis were morally condemned; Palestinian Arabs, now "Jewish" victims, were morally rehabilitated, their terrorist deeds forgotten. In such a politically and morally distorted never-never land, the American media tended to reproduce the old stereotype of Jews as—the "Judeo-Christian heritage" notwithstanding—pariahs.

The inversions, involving associations going well beyond merely credulous sympathy for seeming victims, broke with prior media attitudes and reinforced pre-existing Arab and PLO propaganda. The Palestinian Arabs' self-representation as oppressed "Jews" has been noted as a propaganda tactic. Conor Cruise O'Brien has called attention to a related technique: Arab spokesmen use, for Western consumption, a self-referential political vocabulary rooted neither in Islamic religious values nor in Arab political realities. Phrases like "democratic self-determination" or "secular democratic state" bear no relation to the real nature of universally authoritarian-repressive Arab regimes. The American media's role-reversals, consciously ignoring both Israeli and PLO realities, reinforced this aspect of Arab propaganda, strengthening the "Western" appeal of the embattled PLO and masking its profoundly *anti*-"Judeo-Christian" terrorism. The importance of such media support for a movement that is, after all, a Soviet-armed, trained, and supported client, is obvious: it strengthens PLO efforts to mobilize American public opinion in favor of its recognition (without, of course, having to swallow the unswallowable—recognition of Israel's right to exist).

Much of the moral condemnation of Israel, which was not without its quotient of *Schadenfreude*—delight in "finding out" and "showing up" the Jews' presumed hardness and cruelty—derived its energy from hoary anti-Semitic images. Much media criticism implied a distinction between the Israelis' "Old Testament" tooth-for-a-tooth toughness and a more "just" policy toward the PLO, which would, presumably, display a "New Testament"-like mercy and loving kindness toward these exploited victims. At the beginning of the war, Meg Greenfield (editorial page editor of *The Washington Post*) expressed an "outraged, emotional condemnation" of Israel, an expression of long pent-up anger and resentment, catching in this quite nicely the tone of much media commentary. As Reuven Frank, head of NBC News, rather disingenuously put it: with Lebanon, a former "Holocaust sympathy," as well as the "power of the Jewish community" (to censor the press?), broke down. Anti-Semitic images, long a staple of Soviet, Arab, and West European propaganda, now made their American debut.

The "Old Testament"/"New Testament" juxtaposition touches on an important, if elusive, dimension of the Holocaust analogy. The stereotyping was informed by Christian associations already apparent in the attribution of negative "Old Testament" characteristics to the Israelis-as-Jews. Arafat and the PLO were not only readably "Western," not only—or not simply— "Jews." They were also somehow or other "Christian," almost, one is tempted to say, like Jesus' initial followers, "Jewish Christians," and were persecuted, like them, by the "real" Jews. If the Palestinian Arabs were to be an exploited, oppressed people— alone, abandoned, persecuted—they must, above all, be innocent, Christ-like victims. In the simplistic, implicitly Christian, dream-like associational imagery through which complex issues were conveyed, especially on television, to American audiences, the Palestinian Arabs, hunted down by the merciless slayers of Amalek bent on their extermination, were acting out a transposed Passion. And in the Passion the key player was, of course, Yasir Arafat, the long-suffering Man of Sorrows, repeatedly portrayed as ready—again, the media's term—for martyrdom, in the name of his People.

This paradoxically Christian dimension of the Holocaust screen gave it far greater associational and evocative power than the Vietnam analogy. The Lebanese War was a betrayal by Israel of its Judeo-Christian standing; with it, the mantle of legitimacy passed to the Palestinian Arabs, whose sufferings were an ennobling Passion, and whose leader was a sacrificial Lamb. What else was the PLO's wondrous deliverance from seemingly assured destruction in the supposed "siege" of Beirut—celebrated in full panoply by the media acolytes—than a triumphant Easter, a moral-political Resurrection? Arafat, like a thaumaturgic Christian king, had healed his People by "touching" the formerly scrofulous Western media. And his sudden reappearance a few weeks later, amid speculation about his fate, to be received by the Pope in the basilica of Western Christianity's martyred founder, was an exquisite, if unintended, closure of the Passion-play metaphor.

Media use of the Holocaust analogy worked to empty the "real" Holocaust of its Jewish content (and of its Christian guilt) precisely by applying it to the Israelis *as* Jews. It also energized a Christianizing allegorical thrust insofar as the Palestinian Arabs were concerned. In the process the American media went beyond the rather simple "Jewish" self-image of PLO propaganda, investing it with a new, Manichaean energy in which the complex realities of the Israeli-PLO struggle were transformed into a grotesque morality play. The Sons of Darkness were pitted against the Sons of Light, and the result was a redemptive Transfiguration.

In explaining the American media's attitudinal shift, media dislike of the Right-wing, aggressively "Jewish" Begin government—as well as the post-1973, "oil shock"-induced quest for "more balanced" attitudes—may well deserve privileged status. Begin had invoked the Holocaust in defense of his government's policies; his settlement policy in Judea and Samaria was universally unpopular in the media, and his own supposed "terrorist" background was invoked as a counter to PLO terror. "Israel has changed"—a media attitude reflecting the Likud's non-"progressive," non-Ashkenazi, non-"Western" Jewish support—reflected a view of Begin's government as atavistically Jewish, a setback for progressive, formerly Labor-dominated, Israel. That this view, as well as opposition to the Lebanon war, was shared by many Israelis, served to reinforce the media's moralizing thrust.

Lebanon provided the occasion, an especially dramatic one, for the delegitimation of an already "illegitimate" Begin government, its own democratic imprimatur notwithstanding. Through the Holocaust analogy Begin could be hoisted on his own petard—his resented "Holocaust mongering." But, once introduced, the Holocaust proved not a manipulable metaphor: it probably pushed initial intentions to unwonted extremes. On this reading,

Left-liberal media sympathy for Palestinian Arabs or the PLO and against Begin or Israel were radicalized precisely by the dynamic of the Holocaust analogy and its implicitly anti-Semitic, Christianizing imagery. To the extent that the media campaign was directed against American Jewish solidarity with Israel, it was quite successful. By stressing a supposed Nazi-like oppression by Israelis of a defenseless people, the coverage did drive a wedge between Israel and many American Jews. Precisely the American legitimacy of the Jewish community, a status expressed by the notion of the "Judeo-Christian heritage" (a concept of American provenance), seemed at stake. Put differently, continued Jewish support for an Israel supposedly violating the values binding together Christians and Jews as Americans raised the specter of dual loyalty in the ugliest sense.

The repression of traditional anti-Semitism since 1945 shows how the enormity of the Holocaust has blocked its public expression. The workings of the media's Holocaust analogy validated anti-Jewish sentiments in the name of the Holocaust: not its *denial* (already a current), but its *affirmation*, removed its sting. At the time, Norman Podhoretz and others were right to discern an anti-Semitic thrust in the coverage; but what was involved was not a simple, easily dealt with hatred of Jews, but a much more sophisticated moral stance that singled out Jews by casting them as the negation of supposed Holocaust "lessons." More effectively than the 1975 Soviet-Arab "Zionism equals racism" U.N. Resolution, the media's Holocaust analogy validated anti-Semitic sentiments by associating Israel (and its American Jewish supporters) negatively with the greatest tragedy ever to befall the Jewish people.

Whether this episode represents an isolated phenomenon, a response to a unique conjunction of intersecting elements, or an initial expression of a deeper—and repeatable—process rooted in long-term factors, remains moot. It is important to remember that what is read or seen as "news" is a considered, edited product, right down to the picture-captions and commentators' gestures and facial expressions. How self-professed media "liberals" could have indulged in fantastic and blatantly fictional Jewish/Nazi comparisons and inversions, and with apparently good conscience (as their offended reactions to subsequent criticism indicates), remains an issue. Such people are neither Soviet nor Arab-style anti-Semites, nor fringe neo-Nazis, nor, for the most part, anti-Israel, Left-wing ideologues; they are not, in their own minds, "anti-Semites," nor would one so describe them in ordinary, everyday terms. But the general Lebanon coverage went well-beyond the usual media mistakes, shallowness, hypocrisy, and even dishonesty; by the same token, it went well beyond honest disagreement about the rights and wrongs of the war itself.

Here, use of the Holocaust analogy may well indicate the relative ease with which, in dramatic circumstances, continuing anti-Semitic currents alive within American secular culture can be mobilized. The rabid, unreasoning anti-Israel and anti-*Jewish* reporting and commentary implies the persistence of those dark forces, of ultimately Christian provenance, which made the Holocaust possible. It also underlines the failure of "Western," "Judeo-Christian" civilization, to this day, to learn the Holocaust's hard lessons.

The "dramatic circumstances" of 1982 are repeating themselves today before our eyes. The media are again replete with articles, cartoons, and images imbued with Jewish-Nazi role-inversions and Holocaust analogies. The American Jewish community is once again divided, ever more seriously than in 1982.

This Diaspora division indeed reflects the Israeli division on the territories and their future disposition. But it is reinforced by the media's peculiar representational "spin" insofar as "Jewish" Palestinians and "fascist" (or "Nazi") Israelis are concerned. And, once again, the spin is conjoined to a terrible amnesia, not only about PLO policy and terrorism, but about the basic roots and continuing realities of the Arab-Israeli conflict itself.

The use of Holocaust imagery is particularly effective in dividing the Diaspora. By threatening the "made in the U.S.A." notion of a shared "Judeo-Christian heritage," it threatens the perceived legitimacy of American Jewry. Much more than "legitimate" criticism of Israel's government, as opposed to the state, is involved here. Negative media representation of Israel as a *Jewish* state works to activate, and to validate, a liberal Jewish "universalism" all too ready to proclaim publicly its anguished concern for Israel's "soul." This perceived schism between "true"

Jewish values and Israel's "un-Jewish" actions—quite different from informed, pragmatic discussion of concrete policy alternatives—radically delegitimates the Jewish state. Precisely this delegitimation—the goal of Arab and, since at least 1967, Soviet, propaganda—is a mortal danger for Israel.

The media dynamics clearly revealed in 1982 and now resumed are contributing not only a revival of (often forgotten) pre-1967 Diaspora divisions, but to a possibly Israel-Diaspora split of even greater magnitude. If this happens, and the post-1945 Holocaust blockage of traditional anti-Semitism (already a tottering barrier in Western Europe) is dismantled and paralleled by an intensification of the "Zionism equals racism" theme, we may well be in for hard times indeed. As elections loom in both Israel and the U.S., the implications—for Israel and for the Diaspora—of the current crisis can hardly be overestimated.

More Israel-Bashing at NBC:
Six Days Plus Twenty Years:
A Dream is Dying

by Edward Alexander

NBC's Tom Brokaw served his apprenticeship in Israel-bashing in 1982, during the first months of the Lebanon War. His voice dripped with sarcasm whenever he interviewed Israeli leaders, whom he always described as "hardened," "defensive," "aggressive" and "militant." He called Israeli soldiers cogs in a "war machine" but referred to Syrian troops as members of a "peacekeeping army." He relentlessly complained about Israeli censorship, but had nothing to say about censorship by Syria or by the PLO. Indeed, he could never find anything objectionable in the PLO, and invariably expressed astonishment that anybody should apply the epithet "terrorist" to the world's leading terrorist organization. On August 6, 1982, for example, during an interview with then Foreign Minister Yitzhak Shamir, Brokaw alluded to "the PLO, or the terrorists as *you* call them." Far from being terrorists, the PLO fighters were for Brokaw above all else men of honor. When they were leaving Beirut, Brokaw, though clearly disappointed by their defeat, expressed himself satisfied that they "can leave with honor."

Brokaw's truculence towards Israel and his assiduous praise of the PLO cause in the United States did not go unrecognized. In 1985, the Arab-American Anti-Discrimination Committee, probably the most aggressive promoter of the PLO cause in the United States, chose Brokaw to be its keynote speaker at its annual convention in Washington, D.C. His predecessor as featured speaker in 1984 had been Louis Farrakhan, and in 1985 his star quality earned him pride of place over other speakers renowned as Israel-haters, including Alexander Cockburn, Pete McCloskey, Pete Seeger, Vanessa Redgrave, and Yasir Arafat (who could not appear in person because the American government, unlike Brokaw and most of his NBC colleagues, does still hold the view that the PLO is a terrorist organization). Brokaw did not disappoint his audience. He described the PLO as "reasonable men," expressed what *American Specator's* Tom Bethell, reporting the conference, called "hero-worship of Hafez Assad," the Syrian dictator, urged the U.S. administration to bring pressure on Israel, and voiced the hope that the Soviet Union would become more active in the Middle East.

When Lawrence K. Grossman, president of NBC News, selected Tom Brokaw in spring of 1987 to take the pulse of Israeli society twenty years after the Six-Day War, he was no more innocent of what he was doing than a medical board would be if it selected a well-known advocate of euthanasia to administer a nursing home for the aged. *Six Days Plus Twenty Years: A Dream is Dying*, broadcast on July 1, 1987, was the entirely predictable result of Grossman's decision.

Painful though it must have been for him to do so, Brokaw began the program by devoting all of three seconds to the events leading up to the Six-Day War of 1967, the war that, in his view, instantly turned Israel into a "warrior state." To have lingered over the background to the war might have prompted some curious viewers to ask why it was that between 1948 and 1967 the Arab states never thought to establish an independent Palestinian Arab state in Judea and Samaria. For nineteen years prior to the war these territories were theirs to do with whatever they liked; and not once did it occur to them or to the Palestinian Arabs themselves to pursue the solution now so confidently and stridently recommended by Brokaw and his collaborators at NBC as the only path to peace. For nineteen years there was no Arab move to establish a Palestinian state, no talk of the distinctive national identity and culture of Palestinian Arabs and—of course— no peace.

But none of these embarrassing facts was considered worthy of mention in *Six Days Plus Twenty Years*, for the whole thrust of the program was to imply that the Israeli-Arab conflict is entirely concerned with the territories taken by Israel in 1967 and to obscure the grim truth that Israel is the only country in the modern world whose very existence has for forty years been rejected by all but one of her neighbors. In a part of the program filmed in the Jerusalem classroom of Rabbi David Hartman, Brokaw went out of his way to convey the false impression that all the assembled students, boys about to begin their army service, would soon be patrolling Hebron and other "West Bank" towns, as if Israel had no worries on its borders with Syria, Lebanon, Jordan, or Egypt, and as if the 16,000 Israeli soldiers who have fallen in the country's past wars since 1948 had been in combat against the Hebron schoolgirls lovingly interviewed by NBC rather than defending the country against the combined armies of half a dozen Arab countries. All the other acts of deception and skulduggery committed by Brokaw and Martin Fletcher and producer Paul Greenberg pale into relative insignificance beside this big lie of omission. It is as if some journalistic ancestor of Brokaw's had in 1936 produced a documentary about relations between Czechs and ethnic Germans in the Sudetenland, showing preternatural sensitivity to the Sudeten Germans' complaints about discrimination and mistreatment while blithely ignoring the fact that neither perfect equality of rights for the Sudeten Germans nor expulsion of every German from Czech territory would mitigate by one iota the Nazi campaign to destroy Czechoslovakia.

John Corry of *The New York Times* made this point in his review of the program on July 1. He noted that NBC supplied lots of dramatic shots of Arabs being rounded up and roughly questioned in the aftermath of attacks on Jewish civilians, and then Peter Kent ominously concluded: "This is what the occupation is all about." "Well, perhaps," wrote Corry, "but we'd have a surer sense of what it is all about if NBC... had included an old fashioned map. It is impossible to understand the occupation without knowing about Israel's geography. The West Bank is not just a bank of the Jordan; it is a large piece of territory that extends nearly to the Mediterranean.... If Israel ends its occupation, its borders become considerably diminished; it is more vulnerable to Arab attack."

Jillian Becker, the English expert on terrorism, has said that "to speak of international terrorism without mentioning the PLO would be like describing the circulation of the blood without mentioning the heart." Yet no one who worked on *Six Days Plus Twenty Years* ever used the word "terrorist" in connection with the PLO or failed to express wonderment that, in Brokaw's words, *Israel* "regards the PLO as a terrorist organization." This NBC language rule suggests not only that the program's producer has been remarkably inattentive to world events for the past quarter-century, but that NBC's correspondents in Israel, Martin Fletcher and Peter Kent, were determined not to be unduly perturbed even by spectacular unpleasantnesses that happened at the very time and place in which they were gathering materials for their program, unpleasantnesses that people not working for NBC generally do call "terrorist acts." Among these were the fire-bombing of a car belonging to the Moses family that burnt Ofra Moses and her five year old son Tal to death and badly injured the car's other passengers, and the crushing of little Rami Chaba's skull with a large stone (estimated by police to weigh ten or twelve pounds). NBC took no notice of these murders, because Paul Greenberg's four camera crews had been instructed to scour the land for weeks in search of very different sights, in particular the sight of an Israeli beating an Arab. Failing to find this, they had to use an archive picture of an Israeli soldier shoving an Arab prisoner with a rifle; and even about that they lied. For they gave the impression that he had been arrested for stone-throwing when in fact his offense was assault with an even deadlier weapon. While all Israel was in shock over the burning to death of Ofra Moses (her son died later of his burns) and the crushing to death—with a stone—of Rami Chaba, Paul Greenberg's reporters could only stress how Israeli "military reaction can be ugly" to "children throwing stones."

NBC's policy towards the PLO terror was also evident in its allusion to a 1983 attack that turned a civilian bus travelling along Mt. Herzl in Jerusalem into an abattoir. The allusion was light and fleeting, for this act of savagery served Paul Greenberg's staff merely as a prelude to an interview with an Arab woman—the suspected killer's mother—who says that blowing up her son's house is "worse terror than what they claim we do." None of NBC's intrepid moral inquirers thought to ask her how destroying an empty house could be "worse terror" than blowing up a full bus. Perhaps they were stymied by NBC language rules, which stipulate that the word "terrorist" must never be applied to the PLO. The label was affixed once by NBC in the course of the hour-long program: the Jews who reside in Kiryat Arba were—all of them—labelled as people who "represent extreme views," among whom were "Jewish terrorists."

From the assumption that only Jews can be terrorists, it is a short step to the allegation that "Israel is losing its morality," that it has already made the "choice between democracy and tyranny," and that it is committed to "apartheid." The step was easily made by the standard device of an interview (by Fletcher) with Meir Kahane, the sole representative of "official" opinion interviewed during the program. Kahane's Kach party, it will be recalled, received 1.2 percent of the total vote in the 1984 elections. His presence in the Israeli Knesset has since then been used countless times by unscrupulous journalists as evidence that, in NBC parlance, Israel has lost her morality, corrupted her "dream," and become the devil's own experiment station. By contrast, no NBC journalist has dared to reflect on the decline of the British national character evident in the repeated election of Enoch Powell to Parliament for thirty-four years, until his recent defeat in 1987. Powell, starting in 1968, advocated the repatriation of "colored" immigrants from Britain; in 1983 he received 7000 more votes from his own small constituency than Kahane received in 1984 from the entire state of Israel.

Even the extremist Kahane is, moreover, less extreme than the most "moderate" members of the PLO which is presented throughout *Six Days* as a kind of benevolent fraternal organization. At no point do Brokaw or his colleagues mention that the PLO's covenant unambiguously commits itself to the destruction of Israel and the forcible expulsion of all its Jewish citizens; at no point do they mention that according to a poll taken last year by *Al Fajr, Newsday*, and the Australian Broadcasting Corporation, 78% of "West Bank Palestinians" see the establishment of a state in the West Bank as a mere preliminary stage on the way to full Arab control over what is now Israel, and 88% condone terrorist violence against Israeli civilians.

NBC does deserve some credit for being more candid than it used to be about its Israel-bashing in *Six Days Plus Twenty Years*. Martin Fletcher, interviewed about the program, expressed himself mightily pleased that the Arab lobby in Washington has received the film "very well indeed." "We made this film," Fletcher continued, "as a background documentary so that it would be used." But why should journalists who are supposed to be dispassionate observers and impartial seekers after truth, become advocates of a cause? "It is time that the Palestinian point of view was heard," said Fletcher defiantly.

This is by no means the first time that NBC has advocated what has sometimes been called the "listening" theory of terrorism, which says that to refuse to listen to terrorists is to strengthen their argument that violence is their only recourse. In May 1986 NBC went beyond its journalistic competitors in tortured apologetics for terror into active collusion and criminal complicity. The "NBC Nightly News" for May 5 broadcast a three-and-a-half minute interview with Mohammed Abbas, then under indictment in the U.S. as the organizer of the hijacking of the Achille Lauro and the murderer of the American-Jewish passenger, Leon Klinghoffer. NBC's spokesmen admitted, indeed boasted, that the network had agreed to keep the terrorist's whereabouts secret in exchange for his granting them an exclusive interview. Lawrence Grossman justified the arrangement by claiming, predictably, that he has been acting on behalf of the public's right to know and "understand" the views of "all leaders." Brokaw, just as predictably, said that "It is better to hear him [Abbas] say that President Reagan is public enemy number one and that he shall strike in the United States."

Since no national or ethnic group claiming victimization has ever received more publicity, has ever been "heard" more than the Palestinian Arabs, Fletcher's real meaning in shamelessly trotting out this stale cliche is not that we listen inadequately to the wishes of those bent on the elimination of Israel but that we are inadequately cooperative in helping them to realize these wishes.

246

IV. CRITICISM OF ISRAEL FROM THE JEWISH COMMUNITY; ANALYSES

Norman Podhoretz

Why is it that, in the weeks since the latest phase of the Arab war against Israel first erupted in Gaza and the West Bank, stories about the reaction of American Jews have sometimes seemed almost as numerous as reports from the battlefield itself?

I exaggerate, of course—but not in highlighting the extraordinary degree of journalistic preoccupation with how the Jewish community here feels. For coverage of the clashes between Palestinian rioters and Israeli troops has been so obsessive that it would be hard to find anything which has received comparably prominent treatment.

Take, for example, the violent protests staged by the Tamils in Sri Lanka shortly before the outbreaks in Gaza and the West Bank. Although there are many parallels between the two situations, infinitely less play was given to the one in Sri Lanka. Furthermore, the small amount of attention it did attract was marked by an underlying sympathy for the Indian troops who had been summoned to restore order and who were usually described as "peacekeepers."

No such sympathy has been shown for the Israeli troops in the coverage of the Palestinian riots. Yet the death toll in Sri Lanka was far higher than it has been in Gaza and the West Bank. (All this is documented in a study by the California-based Committee on Media Accountability.)

Even allowing for the fact that there are few Tamils in America, it is remarkable how little time and space could be found by the media for the violence in Sri Lanka. By contrast, an unlimited quantity of these scarce resources has been made available for Gaza and the West Bank—and even then more than enough has been reserved for pieces about the "anguish" of American Jews.

Despite their appearance of "balance" in presenting different points of view, these pieces are anything but neutral. Indeed,
with very few exceptions, they are meant (in some cases, perhaps,
unconsciously) to serve two related purposes. One is to convey the
idea that even Israel's most fervent defenders are turning against
it. The other is to persuade politicians that they can now begin
taking up the PLO cause without necessarily antagonizing the
Jewish community.

These messages are rarely stated explicitly. But through
repeated interviews with American Jews who are only too eager
to denounce Israel, the impression is created that the community
is now split right down the middle. Presumably, then, American
Jews will no longer either be able or willing to work as effectively
as they formerly did against candidates for political office who are
less than friendly to Israel.

Yet as anyone with a real feel for the American Jewish
community can testify, both of these messages are misleading to
the point of outright deception.

It is true, to be sure, that American Jews in general are
deeply upset by the clashes in Gaza and the West Bank. It is also
true that there has been more public criticism of Israel by Jews
than might have been voiced in the past. Yet the fact remains that
very few American Jews are on the side of the Palestinian rioters
against the Israeli troops. Certainly most Jews wish that the
Israeli army could find a gentler way of restoring order. But they
know very well that the riots are nothing more and nothing less
than a new tactic in the continuing war against the Jewish state.

Nor have most American Jews forgotten that it is the Arabs,
and not the Israelis, who are the aggressors in this war. Still less
have they forgotten that what the Arabs want is not to make peace
with Israel but to eliminate all trace of Jewish sovereignty from
"their" part of the world.

Secondly, though most American Jews would certainly re-
joice if Israel could free itself from the burden of ruling over a
hostile Arab population, and though they would favor an exchange of territory for genuine peace, they recognize that under
present conditions the only realistic alternative to the status quo
is a new Palestinian state dominated by the PLO and dedicated
to the destruction of Israel.

250

Thirdly, most American Jews think that it is for Israelis, whose lives literally depend on the answer, to decide which of these bad alternatives is the worse and the more dangerous.

There are, however, a small number of American Jews who think that it is for them to decide. From the comfort and safety of America they presume to tell the Israelis that there is nothing to fear from a PLO state. They also blame Israel for the fact that the Arab world still dreams of wiping it off the map.

Once upon a time, these Jewish sympathizers of the PLO tended to be discreet and indirect. But beginning with the Israeli invasion of Lebanon in 1982 and culminating now with the riots in Gaza and the West Bank, they have grown more and more outspoken.

Thus, taking heart and license from their counterparts on the Israeli Left, they have been dwelling endlessly on the threat to Israel's "soul" of continued occupation. About the threat posed to Israel's body by a PLO state they seem to care less. It is as though they believed that Israel would be better off dead than to go on wrestling as best it can with a dilemma from which no clean escape is in sight.

These are the people who have been interviewed over and over again in the stories about the "anguish" of American Jews. Thanks to the riots, there are a few more such people than there used to be. But any politician who falls for the impression their promoters in the media have created will soon discover that they do not speak for the Jewish community and that following their lead is the surest way to lose its support.

Rael Jean Isaac

To me, the changed attitude toward Israel is typified by the Jewish community's very different response, ten years apart, to two Jewish organizations that publicly attack Israel: Breira in 1977 and New Jewish Agenda today. New Jewish Agenda has gone much farther than Breira, co-operating in activities with the American pro-PLO network. Since I wrote pamphlets (in each case published by Americans for a Safe Israel) on both organizations, I am perhaps specially situated to comment on this phenomenon.

When my pamphlet on Breira was published in 1977 it was only one of a series of "exposes" being published in places as diverse as the Hadassah newsletter, the New York *Jewish Week*, and *Commentary*. In the wake of the storm of criticism from the mainstream of the Jewish community, Breira folded. No similar outcry has attended New Jewish Agenda.

To be sure, it has been easier for Jewish organizations to look the other way in the case of Agenda than it was with Breira. Unlike Breira, Agenda in its first years maintained a low profile. Also, it concentrated initially on building bridges to the pro-Arab network rather than on establishing itself within the Jewish community. For these reasons, Agenda did not attract the attention Breira had drawn in places like the *New York Times*, making it relatively easy for mainstream Jewish organizations to avoid taking a stand on it.

But by 1987, Agenda had shifted its focus to the Jewish community and was thus harder to ignore. It had been accepted as a member of Jewish community-relations councils in a number of cities; persuaded a wide range of national and local Jewish organizations to join it in sponsoring lectures, conferences, and assorted events; taken the lead in promoting the sanctuary movement within the Jewish community; and, by sending a hand-picked delegation to Nicaragua, whose findings were widely publicized in major newspapers, had defused the charge of Sandinista anti-Semitism (the validity of the charge has been documented in "Sandinista Anti-Semitism and Its Apologists," by Joshua Muravchik, Susan Alberts, and Anthony Korenstein, *Commentary*, September 1986). It had even moved into Zionist politics, aligning itself with Americans for a Progressive Israel to participate in the World Zionist Congress elections of 1987.

Nonetheless, when my pamphlet exposing New Jewish Agenda's activities was published in the spring of 1987, to my knowledge, with the single exception of the California Jewish paper *Heritage*, the Jewish press was as critical of the attack on Agenda as it was of the activities that provoked it. The Washington D.C. *Jewish Week* published an upbeat five-page spread on the organization (there was even information on how to join the local chapter). The New York *Jewish Week*, which had been in the forefront in assailing Breira, now openly regretted the role it had taken under its former owner and editor Philip Hochstein. Its article on New Jewish Agenda focused on the organization's serving as a "bridge" between the Jewish community and the Left.

The reaction of Jewish organizations was equally instructive. While several had helped to distribute the pamphlet on Breira, none was interested in the pamphlet on Agenda. The writer of the article on Agenda in New York's *Jewish Week* reported that he asked Jewish organizational officials "in the center" to give their views on New Jewish Agenda. Although this was at a time (September 1987) when many Jewish organizations were rushing to denounce Judge Bork's Supreme Court candidacy, on a subject appropriate to their ostensible concerns they had nothing to say. The *Jewish Week's* writer reported his surprise that the only official from whom he could elicit any comment was from the Anti-Defamation League (the ADL did not think Agenda "speaks" for the entire American Jewish community).

What had happened in the space of ten years? For one thing, Breira had left a legacy. Its very existence dissipated the sense of shock within the Jewish community that previously attended the appearance of an organization of Jews engaged in public attacks upon Israel. Also, Breira had attracted a substantial group of young rabbinically trained Jews who sought positions in Jewish communal organizations partly because they were scornful of the congregational rabbinate and partly because they saw these organizations as having become centers of greater power and influence in Jewish life. Their views were the cliches of the 1960's, with America seen as imperialist oppressor and Israel as its handmaiden in the Middle East. Ensconced in Jewish organizations and federations, they were prepared to accept Israel—if it transformed its society and policies to accord with their "values."

The failure to challenge New Jewish Agenda, then, is partly explained by the influence of strategically placed elites in substantial sympathy with its perspective on Israel. But equally important is the transvaluation of liberalism in the larger society, and the apparent determination of the majority of the Jewish community to remain in the liberal camp even if the policies pursued are antithetical to traditional liberalism. To take only the most obvious example, Jewish organizations, in the name of liberal values, once uniformly and vigorously fought quota systems. Today, in the name of liberal values, a number of Jewish organizations endorse them. This is a perverse tribute to the success of the original struggle, which has produced a generation of Jews so secure that they do not even recognize the dangers to their community, and indeed to the larger society, in such a system.

For much of that powerful segment of the Jewish community that identifies itself as liberal, priorities have changed. Israel's fortunes have taken second place to what have become for many American Jews more burning issues of the day, like abortion rights, school prayer, disarmament, and U.S. disengagement from Central America. It is significant that the articles in the Jewish press on New Jewish Agenda did not exonerate the organization of the charges of anti-Israel activity. Their import was rather that such actions had to be balanced against Agenda's professed noble mission of *"tikkun olam,"* perfecting the world. The anti-Israel activism of Agenda members weighs lightly in an evaluation that sees it as just another manifestation of high-mindedness. Indeed there is a tendency for Jewish community leaders to congratulate themselves on having brought forth "such fine and socially committed young people."

255

Support within the Jewish community for the policies pressed by New Jewish Agenda and a host of "progressive" organizations has been tempered by concern for their impact upon Israel. Perhaps the major danger Agenda presents is in encouraging Jews to believe that the preservation of an imperfect state of Israel is not an end for which it is worth sacrificing the pursuit of millennial dreams.

Irving Kristol

I am pro-Israel not only because it is a decent, civilized country that is a fine addition to our Western civilization—there have not been many such additions since World War II—but because it is today, after the Holocaust, the sheet anchor of the Jewish people. Except among the very Orthodox, it is the existence of the nation and the state of Israel, more than anything else, that today connects young Jews all over the world with one another, with their common past, and with a sense of a common future. Under modern circumstances, a self-sustaining Jewish Diaspora is a highly problematic prospect.

But what does it mean to be "pro-Israel"? It certainly does *not* mean being uncritical of the Israeli government's policies in the areas of economics, religion, or foreign affairs. Just as being "pro-American" is consistent with explicit discontent over American policies, or even over many aspects of American life, so being "pro-Israel" is consistent with a similar discontent. Essential to any such distinction between "pro" and "anti" is not one's critical posture but the point of departure for such criticism. I am "pro-American" because I *like* this country just as it is, because I think this is a *good* country just as it is, a *good* society just as it is—even though I can think of all sorts of ways by which it could become better. I am "pro-Israel" for exactly the same reasons. The fact that one can so easily imagine a better nation is, in either case, irrelevant. People who permit such imaginings to dominate their thinking are in the grip of a political delusion. Similarly, Americans or Israelis who are hypercritical of their countries while pompously proclaiming their loyalty to an ideal version are in fact "anti." Authentic loyalty is to one's incarnate country—as to one's incarnate husband or wife—not to some ideal version.

The most viciously anti-Israel Jews I know are all Israelis (just as the most bitterly anti-Americans I know are Americans). They are, as it happens, left-wing Israelis and this is no accident. Political utopianism used to be as characteristic of the Right as of the Left, but ever since World War II it is overwhelmingly a left-wing phenomenon. To be left-wing these days means to be contemptuous of Western societies, with their emphasis on individual liberty and material prosperity—"consumerism," as it is called—and of Western civilization itself. Left-wing "idealism" is, as it always has been, collectivist and egalitarian. It therefore is sympathetic to, or at the very least indulgent of, collectivist regimes that are ideologically hostile to free-market economies and are also ideologically egalitarian (though in actuality nothing of the sort). True, the type of left-wing regime epitomized by the Soviet Union is by now so discredited that many on the Left feel free to call themselves "anti-Communist." But they keep hoping against hope that newer, "socialist" models of their ideal will be more acceptable. At the very least, they insist on being anti-capitalist, and are therefore hostile to the liberal societies which always are, to a substantial degree, based on a market economy.

In Israel, as in the United States, it is among the Jewish "intellectuals" that one finds the most vociferous and unrestrained "anti" sentiments. Some of the Israelis are disillusioned and embittered Zionists cherishing the original socialist-Zionist vision of a nation that would also be an egalitarian community. Enchanted by such a fantasy, they are repelled by the reality of modern, urban Israeli society and of an Israeli government whose foreign policy is shaped by the necessities of realpolitik. But most are simply modishly left-wing, which is also the case with so many Jewish intellectuals in the United States. Among these American Jewish (along with many non-Jewish) intellectuals, the fact that Israel is a loyal ally of the United States is, by itself, sufficient grounds for disaffection.

Within American Jewry as a whole, however, the situation is more complex. Most American Jews are pro-Israel without qualification, letting their instinctive wisdom guide them. But then there is what is called "the American Jewish community," i.e., the 10 percent or so who are active in Jewish organizations of one kind or another, and who feel compelled to temper their natural pro-Israel sympathies with a more "sophisticated" critical stance. The compulsion flows from the professionals who staff these Jewish organizations. They are overwhelmingly liberal—which means they are hypersensitive to criticism from the Left. They are identical, in their basic political attitude, with their confreres who staff the American Civil Liberties Union, the United Nations Association, various "public-interest" law firms, and who are consumer activists, environmentalists, feminist activists, etc.

All the major Jewish organizations are effectively controlled by these "new-class" types. The businessmen and lawyers who supposedly "govern" these organizations may be conservative or far more moderate in their liberalism, but they are nonideological men and women who are quite impotent when confronted with the ideological professionals they theoretically supervise. Ronald Reagan received approximately one-third of the Jewish vote in 1984, but no major Jewish organization makes a serious effort to reflect this portion of the Jewish political spectrum.

In short and in sum, the emergence of anti-Israel sentiment within the "American Jewish community" has nothing whatsoever to do with what is happening in Israel. It is part and parcel of the same phenomenon which has produced anti-Israel sentiments in all the socialist parties of Western Europe, once a bastion of pro-Israel feeling. Forced to choose between an actual Israel, a Western democracy populated by real (and hence imperfect) Jews, on the one hand, and utopian hopes (mainly focused today on the Third World) for "social justice" and a "new social order" on the other, the Left in all countries (including Israel itself!) has opted for the latter. American liberalism, which has been moving steadily Left over the last fifteen years—Senator McGovern's capture of the Democratic party in 1972 was the watershed—mainly reflects this new ideological orientation. So, to a significant degree, does the "Jewish community."

David Sidorsky

The variety and intensity of the criticisms of Israel suggest
that they are of several types: one type, apparently motivated by
geopolitical ambitions, is a calculated attempt to delegitimate
Israel and erode its political support. Another, apparently motivated by moral expectations, is directed at improving the character of the Israeli state and society.

The geopolitical criticism dates from the Soviet Union's
decision in 1954 to shift its strategy of penetration in the Middle
East away from support of Israel to political backing and arms
supply for Israel's adversaries, especially Egypt, Syria, and Iraq.
As part of that shift, two themes emerged in Soviet propaganda.

The first was that Israel had been misperceived as vulnerable; it should truly be seen as a powerful instrumentality of an
imperial Western out-reach. The image, sketched in bold relief
after the defeat of the Arab aggression of 1967, was of an
aggressor Goliath against Third World victims.

The second theme of Soviet propaganda was that the view of
Israel as a democratic, even pioneering, "socialist" country was
outmoded. In corrected perspective, Israel was a neocolonial
outpost, and hence a tool of repression against a Third World
people. This portrait was accentuated in the 1960's with the
adoption of the new persona of "the Palestinians."

Although at first these themes were confined to the Soviet
press and forums of the far Left, they subsequently became the
accepted truth of the United Nations. And after 1967, they gained
currency in the media of Western Europe. More recently, they
have become a focus for American discussions of Israel and have
found a political base in the left wing of the Democratic party (at
present, even in the spotlight of electoral politics, anti-Israel
views can be expressed in the Democratic party political process,
as long as they are joined by an explicit disavowal of anti-

Semitism). These two themes have helped to define the vocabulary and to set the agenda of Western political discussion on the
Arab-Israeli conflict.

The genesis and goals of the second species of criticism are
very different. The genre of Diaspora criticism, developed from
classic Zionist paradigms of almost a century ago, is directed
toward improving the society of the land of Israel, and there is
usually an objective basis and a measure of validity for each of the
criticisms. Among most of these critics there is as well support for
Israel's security interests and an awareness of the Arab threat.

Some groups who appreciate Israel's desire for peace have
urged that unilateral Israeli initiatives toward one or another of
the coalition of Arab belligerents could be a means of inducing
negotiations. This shifts the focus of the agenda, however, away
from the continuing Soviet escalation of the level of Arab arms
supply or the persistent Arab refusal to recognize and negotiate
with Israel toward a debate on Israel's responsibility for new
initiatives. One result of such a debate is to reinforce the image
of Israel as a new Goliath.

Similarly, groups concerned about the future of Israeli
democracy have argued that there is a negative impact on that
democracy in the need for long-term administration of the Arab
populations of the districts of Gaza, Judea, and Samaria. This
concern has bred the hope that Israeli moves toward unilateral
withdrawal could catalyze a negotiating process. Yet to focus the
agenda of Arab-Israeli peace negotiations on an Israeli change of
policy on withdrawal can also serve to project the image of Israel
as repressive colonial power.

Thus, those who would pursue, in the name of peace and
democracy, criticism of Israel's security policies must bear responsibility for the way in which their views will be interpreted
in the current climate of opinion that is prejudiced against Israel.

In a general inventory of Diaspora criticism of Israel two
facts seem striking. One is the asymmetry of the criticism and the
other is its incredibly high decibel count.

Virtually all of the advocacy for change in Israeli security
policy is in the direction of greater concession. Yet there is a body
of evidence that suggests that the Israeli leadership, in its desire
for acceptance in the region, has not been sufficiently strong in its

insistence that costly victories in the field of battle earn a diplomatic payoff in peace. The recurrent pattern has been for Israel to accept a cease-fire or truce at the point of Arab military defeat, which is then followed by an interim of "no war and no peace" in which the Arabs reserve the right to initiate the next round. For example, four Israeli victories against Egypt were stopped at predetermined lines, and were followed by Egyptian resumption of hostilities. Only the continued drive after the proposed cease-fire to a point just sixty miles from Cairo concentrated the minds of the Egyptian military sufficiently to move them beyond armistice to peace.

It is often stated that the volume of the criticism is justified by the great expectations legitimately demanded of Israel. Yet there is evidence of an escalation, if not inflation, of expectations. For example, I recall vividly the kind of expectations for the new state voiced in the visitor's gallery at Lake Success where I sat during the rollcall vote for the partition plan on November 29, 1947. The expectations expressed, in a moment of great optimism, fell far short of the accomplishments of the ensuing forty years in most of the areas of demographic, political, economic, and social affairs.

My own attitudes to Israel have never been determined, however, by the ways in which it fulfilled any set of expectations, whether religious, ideological, or political, but derive from my sense of its people. The Jewish community of Israel is made up of persons who have endured many vicissitudes and retain great potential for individual expression. They have demonstrated their capacity and will to protect their society. They have also shown their hunger for peace, probably excessively, to the point of signaling vulnerability to a potential enemy. They have developed the juridical institutions that safeguard free expression and the democratic mechanisms for arriving at consent of the governed on the major issues of their policy.

So, as a society, they would appear to have at the least merited a right of democratic autonomy in their quest for security. Actually, my recent concern has not been about these contested issues of life and liberty, but about exploring some of the ways in which the focus might shift to the neglected issues of the individual pursuit of happiness.

Ruth R. Wisse

Most Jewish criticism of the state of Israel is a reaction to anti-Zionism, the anti-Semitism of the late 20th century. As long as Arab states declared their opposition to Israel in belligerent terms, vowing to push the Jews into the sea, liberal sympathies were with the Jewish state. The extermination of the European Jews was still too fresh to admit another such proposal. But when the Arabs, following their unsuccessful war of 1967, accused the Jews of denying *them* their rightful place in the Middle East, they breathed new life into the still potent mythology of the immoral, conspiring Jew. The identification of Zionism as Jewish racism not only deflected criticism from Arab imperial ambitions, but defined the existence of Israel as a crime against the Palestinian Arabs. The prosecution of this charge over the past twenty years has attempted to invert the image of the Jew from European victim to Middle Eastern villain. Some Jews respond to this accusation of their villainy by blaming Israelis for having caused it.

Naturally, Jews who criticize the state of Israel do not feel that they are picking up the enemy's cues. They express their criticism in high-minded concern for Israel's moral health and physical safety. They congratulate themselves for the courage to "dissent" from the imagined unanimity of Jewish support for the Jewish state. But in fact, American Jews during the past twenty years have been unwilling to expose the Arab anti-Zionist campaign for what it is—the extension into the political sphere of the war against the Jewish state. They are reluctant to take the war of words into the Arab camp, challenging Arab rulers to resettle Arab refugees, to accept the idea of regional pluralism, to confront their own racial intolerance. Since the Jews want nothing—beyond acceptance—from the Arabs, they are afraid of adding to the cycle of aggression, and hope that the hostility toward them will disappear if ignored. Unfortunately, recent Jewish history offers the best evidence that anti-Jewish argument rises in proportion to anti-Jewish aggressivity, particularly from sources deemed to be progressive. Anti-Zionism was loudest within the American Jewish community at the height of the Communist campaign against Jewish nationalism in the 1930's. Jewish criticism of Israel has similarly increased at the same rate as left-wing anti-Zionist propaganda. The disinclination of Jews to counter the Arab denial of their national legitimacy means that they must move ever more to the defensive. Thus *Tikkun*, the first American Jewish magazine to revive the old Jewish agenda of the 1930's (as the new Jewish agenda) and to argue the Palestinian case *within* the Jewish community, was founded, predictably, in California, where anti-Israel propaganda is most sustained.

My attitudes to Israel have indeed changed in recent years. I would not have believed that any people could maintain such civilized self-discipline in the face of continuing hostile provocation. I am grateful to an Israel which, by defeating Soviet client states in successive wars (though this was neither its purpose nor concern), did more to extend the hopes of democracy than countries many times its size and strength. I am moved by the reality of ingathered Jews—with all its predictable social unrest—more than by the rhetoric of the olds songs of *aliyah*. My great disappointment is in the Arabs, among whom one would have expected more of Sadat's caliber of statesmanship, more brotherly concern for a least their own people, if not for their fellow Semites.

V. THE JEWISH-AMERICAN COMMUNITY VERSUS THE MAINSTREAM MEDIA: A CASE STUDY OF BERGEN COUNTY, NEW JERSEY

A Reader is Displeased with
The Record's Israel Coverage

by Eli J. Warach

The flood of vitriol that flows from the pages of *The Record*, including editorials, the editorials disguised as news stories, and the columns and Op-Ed pieces—all attacking Israel—are enough to make one sick. The barely concealed venom and malice inherent in these writings is insulting to many of us who live here in Bergen County.

The treatment given Israel in particular, and American Jews in general, is, in a word, despicable. And that's putting it mildly. Frankly, I think that we have reached the point where one must wonder: Why? Why these bigoted attacks on Israel? Why this terrible smear campaign against American Jews? In short, WHAT IS BOTHERING *THE RECORD*? WHAT DOES IT WANT?

Let's look at two recent examples. One was an editorial Feb. 21 called "The Silence on Israel." It condemned American aid to Israel. (Of course, it had the wrong amount—but misinformation never stopped anyone from sounding like an expert.) Then, in vintage anti-Semite-like fashion, the editorial refers to those classics of the bigot, "Jewish political power," "Jewish money." And doesn't that have a familiar ring? All that was missing was a reference to "The Protocals of Zion."

Next case: the sad matter of one Daniel Lazare. Readers have had to put up with his usual ravings (his hatred of Israel is almost classically obsessive). It's easy to see that he has a fanatical hang-up of some kind about Israel and about Jews who speak out in Israel's behalf. Up to now, Lazare has been getting away with "literary" murder, but people generally tended to ignore him. We understood him for what he was—unbalanced and biased where the State of Israel and American Jews were concerned.

Meanwhile, in Bergen County, U.S.A., Jews didn't excuse Lazare, but neither did we pay too much attention to his drivel. We reasoned that even the press has its lunatic fringe—on the left and on the right. But now he's gone too far, much too far.

Comparing Israelis and Nazis in the same breath (in a March 2 column) is more than (to quote Lazare) "waving a red flag." It's the depths of depravity and immorality.

Imagine the gall, the hypocrisy of Lazare when he defends Kurt Waldheim. That's bad enough in and of itself, but Lazare goes on. Yes, indeed he goes on to where it outrages the very concept of decency. He chooses to defend the likes of Martin Bormann, one of Hitler's key aides, especially when it came to the "Jewish problem." Imagine that, if you can—Bormann being defended by Lazare. It shows just how far he will go to make a point. Martin Bormann, he would have us believe, didn't do anything wrong (especially when it came to the death camps). I guess Lazare next will tell us that Bormann didn't even know about the death camps. The next thing I anticipate is the theory that it was all a Jewish plot. Unfortunately, facts are facts. And the terribly tragic fact remains that six million Jews were killed.

Lazare would also have us believe that Hermann Goering, Albert Speer, and Rudolf Hess were poor innocents, just carrying out orders, so to speak. And, he implies, they were tried for crimes that weren't really crimes on the law books. (What's a little genocide among friends?) Well, he has company—no good company, but company—like the anti-Black, anti-Semitic group, The Order, or the Aryan Society.

Among the most insulting and degrading of Lazare's remarks—and it's difficult to find anything that isn't despicable—is the charge that American Jews don't have the right to support Israel. Apparently it's his contention that you play by his rules—or you're one with the Nazis, the Bormanns, Speers, Hesses, Goerings, and yes, the Waldheims. But that just is not so. And we

270

don't accept it. Six million Jews were killed—and these people participated!

The Record column in question stated that the Israeli army is waging war against civilians. That's an absolute lie—period. If Lazare had ever seen the Israeli army at war, he would know that the unrest would have been over the first day.

Comparing Israelis with the Nazis is worse than odious. It is dishonest, and it is deliberately dishonest. It is malicious, and it is deliberately malicious. It is bigoted, and it is deliberately bigoted. It is immoral, and it is deliberately immoral. It is disgusting, and it is deliberately disgusting.

Be assured that Israel will not roll over and play dead just to please someone. Israel will not give up its quest for a secure peace just because some newspaper pundit so wills it. Israel will be secure, will prosper, and will continue to be a light unto the nations. And, frankly, as far as Lazare is concerned, who cares what he thinks?

But, it bothers me; it bothers me tremendously when a newspaper such as *The Record* publishes numerous iniquitous articles, editorials, and columns about Israel and about Jews. But I won't let it erode my support for the State of Israel. If anything, such writings will strengthen that support.

Daniel Lazare: A Candid Conversation with the Controversial Columnist

by Rebecca Kaplan Boroson

The *Jewish Standard*, in response to readers' complaints and its own perceptions that recent editorials and columns on Israel in *The Record* have had a strongly negative tone, asked editorial writer Daniel Lazare to grant it an interview. A transcription of the 90-minute interview, taped March 4th at *The Record's* office in Hackensack and excerpted for reasons of space, follows.

Standard: Many people in the Jewish community have been distressed by your weekly columns, and also by recent editorials that seem to have the mark of your hand.
Lazare: Not all of them do, by the way. The editorial on "silence" [in which a connection was seen between candidates' alleged reluctance to criticize Israel and campaign contributions from Jewish PAC's] was not my editorial, actually.
Standard: The *Standard* felt that it might be useful, instead of talking about you, to talk to you—to find out about your background, what makes you feel and write the way you do, and ask you to clarify some of your stands. We promise no hatchet job.
Lazare: To be truthful and accurate is all I ask.
Standard: We will do our very best. First, would you tell me what your responsibility is on this paper?
Lazare: Well, I'm an editorial writer and columnist... I take part in all editorial board meetings and I have input into all editorials that are written. I'd say I write four to five editorials a week... I

273

write the great majority of editorials on the Middle East; I write the great majority of editorials on foreign policy... I've written the column for about two and a half years. I've been doing editorials pretty close to three years.

Standard: Tell us about yourself...

Lazare: I was born in New York City in 1950. I grew up in suburban Long Island and Fairfield County, CT. I went to the University of Wisconsin—got my B.A. in English in '72, got my master's in English in '82. Before writing editorials I was a reporter for a total of about 11 years—at the *New Brunswick Home News*—and then, since '79, *The Record*.

Standard: We have to ask a question our readers would really like answered: Are you Jewish?

Lazare: Is that relevant?

Standard: Yes.

Lazare: Why is it relevant? And also, what do you mean by being Jewish?

Standard: It's relevant because it's a question our readers have, it's a question they ask. And because they want it answered, we're asking it. You can choose to say, "I'd rather not answer that."

Lazare: My parents are Jewish, I was bar mitzvah. I do not pursue any religion. I think of myself as ethnically Jewish—but we could sit here and discuss for hours exactly what being Jewish means. If I wanted to get an apartment on the West Bank I would get it immediately. Let's put it that way, I would qualify without a doubt.

Standard: You were bar mitzvah in what denomination?

Lazare: Reform...

Standard: If you had children would you provide any religious training for them?

Lazare: No, I would raise kids with an ethnic, ethical, intellectual consciousness of being Jewish, which would mean a decent pride and a critical understanding of exactly what Jewishness means in the late 20th century.

Standard: What does it mean?

Lazare: It's a difficult thing. There's a Jewish religion, of course, which I don't believe in, don't adhere to, and would not raise kids in. But there's a Jewish intellectual tradition, certainly a Jewish ethical tradition. Even to use the word "Jewish" in this context may be misleading, because you're talking about an Ashkenazic intellectual and ethical tradition. Russian Jews came out of a certain period of history, with certain social and political attitudes that other Jews find quite alien. The idea of the engaged, secular, Jewish intellectual is really an Ashkenazic concept.

Standard: Does that appeal to you?

Lazare: Sure, of course. That's one aspect that's been very important to me... The problem [with the religious aspect] is that I don't believe in God. I don't see the need for any religion per se. I'm not religious. I'm just not at all interested. I'm philosophically unsympathetic to religion, actually.

Standard: Where have you been published besides newspapers?

Lazare: I've been published in *The Nation*. I had an article on the 40th anniversary of the Warsaw Ghetto uprising, in 1983. What motivated me to write that article was antipathy for the nationalist explanation of the uprising, the explanation that was in the TV miniseries, "Holocaust," which was God-awful...

Standard: Are you married?

Lazare: Yes. Is my wife Jewish? Yes, she's Jewish. But she's also an atheist, like myself.

Standard: Tell us a little about your political orientation.

Lazare: It's to the left, as you may guess. I don't think of myself as a classic liberal. I'm sort of not a liberal, really. I'm horrified by nationalism or chauvinism of all forms—among Jews, among Blacks, among women, among men. I'm ideologically and philosophically opposed to these sort of things, which of course is at the root of my problems with the State of Israel. I believe in social engineering, essentially, building a better society, in as objective and as forthright a manner possible. Without nationalism, which is an ideology based on the heightening and exaggerating, the mystification of national differences, and that I find absolutely appalling.

Standard: What would your social engineering mean?

Lazare: Toward equality, towards democracy.

Standard: How would you achieve that? You use the word "engineering" to mean altering something in some way.

Lazare: Political action. State intervention. Some of the social democratic countries of Europe are good examples of the things that have been done in this area. Holland... is a strongly ethical country, with a very, very strong egalitarian impulse, and a strong communitarian impulse, an incredible kind of economic regulatory structure, welfare apparatus, and housing subsidies. Actually, parts of Israel are in the same broad social democratic tradition, the European social democratic tradition.

Standard: You are opposed to nationalism. What about Palestinian nationalism?

Lazare: I'm opposed to that as well.

Standard: That doesn't always come across, in both the editorials and the columns.

Lazare: Actually, I have written that. If it doesn't come across, it's only because we operate in such a lop-sided atmosphere in this country. It's very easy to attack Palestinian nationalism. I see Yasir Arafat [being used] as everyone's all-purpose whipping boy. I find the deck is so stacked against Palestinian nationalism that I find myself talking more about Jewish nationalism...

Standard: So you are saying that you may have overcompensated?

Lazare: No, I'm not saying that at all. I dislike all forms of nationalism, I believe in a properly balanced manner, and I'm opposed to Palestinian nationalism. My dream in the Middle East would be an integrated Jewish-Palestinian—Israeli-Palestinian—state in what is now Israel/Palestine. I think actually a separation is not practical. I don't think it will ever work.

Standard: The United States of Israel?

Lazare: Essentially—or the equivalent of what happened in Yugoslavia, what happened in India. Or what happened, say, in the Soviet Union.

Standard: India and the Soviet Union are very good examples of how difficult it is to suppress national urgings.

Lazare: Absolutely. But they're also examples of countries that have made extraordinary progress in the suppression of these impulses...

Standard: You say your dream is for an integrated state—but what if the Palestinians won't and the Israelis won't, but they eventually agree to two separate states?

Lazare: I don't thinks it's viable. I don't think it's practical.

Standard: The other is practical?

Lazare: In a strange way, I think it is more practical. The

Balkans were for centuries just a bleeding ground of ethnic conflict. Essentially Tito came in there and hammered out a relatively equitable federation among all the competing nationalities, and for at least 40 years brought a measure of unforeseen peace to what was previously a battleground.

Standard: It seems a little totalitarian to approve of that kind of peace-making.

Lazare: I don't approve of everything Tito did. Tito was a dictator, and I'd like to see this take place under a democratic framework, but that achievement of his has been undeniable.

Standard: Would you say that if Israel annexed the territories and gave full citizens' rights to the Arabs and everybody voted and elected officials together and created the future of the country— that would be what you'd like to see?

Lazare: I'm not calling on Israel to annex the occupied territories, but if it did, that could be one result. Of course the result of that would be that you'd immediately have a state that was 40 percent Arab, where Arabs would be a controlling bloc in the Knesset, and Israel in a few short years would cease being a Jewish state. It would be an integrated and secular state in the Middle East.

Standard: A consummation devoutly to be wished?

Lazare: I think so, yes. I don't believe in Jewish states or white states or Anglo-Saxon states or Sikh states. I believe in government frameworks which are there to make life as prosperous and democratic as possible for all the citizens within its purview, regardless of their ethicality, religion, or nationality.

Standard: Do you have a good example of such a state?

Lazare: The United States, for all its faults, has made certain accomplishments in this area. This is the great difference between the United States and Israel: The United States is, at least ostensibly, a non-racist state. You saw the Woody Allen article in *The Times*. There was one letter to *The Times* which was condemning Allen, and it called him a "self-hating Jew," because his films are always so self-lacerating. I don't think he is. I'm someone who's been called a self-hating Jew myself, many times, I think that's an offensive thing to say... I think what we're seeing now is a split between assimilationist Jews like Woody Allen and nationalists who are more committed to an Israeli ideal of racial purity.

Standard: I'm not sure what you mean about racial purity.

Lazare: I was using the term "Jews" as a race, for what that term implies.

Standard: Do you accept that Jews are a race?

Lazare: No, of course not. Obviously, there are racial differences among Jews. The term is often used. Sometimes it's used colloquially.

Standard: Have you ever experienced any anti-Semitism firsthand?

Lazare: A few insignificant incidents in grade school...

Standard: What is it that causes you to focus so much on Israel and Jews? You may start something about the Contras and go into free fall and land in Israel.

Lazare: If I do, it's a literary failing... Israel is ideologically important. It's politically, economically, militarily important.

Standard: You don't feel that you have some personal—what's the word—beacon?

Lazare: Or animus?

Standard: No, beacon, that draws you to the subject. Homing device.

Lazare: Well, perhaps. Of course, I'm Jewish myself, so I'm forced to grapple with my own feelings on this thing, so it's a matter of more immediate concern. But I think that's a somewhat minor factor. I think that Israel, the Middle East conflict, is objectively compelling.

Standard: And there isn't a subjective compulsion as well?

Lazare: I think it's less so. I find the topic interesting, because it's important. It's also interesting because it's a topic I grew up with...

Standard: Did your parents do a lot of talking about Jewishness and Israel?

Lazare: Not Jewishness; there was a certain kind of sentimental attachment to Israel in my home. Suburban Jews. Very suburban white bread Jews...

Standard: Have you had a strong response from readers?

Lazare: Of course I have. This is a somewhat heavily Jewish area, and Jews are vocal, passionate people...

Standard: Do you get any "right-on" letters? From Jews?

Lazare: Sure. A lot. Actually, I think that Jewish sentiment in

this country is very badly split. There's a split between the assimilationist-Woody Allen style Jews, for lack of a better word, those who prefer to see themselves as citizens of a multi-ethnic secular society, and those who adhere to a different kind of vision.
Standard: When you get the very negative, passionate letters, do you pay some attention to what the people are saying? Do you have a sense that you have really hurt many people?
Lazare: I think that one inevitable result of slashing, Jewish-style, intellectual combat is that people get hurt. One thing I unequivocally value in the Ashkenazic tradition is the tradition of intellectual street-fighting, the tradition of the intellectual warrior who's never happy unless he's in the middle of a good intellectual fight... Unfortunately, noses may get bloodied, on both sides.
Standard: Do you have any sense that what you write might be misused and turned against Jews?
Lazare: ... I think when you engage in democratic debate, you've got to go out there and flail away and let the chips fall where they may. I think it's highly undemocratic to suggest that people should hold their tongues for fear that somehow the arguments will wind up in the wrong hands...
Standard: The ADL has reported that anti-Semitic incidents are on the upswing, after a period of decrease. It is my feeling that the printed word has power either to reduce or to foster such incidents. And you feel, "let the chips fall where they may."
Lazare: It's highly unfair to suggest that someone who writes frankly about events in the Middle East is responsible for the Aryan Nations.
Standard: Do you write about the Aryan Nations in your free fall?
Lazare: In point of fact, I got off a little swipe in an editorial yesterday or the day before, referring to them as "armed crazies." My anti-fascist fervor is second to none. If you write about the evils that white people do in Alabama in the '60s, you might be giving arguments to a hate-monger like Louis Farrakhan. What can you do when he quotes your article?
Standard: You can strive for balance.
Lazare: I don't believe in balance regarding white racism in Alabama... I wouldn't believe in balance regarding Jews in Nazi

279

Germany either... If I'm going to write a fervent article donouncing the abuse of Jews in Nazi Germany, I'm not going to balance it by giving a couple paragraphs of Jewish abuses of Germans.

Standard: Have you ever visited Israel?

Lazare: No, I never have. I'd like to go, though. Actually, I have a special interest in visiting Israel... One reason I think I might like to visit Israel is that it is famous for its contentious political life, and the debate there has been far fiercer, far wider-ranging, than in the United States today... [But] marriage law is in the hands of the rabbis, immigration law is in the hands of the rabbis, burial law. As a Jew in America, I don't have to contend with any of these things. If I get married I don't have to be married by a rabbi. I don't give a d— what any rabbi says.

Standard: Were you married by a rabbi?

Lazare: Good question. The answer, unfortunately, is yes. But it was a free choice. It was a choice without compulsion. I was [said with a smile] a sentimental young fool...

Standard: We'd like to take you through your March 2 column. You say, "In leading the campaign against Austrian president Kurt Waldheim, the World Jewish Congress may be stepping into the same trap that the United States fell into at Nuremberg." Please explain the word "trap."

Lazare: It was a trap because the United States found itself 20 years later hoisted by its own petard. The United States promulgated a certain kind of ethic at Nuremberg which caused it great discomfort later on, the ethic of individual moral accountability... It made the American government uncomfortable.

Standard: Do you feel that events have shown that the principles promulgated at Nuremberg were appropriate?

Lazare: I believe in the Nuremberg principles 100 percent. It was a trap for the American government. The behavior of the American government was not right in Vietnam. It wasn't even really entirely right in World War II, but it was absolutely not right in Vietnam...

Standard: You wrote, "To be a good German after the war, you were supposed to have been a bad German during it, and vice versa." Do you believe that World War II was a war like any other war?

Lazare: Nothing is like anything else. To some extent it was, but of course in an important way, it was not. There was never anything like Nazism before. Nazism was a phenomenon without parallel... [But] on Sept. 1, 1939, there wasn't a blinking neon sign which said this is an entirely new war; all previous rules are suspended...

Standard: This paragraph seems to say that if you saw your neighbor taken off to a concentration camp, you should say, well, these are the fortunes of war.

Lazare: That was the predominant view at the time. That line, of course, is meant ironically. The irony should be apparent.

Standard: We think the irony is not apparent.

Lazare: That's someone's fault; it may be my fault, it may be your fault...

Standard: "No one has yet found evidence of direct criminal involvement," you wrote about Waldheim.

Lazare: I think that most of the evidence that has come out seems to indicate that Waldheim was in close proximity to the crimes, he knew what was going on and was part of a military bureaucratic apparatus that was carrying out these crimes. But the Austrian commission said it found no evidence of direct complicity. His crimes seems to have been a crime of acquiescence.

Standard: There's another "crime" called lying. For 40 years he said he was invalided out of the army very early on, and he had been invalided out for only a few months and had actually been an officer whose unit was involved in massacres and deportations in the Balkans... Then he went on to become Secretary General of the United Nations and to forbid the opening of the Nazi archives. And he was the Secretary General when the "Zionism is Racism" resolution was passed. That's an abuse.

Lazare: I think it's a question of his complicity or acquiescence with Nazi war crimes, and of course his concealment of that. And then what it says for his U.N. activities as Secretary General and as Austrian president, I agree with that—although I also agree that the Zionism is Racism resolution, although a bit one-sided and a bit crudely-worded, is not entirely false. I believe that Zionism is racism. It's racism insofar as it's dedicated to the extolling of a racial ideal, and that the ideal is necessarily exclusivist. So consequently, it is racist, as much as the slogan

"Germany for the Germans" would be a racist slogan...

Standard: You say Waldheim functioned as a "willing little cog in the great Nazi death machine." The same might be said of Eichmann.

Lazare: Eichmann was a considerably bigger cog. He was the bureaucrat in charge of the "final-solution." It's the difference between a big cog and a little cog.

Standard: The amount of people who die by reason of your having signed your name on a piece of paper makes that difference?

Lazare: We're talking about a difference of quantity, not quality... Don't get me wrong; I think the crime of silence is very serious. I think that bureaucratic complicity and acquiescence should be judged stringently...

Standard: In you column, you wrote, "The Israeli army is currently waging a war against Palestinian civilians," etc. Does not a war have two sides?

Lazare: Every war has two sides.

Standard: Somehow, when you go to write about it, it becomes "The Israeli army is waging a war," not "Israelis and Palestinians are clashing."

Lazare: We have to remember that one side has guns and one doesn't.

Standard: Rocks can kill.

Lazare: Rocks can kill, but guns kill a lot easier. There have not been 73 Israelis killed since the disturbances began in December.

Standard: There had been quite a few killed beforehand...

Lazare: I think this issue should be seen not in one-sided terms.

Standard: You give that impression.

Lazare: I think that you folks give the impression of seeing it in one-sided terms. I think the whole debate in this country has been presented in the most God-awful one-sided manner possible, and I see my little role, my little modest contribution, as trying to rectify that gross imbalance to the way the United States sees events in the Middle East....

Standard: You don't seem, if you'll allow us to say this, to have much familiarity with the debate going on now in the American Jewish community. People want to talk, many of them. They want to exert influence.

Lazare: Many people want them to keep quiet, like Yitzhak Shamir. The World Jewish Congress has not said a word regarding these events. [Congress President Edgar] Bronfman has not said a word.

Standard: The American Jewish Congress is talking...

Lazare: I don't regard Israel as an evil monolith. I see it as a country torn—as worse countries are torn—between conflicting visions. There's a European, social democratic, egalitarian strain, which is very important, and an anti-democratic nationalist strain. I think Israel is in some ways a very vigorous democracy. In other ways, it's not. And I could not say the same for a state like Syria, for example, which is not a vigorous democracy in any sense of the imagination.

Standard: Why is it you don't do a column on the lack of democracy in some Arab countries?

Lazare: It's just not been a compelling issue to address...

Standard: The impression you create with the subjects you use and the ways you go in your free fall is that Israel is this fascistic, vicious state and that the Arab states are clean.

Lazare: I don't believe that. It may be vicious—of course, many states are vicious. It's a violent state, it's a garrison state. It has a vigorous political democracy for many of its citizens, not all. It's unfairly appropriated the mantle of the Holocaust.

Standard: What should have been done with the survivors? Where would they have gone?

Lazare: They would have come to the United States, many of them, given half a chance. And if American Jewish leaders had not opposed free immigration, because they knew very well that most Jews would avail themselves of that option rather than moving to Palestine... If you'd gone through a DP camp in the 1940's in Europe, and you said, okay, everyone who wants to go to America at this table, everyone who wants to go to Israel at this table, I can tell you what would happen. A few die-hard Zionists would go to the Israeli table. Everyone else would flock to the American table, which is the way this thing is happening with the Soviet emigration these days.

Standard: It is true that American Jewish leaders want to encourage [Soviet Jewish emigres' going to Israel], but the reasons behind it, we do believe, are not the reasons you think they are.... The exit would be closed if it appeared that they were all coming to the United States....

Lazare: The great bulk of Soviet Jews are voting against Israel with their feet. They just don't want to go to Israel. They don't want a racial, exclusivist state. They want a state where they can believe what they want to believe without being hassled. And most of them are not terribly attached to Judaism.

Standard: They haven't had much exposure to it.

Lazare: American Jews who have had exposure to it aren't tremendously attached either. Whether you like or not, the tradition is weakening tremendously...

Standard: *The Standard* is here because people have asked it to do something. Before we close, perhaps you can answer them, talk to them. You can have the last word.

Lazare: I talk to them every week. I don't feel any extra obligation to talk to them. The debate is here. They're losing. Zionism has had an easy ride for the last 40 years, and those beleaguered leftists who said that Zionism was somehow undemocratic, that it had an important racist strain, were seen as beyond the pale. Now suddenly we see the evidence before our eyes... The whole thing is that Jews are, in the final analysis, no better and no worse than anyone else. They're subject to the same strains, the same conflicts, the same strain between left and right. And the right-wing element in the Jewish community is on the defensive as it properly should be. And the criticisms of Zionism that were made previously by leftists have been borne out by events.

Editorial Page to Change, Says *Record's* Publisher

by Rebecca Kaplan Boroson

The editorial page of *The Record*, recently under attack by Jewish community leaders as having a pronounced anti-Israel slant, is in for some changes, according to its publisher, Byron Campbell.

"Broadly speaking, it will be more conservative," he told the *Jewish Standard* this week. "The pages have been termed rather liberal, and we'll be changing that some to the right." He declined to elaborate, explaining that "an internal discussion" as to the page's direction was continuing, and adding, "What's one person's conservatism is another person's liberalism."

Campbell, who became publisher of the influential Hackensack-based newspaper about three months ago, insisted that the changes were not being projected in response to the recent criticism. He said he "was discussing this... right after I came here."

Robert Comstock, who had been executive editor, retired about two weeks ago, Campbell said. But he was quick to add that any new approaches *The Record* might take would have "nothing to do with his retirement." Richard Benfield, who was news editor for about 10 years before becoming editorial page editor in late October, reported to Comstock. Until a new executive editor is appointed, Benfield will report to Campbell himself.

Campbell, Comstock, and Benfield met on March 7 with Dr. Leonard Cole (chairman of the Jewish Community Relations Committee), Barry Rosenberg (executive director of the Jewish Federation of North Jersey), and Eli Warach (president of the United Jewish Community of Bergen County).

Last week an account of the meetings, signed by the three Jewish community representatives, Dr. Jim Young, the UJC's executive director, and Alvin Reisbaum, the North Jersey federation's president, was mailed to 500 people. Addressees included board members of both federations, JCRC members, organization and synagogue presidents, and rabbis.

The letter-writers characterized the meeting as "business-like and frank," and said they were "hopeful that the expressions of sensitivity by *The Record's* management will be reflected on news and editorial pages."

Indeed, they noted, "One good sign was an editorial on March 13, six days after our meeting, which deplored Arafat and the PLO violence. That was the first editorial on a Middle East subject in recent memory that was not critical of Israel."

They urged the recipients "to make your views known to the newspaper when you are pleased or displeased by their news coverage or opinion pieces."

Campbell told the *Standard* he had not been surprised to receive the request for the meeting. He said he in fact had welcomed it, because he had been hearing from various sources that much of the Jewish community was unhappy with *The Record's* editorial policy, at least as far as Israel was concerned.

He called the meeting constructive, and said, "Some things were gotten off people's chests, frankly and openly, which I think is good.... We listened more, and heard some things that made some good sense."

"Perhaps there hadn't been as much of a total look at some issues... as might be desirable. Perhaps some comparisons in some writing... weren't fair."

He went on to say that comparing "some of the things that Israel is doing with the Holocaust was just too far out...." This had been done in an op-ed column March 2 by Daniel Lazare, who also writes most of *The Record's* editorials on the Middle East. "The three men weren't saying you've got to agree [with us] about everything," Campbell noted. He said they wanted "a more balanced disagreement," perspective, a sense of history. "There was an emotion, [but also] logic and specifics that we heard, too."

Campbell said that he himself would become more involved in editorial policy-making, although the people who now write the editorials, including Benfield and Lazare, would continue to do so. "I'm very open to many meetings," he went on. "I want as many letters to the editor as possible, on various viewpoints. [This] is particularly important where [the letters] disagree with our editorial opinions.... Listening to others—and vice versa—is terribly important for a newspaper."

Cole told the *Standard* that this was not the first meeting community leaders had held with *Record* editors. He and Michael Greenberg, then the director of the JCRC, met with Comstock and David Corcoran, then the editorial-page editor, roughly a year ago. "A couple of editorials were unpleasant," he recalled, "and Daniel Lazare had written a couple of columns that we felt were biased against Israel."

He added that, "as with the most recent hearing, *The Record* did not acknowledge it had done anything wrong, but they said if we could point out factual errors, they would acknowledge fault and offer apologies."

Still, he said, "I felt we had a reasonable hearing, though we had no assurances that the tone of *The Record's* editorials would change." The newspaper did publish an op-ed piece by Cole responding to Lazare—in tandem with Lazare's own response to Cole—and, says Cole, "during the next seven or eight months, they wrote less frequently about the Middle East, and when they did, their tone was more restrained."

"Following our [March 7] meeting," he went on, "there has been a marked change in *The Record's* commentary, both on the editorial page, the character of the letters that it prints, and its op-ed page columns. They're more balanced, and no longer give an anti-Israel/pro-PLO flavor."

He stressed, however, that he does not think "all of this came about just because we met. *The Record's* representatives acknowledge that they had received many, many letters and telephone calls from readers who were upset by the editorial positions. We were there at the right time."

"They were ready to hear a group from the Jewish community offer a coherent and systematic appraisal of their editorial pieces and of Lazare's columns. They seemed rather surprised when we showed them a dozen editorials and columns about the Middle East, Israel, and American Jews that had appeared during the past two and a half years, all of which were critical of Israel and none of Palestinian terrorism."

Warach, who wrote an op-ed piece for the *Standard* March 11 that was highly critical of *The Record's* editorials and particularly of Daniel Lazare, said he felt the meeting "was worthwhile to convey our extreme distress at the lack of comprehension on the part of *The Record* and its editorial people." I showed them, for example, a newspaper headline that said, 'Arab man lynched on West Bank.' Any reasonable person would have come to the conclusion that that Arab was lynched by Jews, which did not happen to be the case. Everyone at the table agreed the headline was poorly written.

"Speaking for myself, I also informed them that I felt I was at least as patriotic and American as any people at *The Record*, and as an American Jew, I felt my patriotism had been maligned by the editorial 'The Silence on Israel.' That editorial had ascribed candidates' alleged reluctance to criticize Israel to 'the power of vocal American Jewish organizations,' and noted that Jewish PACs had contributed millions of dollars to political campaigns. It went on to indicate that this state of affairs was discouraging "frank discussion of American policy in this vital area," and asked, "Should aid be withheld to show American displeasure over the treatment of Palestinians?"

Warach said that he had noticed a difference in *The Record's* editorial and op-ed pages these few weeks, but "I am not confident that this will continue to be the case."

He noted that his own op-ed piece in this newspaper had prompted a response from Lazare in the March 25 *Standard*. "Three out of four people have pointed out to me that he once again equated Israel with Nazism," said Warach. [Lazare wrote, "As a nation founded on the ashes of Nazism (or so it claims—the truth is another matter).... Like Waldheim and his fellow Nazis in the Balkans, the Israelis face a difficult problem in subjugating and exploiting a rebellious population in Gaza and the west bank. Like the Nazis, their attitude is nationalist, expansionist, and openly racist."] "I think it's absolutely shameful," said Warach. "That is racist, that is bigotry. For someone to say that is absolutely sick."

He noted that " 'the editorials reflect the viewpoint of *The Record*; the columns reflect the viewpoint of the writer.' That's what they told me at *The Record*." But, Warach went on, alluding to Lazare, when an editorial writer also writes columns that he called "one-sided, viperous, and racist,... the twain do indeed meet here. *The Record* continues to print them and must accept responsibility."

"I want the Jewish community to be alert," he added, "to write and call and make themselves heard."

Benfield, who called the meeting positive and "a frank exchange of opinions," acknowledged that there were "things they pointed out to us of value."

But, he stressed, while "we've written only two editorials on the subject since then, [that was] not because of the meeting; it just hasn't come up.

"I don't think I've consciously done anything differently."

He noted that "editorials by definition are judgmental.... Sometimes statements that we make will be viewed as sweeping, sometimes as more qualified."

He declined to discuss directions the page would take. "You react to events," he said. "I don't think it would be fair or accurate" to make that kind of prediction.

Rosenberg, of the North Jersey Federation, said that he had participated in the meeting because feelings in his community, which includes parts of Passaic and Bergen counties, "about the beatings that Israel was taking [in *The Record's* editorials] had reached such a level that it was necessary to communicate with the editorial staff of the paper."

He called the meeting "cordial, constructive in communicating a point of view and deeper understanding of the sensitivities involved in reporting on the Middle East." We got an indication that they would examine their policy and their writing.

"It appears that they have."

Community

by Rebecca Kaplan Boroson

From time to time *The Record* publishes, on its editorial page, a motto: "Friend of the People It Serves." Some of those people visited *The Record* a few weeks ago as representatives of the Jewish community. They expressed some widely-held views and a widely-shared sense of hurt. *The Record*, they said, was showing a strong anti-Israel bias, a bias that was causing Jewish readers distress, a bias that might be caught—bias tends to be caught—by the general reader. They said that bias could be seen in editorials, in op-ed pieces, and even in headlines.

The community representatives showed *The Record's* executives more than two years' worth of column after column, editorial after editorial that were unrelievedly critical of Israel. Nothing critical of Palestinian terrorism had been published during that same time.

They received, they report, a fair hearing. And *The Record's* representatives say they appreciated the opportunity to listen. Some of what they heard, they say, made good sense. They acknowledged the community's wish for perspective, for sensitivity, for, at the very least, "a more balanced disagreement."

We at the *Standard* and the Jewish community at large have remarked on a change at *The Record*. We see greater care taken with language, which can be so misleading, so inflammatory, when used imprecisely. We see an effort to give a more balanced picture of what is happening in the Middle East. We see letter after letter from area Jews expressing views many of us share.

We sense—and appreciate—an underlying respect for the Jewish community. We also appreciate the strength of community itself.

Just how effective would all these very valid—to us—complaints have been if they had been made singly? They might have been disregarded as coming from cranks. But coming from emissaries of Jewish Bergen, Passaic, and Hudson counties, and their over-arching community relations committee, they had credibility. And, seemingly, they have been heeded.

Teaneck Media Watch Group to Monitor Mideast Coverage

Reuben Gross is enlisting recruits for the other half of the battle for Israel.

As the Teaneck psychologist explained Sunday, "The battle for Israel is being fought only in part in the Middle East. At least half the battle is being fought right here in America."

While the Israeli army is concerned with security along the borders and west bank violence, Dr. Gross is calling on Jews and others in the United States to concern themselves with inaccurate news accounts, biased broadcasts, and uninformed commentaries that convey false or distorted perceptions of Israel.

He spoke at the inaugural meeting of a group that is his brainchild, Mid-East Media Watchers. "One of my goals is to heighten the [awareness of the] Jewish community to the need to keep the media unbiased," he said in outlining his plan to five other Teaneck residents gathered in his home.

"My goal, hopefully, is to spread this idea to every congregation in the country," and to create a grass-roots group that will monitor and respond to news reports on Israel.

"People get their ideas and attitudes from the media, and we've learned from the Lebanese war that sometimes [the media] are irresponsible," he said.

The initial gathering was attended by Dr. Stanley Shapiro, Martin Pollack, Arnold Stiefel, Phyllis Goldschmidt, and Dr. Eugene Korn.

Also in attendance was a journalist who declined to be identified but who provided the group with an insider's view of how news is gathered, processed, and disseminated. The journalist also outlined strategies the group could enact in response to biased or undocumented accounts.

"The Supreme Court is not the final arbiter in this country; '60 Minutes' is," the journalist said in emphasizing the media's power to shape people's outlook.

"What you should be going for when you critique the media is to go for things that are really outrageous," the journalist said. He also cautioned the members that they must avoid a hyper-responsive approach if they want to preserve their credibility. "You have to ask yourself, 'Was this a balanced report?' not, 'Did it upset me?' "

The group members also discussed means of responding to objectionable accounts. Suggested options ranged from writing letters to the editor to cancelling subscriptions, but agreement on methods awaits further discussion at subsequent meetings.

Another topic was whether the group should function as an autonomous, expanding organization or become a local affiliate of the Washington-based CAMERA (Committee for Accuracy in Middle East Reporting in America).

Gross explained that while CAMERA and the group he envisions have similar aims, they also have different means. While CAMERA places advertisements in the national press and publishes a newsletter critiquing various accounts, Gross sees Mid-East Media Watchers more as a group that will provide a rapid, widespread response to articles and broadcasts. He noted that he spoke with a CAMERA representative recently and that the Washington-based organization may send a speaker to address the Teaneck group at a later date.

In the meantime, Gross, Korn, and Pollack are serving on a committee charged with better defining the Teaneck group's purposes and objectives. That sharper focus will enable the group to decide how it may best proceed, Gross said.

The psychologist sees a great need for a nation-wide group poised to quickly counter biased reports.

"Every shul in this country—Orthodox, Reform, Conservative, and liberal—should have a unit of this group," he said.

His own experience in replying to unfair stories about Israel dates at least to 1969, as evidenced by a yellowing copy of LIFE magazine that carries one of his letters.

A marital counselor who has lived in Teaneck since 1972, Gross is a member of Teaneck's Orthodox Congregation B'nai

Yeshurun. Formerly the author of *The Jewish Standard's* "Singularly Speaking" column, Gross has visited Israel several times.

Gross said he expects Mid-East Media Watchers will hold its next meeting in about six weeks. Meanwhile, people seeking further information on the group should call mornings.

VI. POLITICAL   CARTOONS

Where to Draw the Line?

by Gerald Baumgarten

Israel's response to Arab Palestinian rioting and civil disorder in the West Bank and Gaza Strip resulted in an outpouring of editorial cartoons in general circulation daily newspapers, large and small, throughout the United States. The volume of cartoons greatly exceeded those drawn in response to the war in Lebanon in 1982 and the picture presented was harsher and more damaging to Israel's image.

The Anti-Defamation League examined 133 editorial cartoons published between December 1987 and February 1988 on the rioting and civil disturbances and Israel's effort to restore public order. One hundred and eight of the cartoons were extremely critical of Israel, 14 presented a generally evenhanded view of the situation and 11 were sympathetic to Israel.

The most offensive were cartoons suggesting that Israel was engaging in a holocaust against Arab Palestinians, likening Israel's actions to the Nazis. Whether or not one views the Jewish state's response to the rioting and disturbances as wise or appropriate, to equate Israel's actions with those of Nazi Germany, which sought the ruthless and systematic annihilation of an entire people, is grotesque and reprehensible. Neverless, such analogies were presented by a number of cartoonists:

—Steve Benson of the Phoenix *Arizona Republic* drew a macabre "season's greetings" card which proclaimed: "Happy Holocaust to the Arabs of the West Bank and Gaza from your friendly occupying forces." The cartoon depicted three armed and grinning Israeli soldiers standing behind a sign marked "No Rocks."

—Mike Peters in Ohio's *Dayton Daily News* showed an Arab Palestinian man in a barbed-wire enclosure marked "Palestinian Camp" baring his outstretched left arm to display a Star of David tattooed on it—an obvious allusion to the tattooing of Jews by the Nazis.

—Syndicated cartoonist Patrick Oliphant showed a freight train taking European Jews to their deaths and, in an adjoining panel, a bus taking Arab Palestinians from their homes. The cartoon was captioned "Deportation—Then And Now."

—Doug Marlette of the *Atlanta Constitution* drew an analogy to the plight of Anne Frank in a cartoon by depicting Israeli soldiers breaking into a hiding place where a child can be seen in a corner of the room writing her diary. In the caption a soldier shouts: "Anne Frank!"

An ADL letter to the *Atlanta Constitution* condemned Marlette's analogy as "inaccurate, grossly distorted and repugnant," charging: "Marlette has the responsibility to distinguish between an excessive reaction to a violent uprising and the deliberate genocide by gassing and starvation of six million Jews, one of whom was Anne Frank." ADL's letter added: "The Nazi Holocaust was the planned physical extermination of an entire people. It was not a dispute or conflict, occasionally turned violent, over a piece of land. The crime of genocide defies comparison."

Similarly, an ADL letter to the *Arizona Republic* said of the Benson cartoon: "On its face, the Holocaust analogy is both despicable and absurd." Criticism of the Peters cartoon in the *Dayton Daily News* from readers also was published.

After printing the Oliphant cartoon, the Bridgeport, CT, *Post* wrote an editorial on the subject signed by Joseph A. Owens, editorial page editor, which expressed regret. Owens said: "Members of the Jewish community believe that it is unfair to suggest that the deportation of Palestinians from Israel might conceivably be likened to the Holocaust." He added: "I do recognize that the interpretation by members of the Jewish community is possible and legitimate. I apologize to everyone who was offended."

Other offensive drawings distorted Jewish religious symbols:

—A cartoon by Don Wright of the *Miami News* showed individuals identified as "The Palestinians" in a concentration camp whose barbed-wire fences conformed to the shape of the Star of David.

—Bill Day of the *Detroit Free Press* presented a prison complex enclosing huts within a barbed-wire fence with observation posts manned by armed guards. Both the prison structure and the barbed-wire fence were in the shape of the Star of David. The cartoon was entitled "Palestinian Refugee Camp."

—Bill Mitchell of New York's *Rochester Democrat and Chronicle* depicted an Israeli soldier holding an automatic weapon, one of whose barrels projected a menorah, which formed a multi-headed weapon.

—Barbara D. Cummings of the *Los Angeles Times* illustrated an article sympathetic to the Arab Palestinian cause by depicting a large Star of David as a spiked juggernaut descending to crush an Arab Palestinian preparing to hurl a rock.

Some cartoons used distorted Biblical allusions to criticize Israel.

Another Mike Peters cartoon showed an Israeli tank with its cannon aimed at a stable. Hitched to the stable's gate was a donkey, and a bright star shone in the sky. From the tank, an Israeli soldier said: "We've heard you've got a Palestinian in there...," alluding to the birth of Jesus. The cartoon, distributed by United Feature Syndicate, appeared in the *El Paso Herald-Post* with a caption reading: "Mike Peters Views A Revised Christmas Story." After the *Nashville Tennessean* printed the same cartoon, Frank Ritter, the paper's "Reader Advocate," wrote: "A lot of people called to voice their complaint that the cartoon was in poor taste and offensive. One caller said: 'The history of Jews and Christians centers around a Christ Child motif. And the problem is that throughout history many people who have called themselves Christians have persecuted Jews in the name of Jesus. The cartoon revives all those thoughts and old prejudices.' "

Mr. Ritter went on to say: "The caller was right—but not everyone is as sensitive... to the issue involved." He said: I'm not Jewish, so I didn't get offended...." He suggested that Peters was "not anti-Semitic" and "merely was trying to make a valid point."

But, concluded Ritter, "Prejudice against Jews exists, it is a fact of life. And Jews are not over-reacting when they see cartoons, however well-intentioned, that might be seen as pandering to that prejudice."

The Biblical edict concerning just retribution, i.e., an eye for eye, was also used by several cartoonists to attack Israel. Jack Higgins of the *Chicago Sun-Times* showed Israeli soldiers, with their rifles smoking, after killing several Arab Palestinians in a village street. The Israeli patrol leader proclaims: "62 Eyes For An Eye... 692 Teeth For A Tooth...."

Similarly, Richard Crowson of the *Wichita Eagle-Beacon* showed an Israeli soldier, holding a still smoking attack rifle, standing near a dead Arab Palestinian. On the wall in the background was written "An Eye For An Eye, A Tooth For a Tooth." The Israeli soldier added: "... And A Bullet For A Rock...."

The right of editorial cartoonists to express their views is not at issue. Furthermore, by the very nature of their profession, cartoonists are given to hyperbole and caricature rather than serious analysis in a historical context. Nevertheless, there is a line between fair comment, whether hostile or friendly to the subject, and repugnant references to the Holocaust. Cartoonists who make their points by comparing Israelis to Nazis or equaling Arab Palestinians with Jewish victims of the Nazis or other such odious references have crossed that line.

"Prisoners of War"

"Knowing the truth is a matter of learning how to read between the lies."

VII. APPENDICES

Code of Ethics of the American Society of Professional Journalists

The Society of Professional Journalists, Sigma Delta Chi, was founded in 1909. Headquartered in Chicago, it now has 28,000 members. Its Code of Ethics, first adopted in 1926 and revised in 1973, is presented here in full:

The Society of Professional Journalists, Sigma Delta Chi, believes the duty of journalists is to serve the truth.

We believe the agencies of mass communication are carriers of public discussion and information, acting on their Constitutional mandate and freedom to learn and report the facts.

We believe in public enlightenment as the forerunner of justice, and in our Constitutional role to seek the truth as part of the public's right to know the truth.

We believe those responsibilities carry obligations that require journalists to perform with intelligence, objectivity, accuracy, and fairness.

To these ends, we declare acceptance of the standards of practice here set forth:

I. RESPONSIBILITY: The public's right to know of events of public importance and interest is the overriding mission of the mass media. The purpose of distributing news and enlightened opinion is to serve the general welfare. Journalists who use their professional status as representatives of the public for selfish or other unworthy motives violate a high trust.

II. FREEDOM OF THE PRESS: Freedom of the press is to be guarded as an inalienable right of people in a free society. It carries with it the freedom and the responsibility to discuss, question, and challenge actions and utterances of our government and of our public and private institutions. Journalists uphold the right to speak unpopular opinions and the privilege to agree with the majority.

III. ETHICS: Journalists must be free of obligation to any interest other than the public's right to know the truth.

1. Gifts, favors, free travel, special treatment or privileges can compromise the integrity of journalists and their employers. Nothing of value should be accepted.

2. Secondary employment, political involvement, holding public office, and service in community organizations should be avoided if it compromises the integrity of journalists and their employers. Journalists and their employers should conduct their personal lives in a manner which protects them from conflict of interest, real or apparent. Their responsibilities to the public are paramount. That is the nature of their profession.

3. So-called news communications from private sources should not be published or broadcast without substantiation of their claims to news value.

4. Journalists will seek news that serves the public interest, despite the obstacles. They will make constant efforts to assure that the public's business is conducted in public and that public records are open to public inspection.

5. Journalists acknowledge the newsman's ethic of protecting confidential sources of information.

IV. ACCURACY AND OBJECTIVITY: Good faith with the public is the foundation of all worthy journalism.

1. Truth is our ultimate goal.

2. Objectivity in reporting the news is another goal, which serves as the mark of an experienced professional. It is a standard of performance toward which we strive. We honor these who achieve it.

3. There is no excuse for inaccuracies or lack of thoroughness.

316

4. Newspaper headlines should be fully warranted by the contents of the articles they accompany. Photographs and telecasts should give an accurate picture of an event and not highlight a minor incident out of context.

5. Sound practice makes clear distinction between news reports and expressions of opinion. News reports should be free of opinion or bias and represent all sides of an issue.

6. Partisanship in editorial comment which knowingly departs from the truth violates the spirit of American journalism.

7. Journalists recognize their responsibility for offering informed analysis, comment, and editorial opinion on public events and issues. They accept the obligation to present such material by individuals whose competence, experience, and judgment qualify them for it.

8. Special articles or presentations devoted to advocacy or the writer's own conclusions and interpretations should be labeled as such.

V. FAIR PLAY: Journalists at all times will show respect for the dignity, privacy, rights, and well-being of people encountered in the course of gathering and presenting the news.

1. The news media should not communicate unofficial charges affecting reputation or moral character without giving the accused a chance to reply.

2. The news media must guard against invading a person's right to privacy.

3. The media should not pander to morbid curiosity about details of vice and crime.

4. It is the duty of news media to make prompt and complete correction of their errors.

5. Journalists should be accountable to the public for their reports and the public should be encouraged to voice its grievances against the media. Open dialogue with our readers, viewers, and listeners should be fostered.

VI. PLEDGE: Journalists should actively censure and try to prevent violations of these standards, and they should encourage their observance by all newspeople. Adherence to this code of ethics is intended to preserve the bond of mutual trust and respect between American journalists and the American people.

Maps

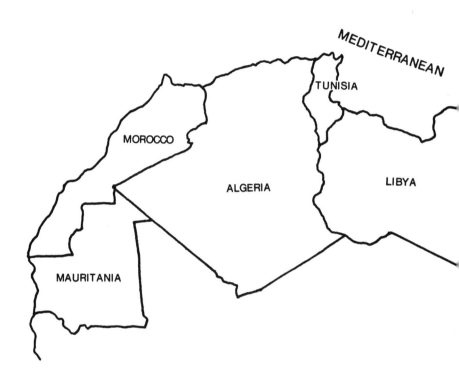

1 KUWAIT

2 BAHRAIN

3 QATAR

4 UNITED ARAB EMIRATES

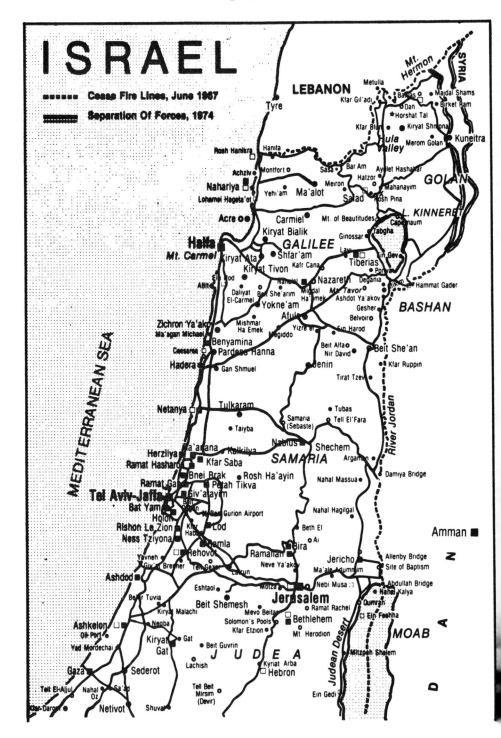

Appendices

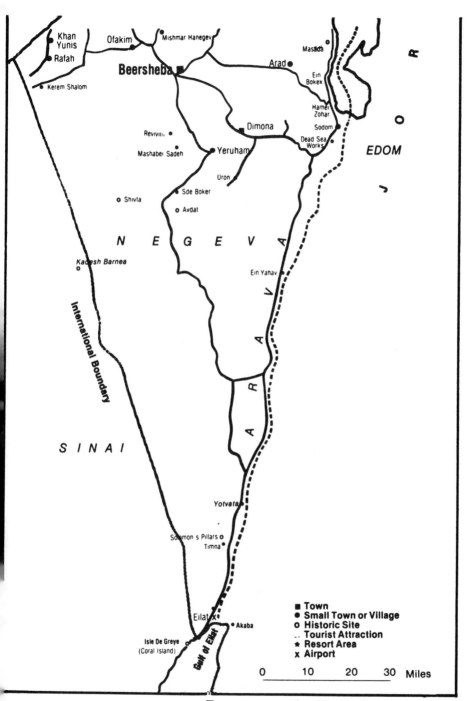

From a map by Carta, Ltd., Jerusalem

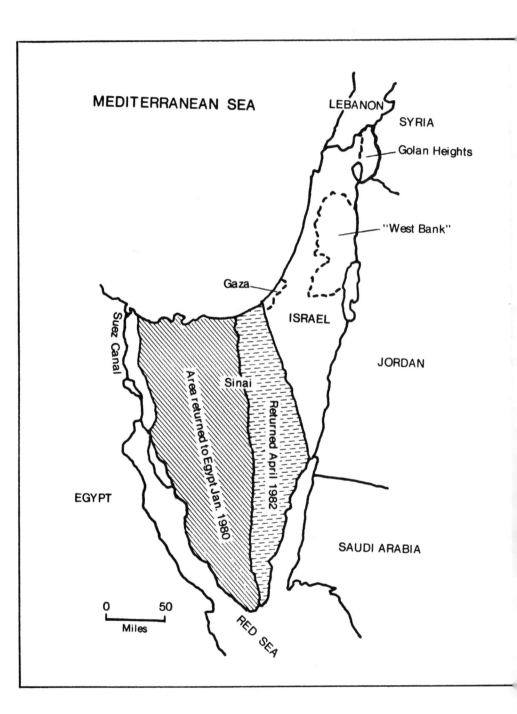

MEDITERRANEAN SEA

LEBANON

SYRIA

Golan Heights

"West Bank"

Gaza

ISRAEL

JORDAN

Suez Canal

Sinai

Area returned to Egypt Jan. 1980

Returned April 1982

EGYPT

SAUDI ARABIA

0   50

Miles

RED SEA

JERUSALEM MEDIA SERVICES

Letter of Introduction

Jerusalem Media Services (JMS), located in the centre of town, provides media services including information and logistic support to local and visiting television networks and newspapers.

JMS is well connected with every city and Palestinian refugee camp in the West Bank, Gaza Strip, and Golan Heights, as well as territories within the Green Line.

JMS provides professional crews, information on current news events, multilingual guides, and any other services you might need in the course of gathering news in the area.

JMS operates out of I.C.T.V, a first rate production house equipped with PAL and NTSC broadcast quality equipment for filming, editing and satellite feeds. Among I.C.T.V clients are CNN, CBC, VIS NEWS, NBC and other foreign news agencies.

JMS's experienced staff will give you timely information, objective analysis, helpful advice, as well as technical assistance in filming and covering current events.

JMS can organize visits to any Palestinian village, refugee camp or city, and put you in touch with individuals, families and organizations.

For furthur information contact:
Rana Ardaji and Kasim Abu Raya at JMS, I.C.T.V, City Tower, 34 Ben Yehuda St. Jerusalem, Tel: 226312, Telex: 26453.

JERUSALEM MEDIA SERVICES

KASIM ABU-RAIA

CITY TOWER 34 BEN YEHUDA STREET

P.O.B 13150 JERUSALEM 94583

TELEPHONE: (02) 226312 TELEX: 26453–ICTV IL

Jerusalem Media Services Business Card

Organizations and Publications which Evaluate Middle East Media Coverage

CAMERA (Committee for Accuracy in Middle East Reporting in America)

1. 2025 I Street N.W.
   Washington, D.C. 20006
   (202) 822-8884

2. P.O. Box 59028
   Philadelphia, PA 19102
   (215) 569-3467

3. P.O. Box 590381
   San Francisco, CA 94159
   (415) 543-7820

The Committee on Media Accountability (COMA)
2210 Wilshire Blvd.
#674
Santa Monica, CA 90403
(213) 938-7111

Zionist Organization of America
4 E. 34th Street
New York, NY 10016
(212) 481-1500

Americans for a Safe Israel
114 E. 28th Street
New York, NY 10016
(212) 696-2611

Midstream: A Monthly Jewish Review
515 Park Avenue
New York, NY 10022

Krantz, Frederick. "The Holocaust Analogy and the Media." *Midstream* (Feb./March 1988).
Podhoretz, Norman. "American Jews and Israel." *New York Post* (March 1, 1988). With the permission of King Features.
Rael Jean Isaac, Irving Kristol, David Sidorsky, and Ruth R. Wisse. *Commentary* 85 (Feb. 1988): 46-47, 51-52, 66-67, 74-75.

From *The Jewish Standard*:
"Teaneck Media Watch Group to Monitor Mideast Coverage." (April 29, 1988).
Warach, Eli J. "Reader is Displeased with *The Record's* Israel Coverage." (March 11, 1988).
Boroson, Rebecca Kaplan: "Drawing Lines" (Jan. 15, 1988); "Daniel Lazare: A Candid Conversation with the Controversial Columnist" (March 11, 1988); "Editorial Page to Change, Says *Record's* Publisher" (April 1, 1988); and "Community" (Feb. 1, 1988).

Baumgarten, Gerald. "Where to Draw the Line?" *ADL Bulletin* (May 1988). With permission of the Anti-Defamation League of B'nai B'rith.

Map of Israel courtesy of Carta, Ltd., Jerusalem.

Political Cartoons:
Conrad, Paul. "Israeli Flag with Guns." Jan. 1988, *Los Angeles Times*.
Conrad, Paul. "Palestinian Homeland." April 1982, *Los Angeles Times*.
Bensen, Steve. "Happy Holocaust." Dec. 1987, Tribune Media Services.
Conrad, Paul. "Free Soviet Jews." Dec. 1987, *Los Angeles Times*.
Conrad, Paul. "Bethlehem Violence." Dec. 1987, *Los Angeles Times*.
Fischman, Shelly. "Shamir and Waldheim." 1988.
Fischman, Shelly. "Reagan, Arab, and Israeli." March 1988.
Danziger, Jeff. "Prisoners of War." Dec. 1987, *Christian Science Monitor*.

Oliphant, Pat. "Israel at Psychiatrist." April 1988, Universal Press Syndicate.

Wasserman. "Goliath's Problem." 1987, *Los Angeles Times*.

Gamble, Ed. "You Can't Protest." Jan. 1988, King Features Syndicate.

Englehart, Bob. "American Tax Dollars at Work." Feb. 1988, *The Hartford Courant*.

Danziger, Jeff. "Jewish Americans and TV." Jan. 1988, *Christian Science Monitor*.

Borgman, Jim. "Dialogue of the Deaf." Feb. 1988, King Features Syndicate.

Gamble, Ed. "The Paradox of the Zionist Dream." Feb. 1988, King Features Syndicate.

Golden, Lou. "Media Map of the Mideast." 1983.